Where Have You Gone,
MICHELANGELO?

Where Have You Gone,
MICHELANGELO?

The Loss of Soul in Catholic Culture

T H O M A S   D A Y

CROSSROAD • NEW YORK

1994

The Crossroad Publishing Company
370 Lexington Avenue, New York, NY 10017

Copyright © 1993 by Thomas Day

Printed in the United States of America

Library of Congress Cataloging-in-Publication Data

Day, Thomas
    Where have you gone, Michelangelo? : the loss of soul in Catholic
culture / Thomas Day.
        p.   cm.
    Includes bibliographical references.
    ISBN 0-8245-1396-7
    1. Catholics—United States—Religious life.   2. Catholics—United
States—Social life and customs.   3. Catholic Church—United States—
History—1965-   4. Pop culture—United States—History—20th
century.   5. Pop culture—Religious aspects—Catholic Church—
History—20th century.   6. Church music—Catholic Church—
History—20th century.   7. Church music—United States—
History—20th century.   8. United States—Religious life and
customs.   I. Title.
BX1406.2.D38   1993
282′.73′09045—dc20   93-20674
                                                                        CIP

Contents

PREFACE

"THIS IS ONE OF THE MOST IMPORTANT THINGS to happen to the Catholic church in its entire history. You must experience it!"

It sounded urgent, and so I went along to experience the experience.

The occasion, sometime about the year 1980, was a Mass at a convention of a Catholic organization. Hundreds of people had come to a large cathedral for what was thought to be the sort of post–Vatican II phenomenon that would change the face of the church, if not the world. Hundreds of people waited eagerly for the experience.

Then, at last, music indicated that the liturgy had begun — and for the next hour or so I had the uncomfortable feeling that I was attending an illustrated lecture on the meaning of the word "decadent." It was like watching all my loved ones and friends disintegrate from a loathsome but unnamed disease, right in front of my eyes.

Maybe it was the music: much strumming of guitars; one "contemporary" song sliding, like warm pudding, into another song of similar consistency. According to the printed Order of Service, nearly the entire liturgy would feature the songs of a famous group of "folk" musicians. Sung prayer, in other words, would also double as a demo-session, a little free advertising for the group.

Pain! Oh, the pain of listening to adolescent self-pity and self-importance in song! It would have been bearable if the congregation, caught up in the fervor of the music, had been carried along in its mighty sound, but very few people in the congregation were actually singing.

I needed distraction — anything to take my thoughts away

from the group's slouching melodies. Like every well-trained
Catholic, I began to look for relief in art, in the building's decorative features, which I "read" as if they were an architectural
prayerbook.

The cathedral, a mountain of stone piled upon stone, suggested a combination of a maximum security prison and a Victorian train station; yet, it was not without charm. Finding that
charm, however, was a little difficult because the building had recently been subjected to extensive plastic surgery in an effort to
make it look more youthful, more postconciliar. During the face-
lift, the cathedral had lost some of its gingerbread ornamentation
and statues that were too cloying for modern taste, but it had also
lost some of its character.

My search for a prayer in architecture was interrupted,
abruptly, by an amplified voice. The presiding priest, holding a
microphone now, began the Mass by telling us who he was and
who the concelebrants and singers were and who we were and how
wonderful it was that we had come. To soften us up even more,
he made a little attempt at humor. (Nobody even smiled.)

This kind of verbal intrusion, the opening warm-up mono-
logue, is, of course, the modern post–Vatican II method for
gathering Catholics together; it is supposed to make everyone feel
at home — but I am positive that the only thing everyone could
feel was a rhetorical cattle-prod being shoved into the ribs. The
man was forcing us to pay attention to him, and him alone. His
warm-up remarks, which warmed up nobody, were really his way
of establishing dominance.

A few minutes later there was a homily whose "style" seemed
to blend logically with everything else. I shall never forget it.

Drifting from one off-the-top-of-his-head thought to another,
the homilist sounded as if he were slipping into a coma. So many
sentences ended with a pause and "y'know" that I started to
count them. All of this semi-coherent mumbling was supposed
to suggest his gift of intimacy and sincerity bestowed upon us, the
grateful congregation; yet, at the same time, the intimacy and sincerity were also suggesting that the man had not really prepared
his remarks.

It was not easy to discern exactly what the homilist was trying
to say with the verbal fragments he was casually dribbling here
and there, but a theme gradually emerged and it was this: "them"

against "us." Out there in the world were "them," the people who just did not understand the revolution that had changed the Catholic church and the way it should worship after Vatican II. They were powerful, these reactionaries, but they would eventually be swept away. The Spirit was with "us," the authentic Christians of the post–Vatican II era, the only people who possess the true faith in Jesus Christ... "y'know."

End of homily. Time for another song by the group, and one with a different mood. The choir, not far from the altar, seemed to be jumping frantically from musical note to note. (All I could think of was galvanized frogs hopping madly in all directions.) Most of the congregation, bewildered by the acrobatics of the melody that everybody was supposed to sing, remained silent.

Right there, on the spot, at that very moment, something hit me. I suffered what a medical doctor would have diagnosed as a massive cerebral conniption. I snapped or, to use a cliché, I hit the ceiling, which was a very high one. I have not been the same since the day I happened to witness that "experience," that celebration of the insipid and the sappy, that marketing opportunity for publicizing the creations of the famous group. I still spend a few of my waking hours trying to figure out why anybody with more than three functioning brain cells would put the label of greatness on something that was so embarrassingly shallow, why Catholic parishes by the thousands would try so hard to duplicate that same "atmosphere" of dense and banal immaturity... and why I reacted so badly, when I should have just walked out.

Why? Some readers are astonished by my inability to grasp the obvious. They tell me why, as if they were explaining to a child. *From the right:* "What shocked you was really the disintegration of American Catholicism. The Modernists, the Marxist promoters of liberation theology, the disobedient theologians, and the Rome-hating liberals have all taken over. If you can't see that, you are part of the problem." *From the left:* "People like you are still looking for the Catholicism of beautiful things, the traditional smells and bells. Fortunately, all that is in the past; the church, alive and open to the world, is creating a new image of itself. Yes, of course, there were awkward moments in that liturgy which you attended, but in the interest of solidarity we are forbidden to mention such failings."

I did not go to that cathedral with the idea that I should be reassured by traditional Catholicism expressing its conservatism, its orthodoxy, in traditional rituals. I certainly was not expecting to be uplifted with ceremonies, music, architecture, and preaching that were all glorious beyond description. I did, however, assume that, in a manner that an anthropologist would describe as a universal human phenomenon, I would be part of a collective, common prayer (an activity that comes in many different forms). Instead, I found myself in the middle of something very . . . *weird*, almost freakish, and it could not be explained away according to the ideologies of conservatism or liberalism. I realize that a High Anglican might find a Cherokee rain dance a trifle weird, just as a Presbyterian might put the same label on a Maronite Catholic liturgy from Lebanon. But the weirdness of that "experience" in a cathedral was something of an altogether different order, and I could not put my finger on it. What was the source of the problem?

The research for this book has been part of my own personal quest to discover what had caused that feeling of being in the presence of ineffable weirdness: something bizarre, neither fish nor fowl, weak, vaguely diseased. Whatever it was, the weirdness had a life of its own and effectively blocked any encounter with theological messages that the ritual was trying to convey.

Writing this book has also been an act of therapy for me, my attempt to come down from the ceiling that I had, as it were, hit. For my own health and faith, I had to analyze the sources of my reaction. Perhaps some of these pages (my therapy) will provide solace and guidance for many other people — Catholic laity, priests, nuns, brothers — who have told me that they, too, have suffered forms of severe agitation while attempting to worship in a Catholic church, and yet they could not name the problem.

This is not a treatise that lays out a hypothesis and then systematically defends it. A large portion of this book is oral history and it frequently takes the form of many "personal" film documentaries — with verbal pictures of events, flashbacks, swift changes of scene, and commentary. As in all oral histories, the language is sometimes colloquial, sometimes blunt. I have tried to be as accurate as possible, but I have frequently had to change details of these oral histories, in order to protect the privacy of the individuals involved. The oral history in this book, I should add, is not predominantly "local." So that I might continue to live in peace with neighbors and colleagues, I generally avoided anecdotal material relating to incidents that took place on any spot within a half-hour's drive from my house.

In parts of this book it may appear that I have, so to speak, brought out an old cigar box, filled with odds and ends from my past, and dumped the contents in front of the reader. Frequently, it looks as if I have borrowed items from the cigar boxes of friends and acquaintances — from their memories. The method to this madness is simple: I want to give the reader a "sense" of history rather than a narration of facts; the cumulative effect of all the information (the odds and ends) might help the reader to understand better the "style" of contemporary Catholicism and explain why the religion that produced some of the world's greatest saints and sinners is now, in so many places, stuck in that deep pit of feel-good sentimentality, the liturgy as weird variety show.

Younger readers — especially Catholics born after, let us say, 1960 — are hereby forewarned. They may find it difficult to "imagine" whole sections of this book. Older Catholics will read a particular sentence and their minds might be flooded with memories (good and bad) of sights, sounds, and even smells. The younger Catholic will read the same sentence and comprehend only words printed on a page. One reason I wrote this book is to give younger Catholics a different perspective, so they could "imagine" a broader Catholic culture that most of them have never known.

Critics should not waste their time complaining about all the things left out of this book. Their best line of attack would be something like this: "The impertinence of this man! He has taken the gift of faith and has reduced it to *style criticism*. He cannot see that a life in Christ and liturgy are more than just beauty, art, and other earthly distractions."

In the Epistle to the Colossians (3:2) it says: "Mind the things that are above, not the things that are upon the earth." Most of the pages in this book are indeed about earthly things, about the Catholic church's public relations with the world — in "style" and in art. This approach contrasts with the innumerable items on the library shelves that exhaustively analyze theological and liturgical aspects of modern Catholicism — "things that are above" — but devote relatively little space to what can be directly observed from on-site inspections. In fact, it is now considered very bad form to examine liturgical and cultural developments in Catholicism after Vatican II as if they were, in any way, the work of mere human beings.

I can respond to criticism of my earthly observations only by saying that for many Catholics today the route to "things that are above" is being blocked by obstacles. In the typical Catholic parish many of these large obstacles happen to be earthly matters of "style," beauty, art, and music. In a sense, this book is a study of obstacles: all the imperfections and foibles that are an inevitable part of anything that human beings attempt to do, even with the most sacred motives.

Part of this book originally appeared in *Homiletic and Pastoral Review:* "The Terrible Latin Mass," vol. 87, no. 6 (April 1987): 15–21. I am very grateful to Father Kenneth Baker, S.J., the editor of this journal, for permission to reprint these passages.

Quotations from the pronouncements of the Second Vatican Council are taken from *The Documents of Vatican II* (New York, 1966), edited by Walter M. Abbott, S.J., and Monsignor Joseph Gallagher.

I wish to thank the following people for the stories, information, and insights that they shared with me: Richard Corliss, Lyle Settle, Elizabeth Maginnis, Jane Bethune, Michael Dimaio, Dan Polino, David Bergeron, Rev. Richard John Neuhaus, Lee Strong, Rev. Michael Barber, S.J., Isabelle H. Penny, Donald St. Jean, Allen Downheiser, Paula Hersh, Sister Anna Marie Flusche, O.P., J. Alfred Thigpen, Thomas Marzik, John F. Quinn, Sister Prudence Croke, R.S.M., Brother James Loxham, F.S.C., Carlton Eldridge, James Wood, Stan Blejwas, Rev. Michael Gilligan, Kurt Poterack, and David Lancaster. Rev. Peter J. Scagnelli provided me with an abundance of material in his article "Liturgical Music: Motto Is 'Anything Goes'" (*Providence Visitor,* April 25, 1991, p. 15). The names of other individuals could be added here, but for reasons of discretion I do not mention them; I thank these people for their sometimes hilarious stories *in pectore.*

I am also very grateful to Klaus Baerenthaler, Justus George Lawler, Michael Leach, Sister Lucille McKillop, R.S.M., Christopher Kiernan, Rev. George B. McCarthy, and Rose Napoli.

And my wife Mary — *sine qua non.*

Chapter One

AN INTRODUCTION TO A STYLE
Never Say Never

FOR ME, THE DECISIVE MOMENT in the oral history came in a display of colors. I remember those colors.

College professors, in their academic regalia, seated in rows of chairs on a dais: black of the deepest blackness, with occasional flecks of gold, red, blue, and yellow. Potted palms and ferns around the sides and back of the raised platform: green. In the center of this setting, a lectern: brown.

A Catholic bishop — purple skull cap, sash, and cape — has just been introduced. The audience claps politely: a colorless sound, but it suggests gray. The purple bishop waits for the applause to stop, and then for a quiet that is the color of sheer emptiness. He gets it. Not a cough is heard. I remember that stillness.

The year was 1964 and the occasion was the commencement ceremony at a Catholic college for men. A few thousand human beings — graduates, faculty, guests — waited for the bishop to begin. Finally, he pierced the silence and announced his topic:

"There has been talk, foolish talk, about changes in the church." He paused; he smiled. "Well, let me assure you, the church will never change."

Oh, yes, *that* sermon. It was a favorite of pastors, aspiring monsignori, and (as in this case) auxiliary bishops. Every Catholic in the audience had heard it before, at least once or twice a year; they knew the whole thing by heart.

"Let these other so-called Christian denominations go off in

1

all kinds of directions; let them chase one heresy after another. We will have none of that. We alone shall keep the faith."

Following the standard formula for this sermon, his tone of voice soon became tense, then angry.

"The church has never changed. The church will never change. We shall change nothing, *nothing!*" He was roaring with fury by now.

Learned professors — theologians and historians seated behind the purple bishop and sweating beneath their academic robes — listened to this address with respectfully attentive expressions on their faces, even though they knew that His Excellency was, with broad and majestic brush strokes, painting himself into a corner. The Catholic church had most certainly changed over the centuries. Its customs and its ritual practices had frequently shifted to meet new thinking, new needs. Its doctrines had always been like ribbons of molecules that remained constant but could be shaped into unexpected forms by competent "scientists," that is, by the church in its orthodoxy. (The idea of Purgatory, to cite just one example, was an evolutionary "change," a medieval way of trying to express older church dogma.) The popular concept of dogma as a statement carved on granite tablets and protected forever in a bank vault (the church) contradicts history. The truth is that throughout the centuries the Catholic church's unchanging, consistent doctrines have gone through all sorts of evolutionary changes — in emphasis and interpretation.

Back to the purple bishop. His demeanor was becoming more and more violent. He seemed to infuriate himself with one indignant sentence after another. His rhetoric was turning crimson, the color of anger. The man, almost out of control, grabbed the lectern. He pounded it. (I thought he would reduce it to splinters.)

Everyone was waiting for him to bring up the subject of the Second Vatican Council, or at least make a passing reference to this momentous gathering of bishops. After all, in 1964 the council was still going on, still in the process of instituting one change after another. But the purple bishop never even mentioned the council. Not a word.

The increase in the volume of the bishop's voice indicated that the finale had arrived. The shouted phrases and the rhetorical fireworks all pointed to what most of the audience knew was coming — the triumphant climax on the words, "The church will never change!" (We could have all recited that same sentence with him in unison.)

It was over. Deafening applause, a hailstorm of sound: perhaps suggesting the color white. A grateful audience gave him a standing ovation.

Reader, please "freeze" this scene for a moment and study it.

The purple bishop, with his message of a church that would never change, defined the Catholic "style," *circa* 1964. The "style" was the man, and it influenced everything from the design of churches to the curricula in Catholic colleges. This, to be sure, was nothing new. From Christianity's earliest years, the correct-thinking, orthodox bishops were always declaring that the church would never change, never accept the new thinking of the Manicheans, Gnostics, and all the other heretics. In the East (among the Greeks, Russians, and so forth), the church established rituals and liturgical arts that gave the impression that nothing would ever be changed. In the West (that is, in Western civilization) the church also used a kind of ritual that created the image of utter changelessness, but it left plenty of room for artistic innovation. Any book on the history of art and any catalogue of recorded "classical" music will offer abundant proof that the Roman Catholic church had (at times) courageously experimented with new artistic styles. The church that would never change sometimes showed remarkable tolerance about changing the style of the art and music that enhanced its rituals. It also had a long history of commissioning excellent architects, artisans, and musicians to create beauty that would symbolize, in the most fashionable style of the time, the community's intense commitment. (We sometimes forget that many revered old works of art, like Michelangelo's frescos in the Sistine Chapel, were once new and almost shocking in their boldness.)

This somewhat odd arrangement — the unchanging faith expressed in artistic styles that went through evolutionary changes — worked very well, as long as artists served the church humbly and demonstrated their devotion by striving for their best standards of craftsmanship. Roman Catholicism had no problem with artistic flamboyance, if it was subtly mixed with humility, restraint, and respect for the church's practical needs. Unfortunately, this tacit agreement between church and artist began to come apart. Modern creative artists, at least since the early nineteenth century, have tended to think of themselves as isolated geniuses obeying only the dictates of creative impulse; such loners usually do not like the idea of humbly serving the church, or anything else for that matter. Modern Catholicism, with much less financial support than it had in past centuries, usually does not like to work with artists, those strange people who want to spend large amounts of money on what are seen as luxuries.

When I heard the purple bishop, in 1964, I knew that "the church will never change" had an unspoken subtext that went something like this: The liturgical arts are symbols of change, disorder, secular interests, and the unpredictable; the church has much to fear from such things. (In 1964, an impartial observer who inspected American Catholic churches built about that time and who heard just one minute of the music used in them would have concluded that most Catholic parishes were energetically engaged in the destruction of these dangerous liturgical arts.)

Not long after the purple bishop scoffed at the idea of any change in the church I again heard that very same topic in a sermon, but this time with a new twist: "Because of the Second Vatican Council, we're making some wonderful adjustments around the edges, but let me assure you, when it comes to the really important things, *the church will never change!*"

A few years later that sermon about the unchanging church disappeared and was replaced by a new indignant speech — delivered by theologians, priests, nuns, liturgists, and others. The new speech proclaimed that the Church of Rome, first cousin of the Whore of Babylon, had been doing things wrong for centuries and should be changed radically, along the lines suggested by the person giving the speech.

In idle moments I sometimes wonder what happened to the purple bishop after that hot commencement ceremony in 1964. How did he react when the policy about eating meat on Friday was changed, when vernacular languages replaced unchanging Latin? What stupendous mental retooling job took place in his mind when annulments became commonplace, when priests began to leave the active ministry by the thousands? How did his brain survive "the changes" without exploding? By all accounts he was a person of kindness and compassion; he was supremely dedicated to his vocation. But, with all that rage and indignation in one part of his psyche, how did he cope? And, of course, what was bothering him (and most of his audience) in the first place?

There are probably no answers to these questions, only insights that tell us something about the sources of Roman Catholicism's angry "style" in the early 1960s. If we have some understanding of where this "style" came from, we will have a better idea where the church is heading and why it occasionally disgraces itself in the way it worships. Probably the best place to begin (the best insight) is with Granny.

GRANNY

At a social gathering back in the 1960s (I cannot remember the year), I was introduced to a young man who had married into one of Philadelphia's Main Line WASP families. Distinguished bankers, lawyers, and businessmen graced the branches of this family tree. They all had prestige and standing in the community; they had money, lots of it, which they spent prudently.

According to this young man, the presiding head of this dynasty was Granny. A lady of great age and even greater dignity, Granny lived a quiet life in the ancestral home. From time to time the grandchildren and great-grandchildren would come to call on her; Granny, delighted with the family visitors, would chat pleasantly. But sometimes the conversation turned to unpleasant matters, and Granny would contribute by imparting wisdom that she had accumulated during her long life. She knew many things about the world, including dark secrets that could only be whispered. One of these secrets, which she told her family on more than one occasion, was that Jewish women had access to a magic ointment that they rubbed upon themselves, in order to make their feminine proportions large, firm, and alluring.

Yes, Granny knew some pretty interesting facts about Jews — and what she knew about Catholics was *even worse!*

My conversation with this young man was interrupted at this point ... and I never met him again. He never finished what he was going to say. All these years I have been left wondering: Just what were these horrid "secrets" that Granny had passed on to her children? It looks as if I shall have to go through life without ever learning the details of her folkloric information on the

Catholic church, but I think I know her sources. In her younger days Granny may have read the "cardinal" or "Jesuit" oath, a seventeenth-century forgery that was, in the early twentieth century, attributed to the Knights of Columbus, a Catholic fraternal organization. In this bogus oath, once widely circulated in the rural parts of the United States, a new knight swears to "make and wage relentless war, secretly and openly, against all heretics, Protestants, and Masons. . . . I will hang, burn, waste, boil, flay, strangle, and bury alive these infamous heretics; rip up the stomachs and wombs of their women, and crush their infants' heads against the walls in order to annihilate their execrable race."[1] Perhaps Granny's mother had read, with a mixture of horror and titillation, Maria Monk's book, *Awful Disclosures of the Hotel Dieu Nunnery in Montreal* (1836). In this lurid work of fiction, passed off as fact, all priests use nuns for their carnal pleasure, nuns hide their pregnancies underneath their flowing garb, and murdered babies are buried in the basements of convents. It is quite possible that Granny's own grandmother, like many loyal American Protestants, was absolutely convinced that the pope, aided by reactionary monarchs in Europe, was plotting to take over the Mississippi Valley. Whatever the case, Granny and many of her ancestors — the kind of people who checked the butcher's bill carefully before they paid it and who read the newspapers to be informed — were prepared to believe any preposterous fabrication about the Catholic church or Jews or other unfamiliarities.

Now, it is to be understood that some Catholics, throughout history, have been quite capable of believing outlandish lies about their non-Catholic neighbors; and some Catholics have made contributions to the sickening history of anti-Semitism. In addition, the Catholic church and its agencies, like all human institutions that go back for centuries, have had their bad moments when they committed all manner of monstrosities. But still — the church really did not deserve the kinds of preposterous falsehoods that were once repeatedly flung at it in the nineteenth and early twentieth centuries.

The Jews of the United States founded the Anti-Defamation League in order to stop the spread of lies and bigotry. Catholics responded differently. They had lots of babies. They filled convents and seminaries with celibates who dedicated their lives to the faith and its protection. They took great pride in their priests, who stayed priests forever, and celibate too. (Now, could Granny's church duplicate something like that?) They boasted that they belonged to the church that never changed — unlike Granny's church, which was the result of revolt and incorrect changes in Christian theology. They became exquisitely, perhaps neurotically sensitive to anything that looked like the slightest criticism of their church. They produced bishops who defended them against calumny, against change. (Change, in any form, could mean that somehow you were wrong and Granny had always been right.)

In 1907 Pius X condemned Modernism, the proposition that the Catholic church should change its doctrines in order to conform to the times. He even set up an efficient policing system to make sure that seminaries would not be polluted by this heresy. There could be no dialogue with the Modernists, just as there could be little reason for social interaction with the likes of Granny. Enemies were enemies, and they were spreading untruths.

On the eve of the Second Vatican Council, the mood in Roman Catholicism was sometimes as irritable as it was in the days of Pius X. So many of the sermons that I can remember from pre–Vatican II days sounded angry. Maybe the crankiness and anger were justified, since the previous two hundred years had been especially difficult for the church. As far as the purple bishop and many of his fellow Catholics were concerned, it was only yesterday when the French Revolution broke out; in the name of progress and liberty, the church was violently persecuted; cathedrals and monasteries were demolished. Napoleon came next. He invaded Rome, confiscated the pope's archives, and sent them to Paris; then he practically made the pope his prisoner and brought him to France as a war trophy. It was also yesterday when Bismarck launched his campaign to create a modern and culturally unified Germany, in which there could be no place for an independent Catholic church; bishops were arrested or forced into exile. The history of Catholicism in modern France ("the eldest daughter of the church") was largely about the government expelling monks and Jesuits or confiscating church property; in 1871 (not far from yesterday) radicals, determined to change society, took over Paris, desecrated churches, and killed the archbishop. Older Italians could remember (as if it were yesterday) when the Italian government and the papacy were not on speaking terms; they also remembered that the great national heroes who united Italy wanted to reduce the pope to the level of state employee. When the Mexican government brutally suppressed the Catholic faith and when some leftists made every effort to exterminate the church during the Spanish Civil War, there were many influential people in the world who applauded such activity as a necessary phase in the march of progress; that was yesterday, too. And if you were of Irish descent, the centuries of English misrule, the suppression of the church, and the Potato Famine were not yesterday, they were now!

The above is not an effort to portray the Catholic church as a blameless collection of angels, an innocent victim caught in the cruelties of history. In many cases, the church "was asking for it." The Roman Catholic hierarchy was fond of cozy relationships with dictators, wealthy landowners, and reactionary monarchists. Popes and theologians confidently taught that the divine plan — the unstoppable course of history — is a political situation in which an established Roman Catholic church and the state work together as equal partners; in this type of perfect political environment Roman Catholicism should be proclaimed as the state religion, but other faiths should receive only the amount of "toleration" that is expedient. (The ideal of a triumphant state religion that supersedes all other religions was once common in Protestant countries.) Roman Catholicism did not officially repudiate this proposition — really, this craving for political power — until Vatican II's Declaration on Religious Freedom (1965).[2]

To make a long story short: If the Catholic church had enemies, it richly deserved some of them. In 1964, a Catholic bishop knew that these enemies (deserved and undeserved) were everywhere — other religions, intellectuals, communists, radicals, and people like Granny, but also some governments and entire countries — and they all wanted the church to change, or maybe perish utterly. If a bishop and many of his flock were a little paranoid about their religion's survival in a changing world, they had a right to be.

In the United States, Catholicism's paranoid "style" was complicated by a slight case of schizophrenia.

On the one hand: The patriotism of American Catholics ranged from the fanatical to the hysterical. They loved their country. They were as American as anyone else, even though their grandparents or parents spoke with accents; maybe they were even more American than some of their neighbors. They bristled at the suggestion that they really owed their allegiance to a "foreign prince" (the pope). American Catholics would show their loyalty and patriotism by putting the nation's flag (an "idol" of a secular entity) right inside the sanctuaries of churches, right behind the altar railing — a practice that was once considered a radical departure from ecclesiastical tradition.

On the other hand: That great and attractive phenomenon called "American culture" — it looked so Protestant — was a constant threat. If Catholics were lured into it, the result would surely be assimilation, apostasy, and the eventual extinction of the church. The only way to survive was to follow a strict code of segregation from the temptations of "American culture" while, at the same time, remaining unswervingly loyal to the nation that produced that culture.

* * *

"The town was a whole." In her memoirs, *Ohio Town*, Helen Hooven Santmyer used those words to describe the social life in the place where she was raised at the beginning of the twentieth century.[3] Families knew one another; they even knew who lived in what house. Maybe the United Presbyterians could be a little "stiff-necked and ungracious" when it came to religion. (They did not mind if you came to their church and sang their hymns but "they came to yours and stood through hymn-singing — a whole line of your friends and contemporaries — not only mute, but with mouths clamped shut in hard stubborn lines.")[4] Maybe there was a problem here and there but, in general, the town was a balanced unity. Even race relations between black and white were "so easy and comfortable." The town was "not two communities, but one."

Then the author pulls back a little from this bold assertion.

"That statement," she adds, "is not quite accurate, since Roman Catholic segregation-by-choice has always made us in practice two towns. Growing up, we knew far fewer Catholics than Negroes." The area where these Catholics lived, "might as well be a part of town twenty or thirty miles away: it is as strange as that. I could not write about it. We never walked there, and never knew whose house this one was, or that one."

Santmyer broadly identifies the town's Catholics as Irish immigrants, who represented a threat to the established order. They competed for jobs with those who had lived in the town all their lives; they wanted political power, and this necessarily involved taking that power away from somebody else. If they chose to live in their own separate enclave, maybe it was partly because the rest of the town did not exactly welcome them.

This Catholic "segregation-by-choice" was not unique to Santmyer's town. All across the country, many Catholics would have been the first to admit, with pride, that they were a little isolated from the mainstream "American culture," because of their specialness. If they were so sure of themselves and set apart, it was because Roman Catholicism was the true religion ("the *the* church," as the comedian Lenny Bruce used to say) and all other creeds were denominations, in various stages of error.

Protestants, noting this grand self-assurance in their Catholic neighbors, invented a whole repertory of jokes about Catholics in heaven — who lived in a separate part of the celestial realm and were allowed to maintain the illusion that they were the only ones up there.

"Stick to your own kind" is a way of life followed by the Amish, by Hassidic Jews, and by all minorities that want to preserve their distinctiveness. It has many advantages. But there can be no "sticking together" and no distinctiveness without a *cultural* heritage that defines just how one group is not the same as another. (Customs, traditions, food, art, music, poetry, literature, and other cultural expressions all tell the group how it fits into the order of things.) Moreover, this "sticking together" can be effective only when it is coupled with another piece of advice: "Don't start envying and imitating attractive *cultural* features of another kind."

This discussion is becoming rather abstract. The time has come to switch from abstractions to the one concrete reality that brings everything together: education.

SEPARATE BUT EQUAL

In the early part of the nineteenth century, Catholic youngsters could go to their local public schools. There they learned how to read and write, how to do arithmetic. At these same institutions they also heard readings from the Bible, in the King James Translation, and prayers that were decidedly Protestant; some textbooks contained anti-Catholic passages; the history classes always seemed to emphasize the glorious victories of Protestant leaders over evil Catholic individuals and governments. What was called a "public" school tended to be, in effect, an interdenominational Protestant establishment open to all. Catholic parents and their clergy found this situation intolerable.

The leaders of public schools, oblivious to any problem, maintained that they were only doing their duty, only conveying the essence of "American culture" and citizenship to the nation's youth. Many Catholics saw things differently; they detected a plot to undermine their religious distinctiveness by homogenizing them in an American cultural sameness. They estimated (with wild exaggeration) that millions of Catholics had left the church because of an exposure to public schooling. German-speaking Catholics were especially alarmed by a public educational system that wiped out their language and *Kultur*; they were determined to support their own ethnic/religious schools. The situation became so critical that the Catholic bishops, meeting in 1884, decided on drastic measures. They declared that "indifferentism," the belief that one religion is as good as another, is the "actual and necessary fruit of the public schools as conducted" in the United States.[5] With this in mind, the bishops decreed that each Catholic parish, with rare exceptions, was to support its own parochial school; that Catholic parents were required to send their children to these schools or other Catholic schools; that Catholic children could not attend public schools, except for sufficient reasons, approved by the local bishop. There were over two thousand parish schools when the bishops made these pronouncements in 1884. By 1960 there would be more than ten thousand such schools.

Roman Catholics had never, in any part of the world, attempted a privately financed parochial school system on such a large scale; the entire concept, the sheer ambitious confidence of it all, was astounding. But, at one time, Catholics thought they had no choice. The creation of the parochial schools — and, indeed, an educational system that continued through graduate school — only makes sense when we realize that it was partly an act of desperation. Non-Catholic education meant assimilation, and educational assimilation meant extinction.

Was the Catholic population overreacting? Creating an educational ghetto? Perhaps, but just consider this. In 1920 the Masons of the Scottish rite in Oregon organized a campaign to restrict private schools, and this would have included all parochial schools in the state. The promoters of this campaign bypassed the state legislature and gathered enough signatures to put a voter initiative on the ballot; this proposed law, on the November 1922 ballot, compelled children between the ages of eight and sixteen to attend public schools. All other schools for these children would be illegal. The measure, actively supported by the Ku Klux Klan, was passed by the voters and was scheduled to become law in 1926. Other states were in the process of passing similar laws.

Roman Catholics, Episcopalians, Presbyterians, Lutherans, and others protested the Oregon law but their arguments about the rights of parents seemed to contradict the most progressive ideals of American patriotism. Supporters of the new law claimed that the public schools would preserve the nation by educating children to be true Americans; this law would prevent immigrants from bringing up their children in environments that were a threat to principles of the American government; dividing the schools would only Balkanize the nation and lead to its destruction.

In 1925 the Supreme Court listened to these convincing arguments but still ruled, unanimously, that the Oregon law was unconstitutional. Religious schools had a right to exist.

Historians can look at this episode as an example of American nativists against immigrants and Catholics, or populists against the rich (who would have the advantage of private schooling). Lawyers could find enough legal intricacies to occupy themselves indefinitely. The purple bishop, however, would have focused immediately and intensely upon one point here: compulsory homogenization. The Oregon law was plainly intended to be an instrument for making "American culture" the state religion. Individual creeds would only supplement the great worship of the nation.

Sometime in the early 1960s I got into a long conversation about religion with a gentleman who was a fervent Mason and a one-size-fits-all Protestant. In reference to my Roman Catholicism he made the following point: "Remember, you are an *American first.*" I think I responded by saying, "Huh?" or something equally brilliant. My mind went blank. Later, I began to realize that this man's priorities were indistinguishable from those of totalitarian regimes. But I did see his point. He imagined that out there in the fields of wheat or beneath flags fluttering in the wind was this great phenomenon called "American culture," a national *style* — which included everything from the ideals of democratic government to picnics on the Fourth of July, from social behavior to matters of taste. That set of values came first, and your other set of values came second. It did not occur to him that both could be parallel.

I never attended a parish school, but I did go to Catholic private schools, which usually had a lot in common with the diocesan institutions. I remember that there were moments when the "Catholic culture" in the school and the "American culture" outside had to be reconciled.

For example, we learned all about the Declaration of Independence and the Constitution of the United States, but we were also reminded that a prominent Catholic signed the former and two other Catholics signed the latter. This would counterbalance any false notions (in "American culture") that the Catholic population had contributed nothing to the early history of the nation.

In "American culture" it was commonly believed that the Middle Ages were a time of monkish superstition and ignorance; rays of light and learning supposedly did not dispel the darkness until the time of the neo-pagan Renaissance and Martin Luther's Reformation. Young Catholic students would be given an antidote to such poisonous falsifications by reading *The Thirteenth: Greatest of Centuries* (1913) by James J. Walsh — about five-hundred pages of ecstatic and uninterrupted propaganda in honor of the Catholic church's glory during the Middle Ages.[6]

In elementary school we sang all of the famous Christmas carols, the kind of music heard everywhere during the holiday season, but most of that music was rigorously excluded from the liturgy because it was Protestant in origin (or Catholic but filtered to us through Protestant sources). With very little mental effort we managed to live with the contradiction that this music (from "American culture") was simultaneously beloved yet taboo.

One widely used set of textbooks took Catholic high school students on long voyages through the great accomplishments of English literature, including Catholic contributions. These textbooks contained plays by Shakespeare. (Maybe he was a secret

Catholic. His parents certainly were Catholics.) They also contained approved poetry by the masters — and by Catholic lesser masters: "The Hound of Heaven" by Francis Thompson, "Trees" by Joyce Kilmer, and poetic efforts by a few priests and nuns whose reputation has now plunged into oblivion. There were short stories by famous authors, including a memorable one by the Catholic J. F. Powers on racial injustice. I remember a reading that made us aware of the moral dilemma of nuclear war.

A real crisis must have occurred when the editors of this voyage through English literature came to the conclusion that they could not ignore two of the supreme monuments of the English language: the King James Bible and the *Book of Common Prayer.* In those days it would have been an offense punishable by excommunication for Roman Catholics to contaminate the pages of a Catholic textbook with quotations from such documents of Protestant heresy. But, according to "American culture" and impartial opinion everywhere, these two works were masterpieces of literary style and highly influential. So the editors of this high school anthology resorted to a most peculiar compromise: A brief commentary mentioned the *literary* importance of this Protestant Bible and prayer book; then, as an "illustration" (to make the point), the textbook included a translation of the twenty-third psalm by Monsignor Ronald Knox, a twentieth-century British Roman Catholic priest. (Our teacher, Mr. Barton, drew our attention to the absurdity here.)

In 1956 my parents received a letter that notified them that I had been admitted to a Jesuit preparatory school. Tuition would be $125 per semester (an amount that was practically a gift of the Jesuits to the Catholic community). The author of the letter, the principal, ended by emphasizing the purpose of the education I would receive:

We are trying to the best of our ability to train boys for CATHOLIC Colleges. We believe that the final product of . . . [our high school] does his best work in a college which is integrated by sound Catholic Philosophy. On the contrary, we believe that the present day teachings in the majority of secular institutions, based on chaotic philosophies, defeat the purpose of our existence. Any parent who thinks that a boy who goes to a Catholic High School is by that token able to attend any secular college, shows a lack of understanding of the mental ability of the adolescent boy. To place him at the mercy of atheistic or agnostic professors at a time when his mental habits and spiritual values are just forming is unfair to him, and unnecessary, when one realizes the excellence of the Catholic colleges in the vicinity, and indeed, throughout the country. Hence, we urge you, even now, to give serious thought to the CATHOLIC College to which you wish to send your son, so that we can work together to prepare him for a future that will be blessed in all its events.

The principal was grimly serious about this. Not long after he signed the above letter, a senior (an outstanding student) applied to an Ivy League university, where he wanted to study an obscure branch of archeology — something that was not available at any Catholic institution in the nation. The principal refused to cooperate, refused to supply any letters of recommendation. Angry words were exchanged. The boy's parents retained the services of a lawyer and threatened to sue the school. Only then did the principal relent and forward the appropriate documents.

The administration of the high school did not object if a student planned to attend one of the military academies, such as West Point, or an institution that specialized in something like forestry or music, but applying for admission to an undergraduate program at a non-Catholic college or university was strenuously discouraged. The thinking was that only the most shabby sort of Catholic parent or student would be attracted to non-Catholic institutions for an undergraduate education; in such places danger lurked everywhere. The fraternities were cesspools of sexual corruption; Anti-Catholicism, the "anti-Semitism of the academic establishment," was rampant; and the whole disorderly educational process left the student confused and spiritually impoverished. (The reasoning here tended to combine truth and exaggeration.)

My high school was not unique in its attempt to segregate its graduates into Catholic institutions. Many other Catholic schools had similar policies. One member of the hierarchy whom I know about, Russell J. McVinney (bishop of Providence from 1948 to 1971), put out the word that the Catholic high schools in his diocese were to give absolutely no assistance to any student who applied to certain non-Catholic institutions (generally the places that represented the most prestigious ideals of "American culture").

Behind the concern for the spiritual welfare of youngsters there was also a concern for money. By the mid-twentieth century the religious orders were giving gainful employment to their members by running colleges and universities. They did not want to compete for "customers" with the better endowed non-Catholic institutions.

The attempt to isolate Catholic undergraduates in Catholic institutions was never a national policy of the bishops, but it was somewhat successful. Thousands of bright youngsters were guided into Catholic undergraduate schools, which grew and prospered. These institutions turned out fine lawyers, doctors, businessmen, and, in numbers beyond calculation, politicians. Yet something was missing. Where was the intelligentsia? Where were the scholars, scientists, statesmen, and writers, the sort of people who supplied the new ideas that changed the direction of history? Where were the individuals who would help to shape "American culture"? For a long time it looked as if the self-segregated Catholic institutions would produce a few, but not enough to make much of an impact.

*   *   *

"Have we any scholars?" That was the title of a provocative article published by George N. Shuster in 1925 in the Jesuit journal *America*. He did not give a reassuring answer to his question: "If we try to view Catholic academic life [in the United States] as a whole, we shall find that during the past seventy-five years it has produced not a single great literary man or writer on literary subjects" or, with a few exceptions, a scientist "who has made an original contribution." He cannot name a single historian "whose study of a definite field has resulted in a new orientation of our minds toward the past." He can think of only one important economist. "If we are honest," he continues, "we must admit that during seventy-five years of almost feverish intellectual activity we have had no influence on the great culture of America," other than some small endeavors to spread old knowledge from the past.[7]

Shuster, a devout Catholic and associate editor of the Catholic journal *Commonweal*, again examined the same issue in his book *Catholic Spirit in America* (1928).[8] In it he described some of the great cultural contributions that European Catholics have made over the centuries. He wondered why it was hard to find similar accomplishments in the United States. "Among those who are creating public consciousness in contemporary America," he wrote, "for better of worse, singularly few stand inside the pale of the Church. So limited is Catholic force in the long cordon which stretches from the sonnet to the machine-gun that if it ebbed away entirely the loss would hardly be discerned." Shuster noted that America's industrial growth "lay heavily upon Catholics. They were poor and weary, they had little time" for cultural expression. The Catholic school system — made possible by the heroic sacrifices of nuns, brothers, and priests — "has cost more than anybody can estimate," because those who worked in it had little time for intellectual development. This "tremendous enterprise of parochial education harnessed the Catholic elite to a treadmill and drank in fruitful energies like some invisible giant sponge." To make things worse, Catholic elementary and high schools were offering "a form of training different from, even isolated from, all that was being employed . . . in the world outside." These schools were not offering "opportunity for social contact of the invigorating and informing kind." All of this isolation, Shuster complained, "to a considerable extent cut Catholics off from natural participation in the general cultural development."

But that was the point of the educational system — to cut American Catholics off from the "general cultural development," which was filled with danger and all manner of implications that the church should change, like everything else.

Shuster went right to the source of the problem, to the origins of the "Catholic style" that he knew in the late 1920s: "The Catholic Church stripped bare, which one confronts in this country, is the outcome of martial conditions imposed by environment." The American church was a fortress under siege. "The leisurely, wise Old World Church," however, had developed a culture that used liturgy as a highly effective way of "educating" the laity. "In this marvelous, symmetrical blending of dogma and mystical insight, of sacrifice and prayer, charity and intelligence," there is a wholesome way to express the faith. But the quasi-military American church was putting excessive emphasis on defending the faith with cold logic, with memorized formulas from a catechism.

In 1938 another grenade of this sort was tossed into a complacent American Catholic church — a book entitled *Catholics and Scholarship: A Symposium on the Development of Scholars.*[9] An archbishop, a bishop, priests, and laymen contributed to this blunt and candid symposium whose persistent theme was, No, we still do not have enough "scholars" — the scientists, writers, professors, and so forth who would contribute something to "American culture."

Father John A. O'Brien, Ph.D., editor of this book and the principal organizer of this "symposium," wastes no time getting to the center of this issue.

> The task facing the Church in America [in 1938] is that of carrying the leaven of her social philosophy, her ethical code, her deposit of divine truth, to the hundred and ten million citizens outside the fold. The penetration of this vast zone of thought and influence... calls for a vigorous Catholic press, articulating the thought of the Church on all the stirring questions of the day. Not less does it clamor for the leadership of Catholic scholars, lay and clerical, who will point the way out of our groping confusions and disturbing dilemmas without compromise of principle.... Hence the Church's need for scholars of eminence — scholars who will win for the Church her intellectual and cultural leadership of American life.[10]

Another way of putting it: Catholicism in the United States could do little to shape "American culture" because (in 1938) it lacked intellectual clout. In Father O'Brien's opinion, "To great masses of people we are still the hewers of wood and drawers of water — just a step higher in the intellectual scale than the Salvation Army."[11] He intimates that it is hard to convert people when they have a low opinion of the church's intellectual life.

O'Brien cites statistics. He refers to studies (from the 1920s) that showed that only a relatively small number of the people listed in *Who's Who* or *American Men of Science* identified themselves as Roman Catholics. He examines data from state universities. In O'Brien's home state of Illinois, for example, there were over two million Catholics, one-fifth of the population. Yet, at the University of Illinois, out of an instructional and research staff of 1,101 there were, by O'Brien's calculation, only 34 Catholics. "Instead of one out of five, it is one out of 32." This was not because of rampant anti-Catholicism on campus or because of compulsory attendance at interdenominational Protestant chapel services (as was the case in the nineteenth century). In O'Brien's analysis, the reason why a Catholic presence was so small on the state university's faculty was "Catholic aloofness" — an almost aristocratic indifference to the whole enterprise. "We seem," O'Brien writes, "to have a rare genius for aloofness from the public tax-supported institutions which are so largely directing scholarly thought in America." He warns that this policy (this "style") of "isolation and aloofness . . . has cost us dearly in prestige, in influence upon scholarship and in public opinion."[12]

Bitter words and, as one contributor to this symposium/book observes, not quite the truth. But perhaps O'Brien could be excused for a little bitterness, expressed in overstatement. He had scars and bruises from his years of battle to get an isolated and aloof American Catholicism interested in public-supported universities.

In the 1920s O'Brien had worked tirelessly to form what he called a Catholic Foundation at the University of Illinois — a place where Catholic students could come together and perhaps even take religion courses that could count toward their degree.[13] He wrote strongly worded articles and pamphlets to raise money for the foundation. (Much of what he says in *Catholics and Scholarship* is based on his writings from the 1920s.) A number of bishops supported the project — it was similar to the "Newman clubs" for Catholic students at other secular campuses — and the university's administration was unfailingly helpful, but there were many in the church who thought that a "Catholic presence" on the campus of a nonsectarian state institution was a damnable proposition, a flagrant act of disloyalty. The National Catholic Educational Association was extremely hostile to O'Brien's plans and at its annual meeting in 1926 passed a resolution declaring that attendance of a Catholic student at a non-Catholic institution was "not at all desirable, but at most tolerated." The Jesuits, even more hostile, took every opportunity to condemn O'Brien's Catholic Foundation and what was seen as his attempt to lure students away from Catholic colleges and universities. In the pages of *America* and other forums, one Jesuit after another vividly denounced the whole concept of Catholic students submitting themselves to the evils of a non-Catholic university, where education consisted of mere information separated from spiritual values. Archbishop Michael J. Curley of Baltimore joined in the condemnation of the Illinois project; so did prominent Catholic laymen.

It is important to remember the "context" here. At that time, public education could be an emotional issue among many Catholics. In the 1920s some state legislatures were trying to force all children into public schools and, in effect, shut down parochial schools. As far as many Catholics were concerned, this attempt to enforce educational uniformity proved that "public school" meant the same thing as "anti-Catholic school"; the purpose of these institutions was to destroy Catholic identity by submerging it in a generalized "American culture." Monsignor Matthew Smith, a contributor to *Catholics and Scholarship*, described just how emotional this issue could become: "Catholic parents sometimes denied a higher education to their children because of carrying the virtue of faith to an extreme limit that, occasionally at least, made it cease to be a virtue. If a Catholic school was not available, they often denied their children other schooling."[14] And then, in this "context" of anger and suspicion, O'Brien was proposing to set up a "Catholic presence" at a public university, right in the belly of the beast.

O'Brien — vilified in the Catholic press, considered by some to be a traitor to his church — had made "diplomatic" errors that only increased the furor surrounding his plans. In all of his published works, going back to the 1920s, he may have praised Catholic colleges and universities, but he did not give them a prominent place in his grand vision of a future dominated by state universities; like all the great fundraisers of history, he exaggerated; and he could sound arrogant. But, whatever his faults, he knew what had to be done and he eventually saw his dream become a reality.

In 1928 a large chapel for Catholic students at the University of Illinois was dedicated; bishops and clergy representing the dioceses of Illinois attended. Within a year, the rest of the complex, now called the Newman Foundation, was ready for use: an auditorium, dormitory, dining room, reading rooms, and social center for Catholic students. The facilities are considered to be the most impressive of any "Newman club" in the nation.

A few years later the apostolic delegate, the pope's ambassador to the church in the United States, visited the new buildings for Catholic students at the University of Illinois and had nothing but praise for the whole undertaking. He hoped that similar Newman Foundations would be opened at every state university across the nation.

Controversy? What controversy?

CONTRADICTIONS

More intellectual grenades would be lobbed into the educational division of the American Catholic church. Monsignor John Tracy Ellis in 1955,[15] Thomas F. O'Dea in 1958,[16] and others would stun Catholic audiences with the bad news that the American church's intellectual life was not a brilliant beacon upon the landscape. "Outsiders" and "insiders" (like Ellis, a priest) were observing the obvious: that something was wrong when an organization with so many people was producing so few illustrious "intellectuals" with a national reputation. Why was there so much intellectual, theological, and even artistic ferment in European Catholicism and, by comparison, relatively little going on in the United States?

Much blame was heaped upon anti-intellectualism and stultifying traditions brought over from the peasant societies of Europe. Relatively little attention was given to another factor: a behavioral "style" based on self-segregation and aloofness.

"Mr. Day, please permit me to stop you at this point. It seems that you are just picking at old scabs. Get to your point. What are you trying to say?"

I am trying to bring the reader back to a "style," a "mood" that characterized American Catholicism before Vatican II. That "style" — which showed itself in education, politics, the liturgical arts, and a whole way of life — was full of contradictions. For example: The American church, true to its best missionary instincts, wanted to reach into the modern world and become its inspiration (spiritually, intellectually), but it also behaved as if it wanted to retreat into a large, self-sufficient ghetto, an enclave quarantined from the rest of the world, with separate schools. The church was unsurpassed in its serenity and confidence, but it was also angry, throbbing with resentments — a huge Anti-

Defamation League. It spoke haughtily of its great intellectual traditions, its liturgical traditions (which included great art, architecture, and music) — all symbols of an unchanging spiritual tradition — but, after a visit to the local parish or Catholic college, it was often hard to believe that the American church was the heir to those vanished glories. American Catholicism was bulging with confidence in its own accomplishments, but just one furtive glance at the "outside world" (perhaps a powerhouse nonsectarian university or Protestant biblical scholarship or what some Protestants were doing with the liturgical arts) proved that the church was really not at the top of the heap in all things. Roman Catholics were supremely patriotic and all-American, but they feared (with some justification) attempts to "Americanize" their children through non-Catholic schooling.

Underneath the "style" of aloof imperturbability those contradictions were causing discomfort, yet it was considered slightly treasonous to mention them, *because Granny was watching.* With her over there — disapproving and just waiting for the Catholic church to make a fool of itself, to lose face by admitting a mistake — no loyal Catholic would concede for an instant that something needed to be improved (changed). An even higher degree of loyalty required a form of contemptuous secession from a world gone mad with change.

SEPARATE BUT WEIRD

About a year before I heard the purple bishop blast away at the concept of change, I visited a new Catholic church in the suburbs. But was it a church or an "attitude," expressed in building material?

The structure was almost crushing in its ugliness. Neither traditional nor modern, it seemed to enclose a space that was large and unsure of its identity. In what looked like a clumsy, last-minute attempt to hide the ugliness, slabs of marble had been affixed to some of the walls; marble statues (one of them enormous) were placed here and there.

Parishioners heard liturgical music at just one of the six or seven Masses in this church on Sunday; like the building's architecture, the music was not really "traditional" or "modern" but in a style that could be described as "neither here nor there." Usually, an organist just played what sounded like unarticulated vibrations as a soothing background noise; sometimes a soloist sang. There was no real choir and no attempt to bring the musical talents of the parochial school children into the church.

The distinctive feature about all the Sunday Masses was their speed, which could be measured only by a stopwatch. (The pastor and his staff had no choice. Thousands of people had to be processed in the church every Sunday morning.)

Just a few minutes of looking at the interior of that new church gave me the strange feeling of being in the presence of something inexpressibly weird — the same feeling that would hit me years later when I attended that "relevant" liturgical "experience" in a cathedral. (I describe it in the Preface of this book.) The building had cost a fortune to construct. It had so many chunks of incongruous marble decorations and statues that it looked like an indoor cemetery. It was expensive, lavish, and yet the basic construction was cheap looking — a strange combination of gymnasium architecture and pretentious marble *appliqué.* It contained many things to look at, and yet all the separate things, taken as a whole, had no character, no style.

This building, and the kind of worship conducted in it, offered documentary proof that a large portion of American Catholicism, just before Vatican II, had separated itself not only from "American culture," Modernism, public schools, non-Catholic colleges and universities, the changeable world, and other spiritual dangers but also from the church's very own roots in cultural history. In a sense, the building, which was not traditional or modern or a synthesis of both, was also not even Catholic. I explain in the following paragraphs.

Decades before the plans for that weird church took shape, there were many Catholic bishops and pastors who tried to build churches that suggested acquiescence to the canons of taste or the logic of a particular style; in some cases they even hired a fine architect or artistic consultant to help with the planning. The result may have been a marvel to behold or just a useful space or a visual junkyard, but at least there was an attempt to show that God's goodness could be an inspiration for human endeavors, even for a good building. In contrast, the pastor who built the weird church and the archdiocesan building commission that supervised him did not have to worry about the inspiration of God's goodness or enduring artistic values or Catholic "History" looking over their shoulders. After all, the secular world had assured them that such ideas were finished — hopelessly old fashioned and meaningless to modern people (*circa* 1960). Scientifically trained architects — those cultural pioneers who were going to improve the human race with brutally functional buildings — had convinced thousands of admirers that architectural traditions and the quaint notions about a "sacred" art were dead.

Thanks to these developments in modern architecture, as well as art, the clergy who made the decisions about the look of that weird church would not be burdened by any anxieties about measuring up to the church's artistic past. They saw themselves as free, independent agents — pioneers bringing a new spirit of Christianity to new suburban territory. They had left the liturgical arts back in the big city, where the museums were. They were very proud of being *contemporary* Catholics, who had gone beyond the use of mere "art" in church and progressed into a more modern form of Christianity. They described themselves as conservative but their attitude toward the church's historical understanding of liturgy and the arts in church was quite radical; in a sense, they were "anti-Catholic" secessionists who were breaking with their past.

Yes, to be sure, the faith could be found in that weird church — in cement underneath the foundations, in the catechism answers parroted by children in the parish school, in the quiet piety of the priests and parishioners. But this new brand of "contemporary" Catholicism had no artistic beliefs to follow — no artistic "faith." By the early 1960s, aloof "contemporary" Catholicism (American-style) had, to a very large extent, cut itself off from the liturgical arts. Rising construction costs and the pressures of supporting a large school system had convinced many Catholics that the arts for a church did not exist any more, at least for them. Of course, American Catholics remembered bits and pieces of their artistic heritage — polished marble surfaces, gold vestments, stained glass, a few Latin songs, and other "Catholic decorations" — but, when it came to the question of how those bits and pieces would fit into a unified statement of faith, many of them had become agnostics.

Here was the problem: The arts (architecture, sculpture, music, and so forth) depend on a ruling sense of coherence to make them beautiful and to justify their presence in church. This artistic coherence accounts for part of the "power" we see in a Renaissance portrait and a twentieth-century canvas by Picasso, in Gothic stained glass and rural churches made out of wood, in a Gobelin tapestry and a patchwork quilt. Gifted, trained "artists" (and this includes architects and musicians) possess the key to this coherence. (Does the artistic logic mirror a theological logic concerning the meaning of life?) Over the centuries, the church had worked with "artists" to produce liturgical arts that could somehow communicate a sense of prayer to the faithful — with pleasing architectural proportions, with traditional designs that had withstood the test of time, but also with modern innovation. In the best examples of church art (something simple or magnificent) you will always find a disciplined coherence, the impression that the "artist" — just like the priest and loyal parishioner — has happily submitted to the rules of a "higher authority." (In the case of the "artist," the rules happen to be the coherence of a style.)

This working arrangement between church and artist was on the way to extinction about the same time the weird church was being built. Modern artists and composers were isolating themselves from the needs and tastes of ordinary people. Roman Catholicism was isolating itself from the dangers of the modern world and from those practitioners of cultural change, those disciplinarians of coherence: talented "artists." In places where an aloof clergy and laity had little to do with knowledgeable "artists," the church building and the art and music in it often appeared to be the result of one *impulsive* decision after another (artistic items chosen, on a whim, from the catalogue of a church decorating company, songs chosen not because they related to the liturgy but because they sounded nice). If an artistic "faith" is dead, if impulsiveness is all that matters in the choice of church art, the way is open and clear for that quick-fix of the emotions, that delight of self-centered and cynical types: sentimentality.

The weird church in the suburbs may have had no style whatsoever (i.e., no coherence), but there was a deliberate program of kitsch sentimentality behind everything. The parishioner was supposed to encounter lovely detached items — a marble surface or a statue or a sentimental hymn — and respond by thinking, "Aw! How pretty." (In television situation comedies, a technician can press a button and produce canned laughter. There must be another button to play what sounds like a canned "Aw" from the audience — when, for example, the little girl, age three, appears on the set in her new gingham dress and bow in her hair and says sweetly to her father, "Hawoe, Daddy." Audience: "Aw.") The weird church was a building dedicated to the "Aw" response.

If a good, conscientious architect had designed this church, he or she would have made sure that the parishioners encountered something nobler, something higher than the low "Aw" reaction (and the building might have cost less). If the music director at the weird church had been someone with good musical training and sensitivity for the church's liturgical needs, he or she would have helped to give the parish a kind of musical expression that was more profound and more coherent than the ragged assortment of sentimental "Aw" songs that dominated the repertory (e.g., "Mother, at Your Feet Is Kneeling"). But, in those days, many Catholics kept aloof from "artists," or anybody else who would take away delicious sentimentality and replace it with something more coherent, more disciplined.

*   *   *

An imaginary incident about the planning of that weird suburban church, back in the late 1950s: An informal building committee, which consists of the pastor, other priests, and a couple of contractors, is meeting to look at possible options for the new church. An idealistic curate appears before the group. He shows them some photographs of modernistic churches built in France and Germany after World War II — bold, "original" structures, yet somehow part of a long traditional continuum. He mentions that most of these new churches, with their emphasis on simplicity, were not that expensive to build. He stresses that the new parish church should be constructed with musical needs in mind because, someday, congregations will sing more parts of the High Mass. (He shows the group some publications with chants and hymns for the congregation to sing at Mass.) He describes something called Liturgical Renewal; he predicts that it and the liturgical arts will flourish together.

Later that day the pastor calls the archdiocesan chancery. The following week the curate is reassigned to a new rectory, which is really an igloo very close to the Arctic circle. *End of imaginary incident, Part I.*

That poor, naive curate. The man did not realize that the committee was incapable of even listening to his gentle enthusiasms. Where he saw the possibility of deepening the awareness of the faithful by using the best liturgical traditions of Catholicism, the beauty of holiness, and the holiness of beauty, the committee only saw Granny. This was their reasoning, which I put in quotation marks: "Protestants build distinctive new churches as a form of advertising, to get members; Episcopalians, Lutherans, and other denominations have to fill up their services with fancy singing, choral and congregational, because they do not have the Blessed Sacrament. Maybe a few generations ago Catholics did that sort of thing, but we modern American Catholics have broken away from such wasteful extravagance. We can't imitate Granny's high-class cultural values; we can't insult our suburban, proletarian parishioners with things that appeal only to intellectuals, artists, and old-fashioned Catholics."

That was certainly not the reasoning everywhere, but, as I recall, it was the direction of the prevailing winds.

On January 25, 1959, Pope John XXIII made the completely unexpected announcement that he was calling an Ecumenical Council. But why? There was nothing that needed to be discussed or changed. Perfection does not need improvement.

A continuation of an imaginary incident, or Part II: In 1964, after a long ride on dog-sled, through a blizzard, the naive curate arrives at the post office and picks up his mail, which includes a copy of Vatican II's Constitution on the Sacred Liturgy. He reads it right there, beginning to end — and he is stunned, overjoyed, vindicated. Now, please be assured that he does not begin to daydream about a great High Church revival, with basilicas all across the landscape and picturesque ceremonies amid clouds of incense. Rather, he recognizes that this document, among many other things, invites the majority of American Catholic parishes to rejoin the family, to worship like Catholics once again, without feeling guilty about it. He concedes a point: In the weird suburban church and others like it, they worshiped like Catholics; they always scrupulously observed the letter of liturgical law, but the spirit behind that law had been lost somewhere in the pile of bills for the parochial school. And now all of that would change, he reassured himself. Heaven be praised!

At the very moment the naive curate is reading the Constitution on the Sacred Liturgy for the first time, a copy of the same document is passed around the rectory next to the weird church, that architectural freak in suburbia. The document causes bewilderment, but there is a sense of relief when someone explains as follows: The constitution is really a repudiation of the church's liturgical past. The church, which will never change, is in the process of scraping away all the artistic and ceremonial barnacles — *changes* — that have attached themselves to the Mass and almost obscured its meaning. These useless disfigurements, largely European in origin, were for the sort of people who go to museums (i.e., Granny). It is now permissible to replace this foreign style of worship with something more like our own "American culture." The isolation and aloofness are over; we can come out of the bomb shelter now and, when it comes to worship, behave just like everybody else.

A DIGRESSION

It would be misleading to continue with a discussion of how this Catholic "style" *before* Vatican II evolved into its *after* form without first tieing up some loose ends:

Loose End #1: Statistics cited by Father John A. O'Brien in *Catholics and Scholarship* did indeed seem to show that, during the 1920s, relatively few people who identified themselves as Catholic were in the upper echelons of business, science, and education. When some Catholics were wringing their hands over these statistics, I wonder if they ever noticed the relatively low representation of women and nonwhites on various lists of accomplishment or the virtual exclusion of Jews from important teaching positions in so many colleges and universities.

Loose End #2: In 1977 Andrew Greeley published *The American Catholic: A Social Portrait* — a thorough statistical analysis of the Catholic population of the United States. He and his colleagues at the National Opinion Research Center discovered that, on average, Catholics in the United States, by 1977, were doing very well financially; in fact, the statistics for non-Spanish-speaking whites showed that Catholics were earning more money than other Christians. The educational mobility of Catholics was second only to Jews. At elite colleges and universities, there were many more professors who had been "raised as Catholics" than in the past.

The statistics show that there has been an immense change in the character and culture of the American Catholic population (broadly defined). Just in the areas of economics, education, and social standing, the Catholic population had made considerable "improvements" between, let us say, 1925 and 1975. Catholicism is still the religion of the poor, middle class, and rich; it still has its intellectuals, anti-intellectuals, and more ethnic groups than it can keep track of, but its adherents (and its former adherents) are now more fully integrated into American society: top to bottom, successes and failures. Perhaps part of this American success story could be attributed to the unprecedented educational opportunities offered to veterans after World War II. Perhaps the ambitions of "immigrant overachievers" (and their children) had something to do with this. Perhaps Catholic schools and institutions of higher learning contributed a great deal to this general "improvement."

By coincidence, the dividing line between the "old" church and the sociologically "improved" one appears to coincide with the Second Vatican Council and its aftershocks. For this reason, many American Catholics now have developed a tendency to see the era of the "old" church — with its pre–Vatican II "style" — as a time of immigrant alienation in a strange and suspicious new environment. The "improved" Catholic does not always know what to do with the heritage from this "unimproved" church — including the arts connected with worship (architecture, art, and music).

A hundred years from now, another researcher will put together a large statistical/sociological profile of the Catholic church in the United States, and it will again show enormous change. The figures will most certainly go up, as well as down.

Loose End #3: In the newspapers you will now find the names of all sorts of Catholics — within the pale of the church or just a few paces outside of it — who are vibrantly "creating public consciousness in contemporary America" (something that George N. Shuster could not find in the 1920s). They are in politics, business, literature, film, communications, education, entertainment, law, criminal enterprises, and so forth. Of course, the "public consciousness" created is sometimes quite distant from orthodox Catholic dogma and values.

In the same newspapers and in library catalogues you will find the names of influential American Catholic "alumni and alumnae" — ex-Catholics, Catholics on an extended leave of absence, and fallen-away but never quite fallen-off Catholics who have all made significant contributions to "American culture." Without their experience in the church — benign or malignant — many of them would have turned out to be quite dull people.

Loose End #4: Parochial schools in big cities, especially the inner-city, are a huge success. They offer hope and a chance for advancement to thousands of youngsters from poor families, and in many cases these students are not Catholic. These schools do a much better job than some nearby public institutions in promoting the virtues and values of "American culture." A hundred years ago, who would have ever predicted that?[17]

Loose End #5: In 1969 I was enjoying a friendly lunch with a group of foreign students. For some reason, the conversation turned to the matter of science: how important it was and how it was influencing the whole world. Then, suddenly, without warning, an African student broke into the discussion with a conversational karate chop: "You white people and your science!" he said with barely controlled anger, "You think science is so great and it belongs to you. Well, all of it, the whole thing, was invented by St. Augustine, who was a black man."

Lunch resumed quietly.

The African student and I came from different parts of the world and different cultures, but I recognized something familiar in him, an attitude I remembered from my past: that "style" of Catholic resentment disguised as aloofness, that feeling of being an outsider watching people, another "kind" of people, having fun at the biggest party in town. Anybody can walk into the party but you are afraid, with good reason, that you might be treated rudely, or maybe you will not know how to act and thereby suffer a lowering of your self-esteem. And so, to save your tender pride, you affect aloofness, you segregate yourself, and you pretend that your ancestors had really invented the party centuries ago.

Many colleges and universities now provide separate "ethnic theme" dormitories for African-American students or other groups; there may also be separate territories in dining rooms for African-American students, separate student activities, and even separate graduation ceremonies. This policy of self-segregation only reflects a segregation that is inserted into the curriculum: separate courses that extoll the accomplishments of Africans and African-Americans, separate departments, and separate faculty. In a few cities there are special tax-supported academies that emphasize an African-American curriculum and black achievements. There is talk about setting up separate black colleges within state universities. African-American Catholics are now demanding that the Vatican give them their own rite, bishops, and dioceses.

Anyone for a game of *déjà vu*?

In the nineteenth century, German-speaking Catholics in the United States were demanding the right to have their own bishops and parochial schools where instruction would be largely in German. Well into the twentieth century some Polish parishes supported an educational system (right up through high school) that preserved the Polish language and emphasized the glories of Polish culture. In Catholic schools where Irish Catholics predominated, students might just get the impression, from the way the curriculum was taught, that God really did make the Irish Number One.

People cannot live as abstractions. Usually they want to identify themselves with the specifics of a tribe and all the wonderful things that the tribe has accomplished. (The "tribe" could even be atheists or "free spirits" or whatever.) Sometimes people of one tribe do not want to be absorbed into another tribe, which is perhaps bigger or enjoys a higher standing in the community, because the assimilation process involves a painful renunciation of a personal identity shaped in a tribal past.

"Ethnic Catholics" in the United States were fighting ugly battles with their church over this same problem — tribal identity versus assimilation — for well over a hundred years. The compromise was the separate but equal national parish for the "ethnics" who wanted to keep their own religious culture and heritage alive. A regular American (i.e., predominantly Irish) Catholic parish would be on one corner and maybe right across the street would be the Catholic parish for the Germans or Poles or some other nationality. Then, over and above this, there was the whole network of Catholic colleges and universities, enclaves of separation, where "Catholic pride" was taught.

Angry African-Americans, Latino-Americans, radical feminists, and so many other separatist groups should take some time away from their identity studies and learn lessons from American Catholicism's own experience with self-segregation and an early form of multiculturalism — an experience that may have been fundamentally healthy but that easily slipped into sickness. By the time of Vatican II, American Catholicism's version of ethnic/religious studies was in danger of becoming a form of stroking. The aloofness was leading to delusions of grandeur. The segregation-by-choice meant isolation from important networks of power and influence. Catholic self-esteem was in great shape, but only as long as the church could pretend that the outside world and its culture really did not exist.

Years ago, the Irish immigrant, right off the boat, could blame anti-Catholicism if he could not get certain kinds of jobs. After all, there were signs in front of some businesses that read, "Irish need not apply." But if the lightbulb burned out, he could also comfort himself by blaming that, too, on anti-Catholicism. Nothing was his fault; and his church — aloof, proud, self-segregated, not about to change by assimilation — assured him that he was right and the rest of the world, largely anti-Catholic, was wrong.

I get the feeling that "I have seen this movie before" when I hear African-American leaders blame racism for everything from urban riots to lightbulbs that burn out. Yes, indeed, racism, both in vile and subtle forms, exists, and blacks still suffer the cruel consequences of a racism that has persisted for hundreds of years. All of that is absolutely certain, but I must confess that, when I hear these spastic invocations of racism (or sexism) as the cause of any and all evils in the world, I sometimes close my eyes and see, once again, that purple bishop ranting against change. The message is the same: everything wrong in society is somebody else's fault; the whole world has to change, but not us. *Mutatis mutandis*, the purple bishop was American Catholicism's version of a Malcolm X.

Students at a prominent Catholic university used to be able to take an elective course called something like "Great Catholic Novelists" (all of them European). Then, sometime in the 1960s, many in the Catholic laity changed their minds about this type of ethnic/religious knowledge. They began to murmur thus: Look at John F. Kennedy; his rise to prominence was made easier because he was not "limited" by the constant defensiveness of a Catholic education; he probably studied the great novelists, not just the Catholic ones; let us do likewise.

Students at innumerable colleges and universities can now take courses in Great African-American Literature, under various titles. But someday there will be murmurings within the black community, complaints that you really cannot bring that kind of soft currency to the bank, or at least not a lot of it. The world recognizes the hard currency of great novels, especially the classics that have not lost a cent in value over the years — books by men and women of all races and creeds.

The bank will usually accept the gold-backed currency of knowledge about medicine, science, engineering, computers, social science, the fine arts, and so forth, but everything else — for example, constant reminders that Louis Pasteur was a Catholic or constant assertions that Egypt (an African land) is the only real source of civilization worth studying — is loose change. Knowledge ("pure" and as "objective" as possible) is power. Knowledge of authentic cultural "roots" is helpful for inner strength and self-esteem. Knowledge corrupted as dishonest religious or ethnic propaganda is a form of thumbsucking.

BEFORE AND AFTER

Granny disappeared! (Well, sort of.) It happened sometime in the 1960s. She is certainly alive somewhere and the Anti-Defamation League still has much work to do, but she is weaker and in hiding. Ecumenism had a great deal to do with her (partial) disappearance; so did the vast increase in the information that we now have on one another. (It is hard to demonize your neighbor's church when the media report daily on just how imperfect your own church really is.)

Soon after Granny became a missing person, the purple bishop began to sweeten up; his speeches and sermons lost some of their stridency. It was as if he had been walking around all his life with a pebble in his shoe and, when Granny disappeared, the pebble also disappeared. At about this same time, priests began to leave the active ministry by the hundreds, fewer seminarians were preparing for ordination, nuns were quitting, parochial schools were closing every day — in part because Granny was staying out of sight; the danger had diminished and the religious tribe no longer needed a phalanx of professional protectors.

I realized just how much things had changed (sweetened up) when the alumni bulletin from my Jesuit high school began to list, with pride, the numbers of students who had been admitted to Harvard, Yale, Princeton, and other top nonsectarian institutions. (Outstanding Catholic colleges and universities were also on the list.) The angry separatism was over; the rush to become assimilated had begun.

I belong to what I call the Contingent of Before and After Catholics, people who have experienced the pre- and post–Vatican II church. We have many stories to tell about before-and-after changes — not necessarily "technical" changes, such as a repositioning of the altar in churches, but a whole new set of attitudes about Catholicism's idea of itself and its "assimilation" with the world around it. Here are just a few very instructive before-and-after stories about the Catholic "style" (U.S.A.), about an institution that will never change being shaken by change, down to its foundations:

Before: "How Catholic are America's Catholic Colleges?" In 1992, a senior at Holy Cross College, a Jesuit institution, asked that question in an article published in a conservative journal.[18] The article contains the following description of the Theology Department at Holy Cross, as found in the 1960 course catalogue: "[The purpose of the study of theology is to] make each student alive to the fact that Catholicism is not merely a Creed but a culture; that the study of theology is not merely an intellectual discipline, but the charting of a way of life, a program; that the appended courses outline not merely semester hours, but italicize an attitude towards life as a whole."

After: Thirty years later, the course catalogue at the same institution describes the Religious Studies Department (formerly the Theology Department) as follows: "Since Holy Cross is a Jesuit college and the majority of its students come from the Roman Catholic tradition the department believes it is necessary to provide them with an opportunity to know and understand this tradition as well as to situate it in the larger context of other religious traditions and in the broader cultural context in which they live."

The student who writes this article on Catholic colleges goes on to complain that Holy Cross now offers politicized courses in feminist theology and liberation theology instead of Catholic theology (which is now called a "tradition," rather than a way of life or "culture"); students can even fulfill a requirement in Religious Studies by taking a course like "Aboriginal Religions."

Holy Cross may not offer the same total immersion in Catholic dogma and culture as it once did but it is now, by any academic measurement, one of the best colleges in the nation; it has a far more impressive academic reputation than it had in 1960.[19] It slips in Catholic "values" where it can. If Holy Cross and other Catholic colleges and universities ever decide to go back to their 1960 curricula, a career-conscious laity would shun them; these schools would soon be out of business.

Before: In the 1920s, the Ku Klux Klan had made its presence felt in the area around the University of Illinois. Cross burnings and parades were a way of showing that blacks, Jews, and Catholics were not welcome in that part of the country. This was one of the reasons why Father John A. O'Brien wanted to establish a Newman Foundation at the university and show that Catholics had a perfect right to be there.

After: In 1986, for the first time in its history, the Klan elected a Northerner as its Imperial Wizard, a man from Connecticut who says he is a Roman Catholic.[20] Roman Catholics are now welcome to join the Ku Klux Klan, according to a Klan leader in Colorado (and an ex-Catholic himself). "This isn't the 20's," he says.[21]

Assimilation victorious!

Before: Nineteenth-century Catholic bishops shouted themselves hoarse in their denunciations of public schools that made Catholic children listen to Protestant prayers and readings from the King James Bible. And they would certainly not let any of their priests offer wishy-washy, nondenominational invocations to some nondenominational deity at a public school graduation ceremony.

After: Bishops sharply criticize courts for decreeing that public schools should not force children to listen to prayers or Bible readings. This is a country founded on Judeo-Christian principles, bishops say. (But neither the Declaration of Independence nor the Constitution makes any reference to a Jewish or Christian heritage.)

This issue would take on a whole new character if an area of the nation became predominantly Moslem and the local school board decided that the school day should begin with the students facing Mecca and saying: "There is no God but Allah, and Mohammed is His prophet."

Before: A university professor at an Ivy League institution told me that sometime in the 1950s he was teaching a music history course about the composer Johann Sebastian Bach. He happened to mention that Bach was a Lutheran and that one of his sons, Johann Christian, converted to Roman Catholicism and became a priest. "I suppose," he said to his class as an aside, "this made Johann Christian the black sheep of the family." A day later he received a stinging letter from someone in the Newman club, the association for Catholic students on campus. He was rebuked for this outrageous slur against the Catholic church. (Very tense times. A criticism of anything remotely connected with the Catholic church, no matter how reasonable, would not be tolerated. Anything perceived as an insult to the majesty of the institution might bring out the picketers.)

After: A man who looks just like Pope John Paul II is a guest on the "Tonight Show." Dressed in white pontifical robes, he smiles and makes appropriate gestures of pontifical kindliness, but he does not utter a word. The audience laughs. No angry protests. No pickets.

Before: In 1903 there was one Roman Catholic priest for every 871 Catholics in the United States. In the 1920s and '30s the number of priests serving the Catholic community grew substantially until the year 1942, when there was a ratio of one priest for every 617 Catholics. After 1942, however, the curve on the chart turns downward. More priests would be ordained but not enough to keep up with the expanding Catholic population, which would grow 90 percent between 1942 and 1962. When the bishops from the United States were in Rome for Vatican II, they may have had in the back of their minds the reality of worsening ratios (1/617 in 1942, down to 1/771 in 1962).[22] In addition, the "ratio statistics" for religious sisters were not good: one sister for every 188 Catholics in 1952, down to one for every 247 in 1962). The parochial school system was also on a downward curve; it may have been expanding triumphantly when Vatican II was in session, but a closer look at the statistics shows that the proportion of Catholic youngsters attending these schools had been steadily declining since the 1930s.[23]

After: More of the same, only worse. Perhaps the Second Vatican Council just accelerated changes that were well under way even before Pope John XXIII called the council together.

* * *

A few years ago, a friend of mine told me about the time he was having a conversation with his son. My friend, who considered himself a staunch Catholic, was speechless for a moment when his son, age thirteen, said in honest confusion, "Daddy, what religion are we? Catholic or Protestant or Lutheran?" The boy had attended public, private, and (for a year) Catholic schools. Most of his friends were Catholic. He faithfully attended his parish's religion classes offered for youngsters. He attended Mass weekly. Along the way he was picking up the facts and formulas of the Catholic faith, but all of that was being presented in a *cultural* ambiance that resembled "American culture" at its most bland. The parish churches he had known — in architecture, song, and "style" — looked like every other church in town. (Yes, there was the matter of abortion, which separated Catholicism from many other churches, but that always seemed to come across as a *political* issue involving the intimidation or election of certain politicians.)

My friend explained to his son that, according to old and orthodox Catholic dogma, the peoples of the world can get into heaven, regardless of their religion, as long as they follow the best dictates of their conscience. Then he went on to describe the Catholic church as the authentic perpetuation of faith in Jesus Christ.

The boy listened to all this. He knew what his father was saying; his religion teachers had certainly instructed him in the dogmatic workings of his faith and about good works as a sign of good Christianity. But, unlike a boy of 1650 or 1950, he had very few "tangible" cultural symbols — matters of style — to show him that his church differed from others.

This is a book about Roman Catholicism's change since Vatican II, with emphasis on change in its liturgical life and in the United States. The Latin Mass, church art, and church music — cultural symbols and the topics of the following chapters — may not shape the destiny of the human race in the future but they are useful as "windows"; they allow us to look through them and see how a whole complex of seemingly disconnected details fits together. At the same time, looking through these "windows" is a little embarrassing — like watching a domestic dispute in the neighbors' house through their dining room window. In this case we are observing contemporary Catholicism have a furious argument with itself over these questions: "What were we?" and "Where do we go from here?"

Chapter Two

THE LATE LATIN MASS
Abolished Forever

METEOROLOGISTS SHOULD INVESTIGATE a very bizarre phenomenon: During a polite, ordinary conversation among a group of Catholics, someone casually slips in two words, "Latin Mass." Suddenly, there is a chill in the room. The barometer falls. Negative and positive charges begin to gather in the air. You can almost feel the tension and uncertainty forming. Some older Catholics will sigh wistfully about the inexpressible beauties of a Latin liturgy they attended in a monastery long ago. But that drift of the conversation will be quickly halted by someone who, with cold reasoning, denounces the utter wickedness of worship in Latin. The church, this person will righteously assert, was wrong to use Latin in the first place (for approximately one thousand and six hundred years) and, besides, the Second Vatican Council abolished it forever.

Thundershowers. High winds. Run for cover.

The Latin Mass is a very touchy topic, and the controversy it sparks tells us a great deal about the mood of Catholicism in the United States today. In fact, it is impossible to gain any real understanding of what has happened to the church in recent decades without first examining the strange fate of something that Catholics, well into the 1960s, considered to be as normal and as self-evident as the pope: worship in a dead language.

One place to find information on this subject is the newsletter of the Latin Liturgy Association (LLA) of the United States. I should add immediately that the LLA is a worthy, thoughtful Roman Catholic organization that promotes the use of Latin in the liturgy; it is fully in accord with the work of Vatican II, and some bishops are included among its members. The LLA's newsletter is well-written, informative, politically neutral, and sometimes witty. With that said, it should nevertheless be noted that this association's dignified newsletter sometimes has to report on matters that resemble a very undignified brawl.[1]

The brawl over Latin (at least in the United States) looks something like this. On one side of this fight we have the LLA and all those who would like more opportunities for Masses celebrated in Latin — according to the Rite of Paul VI (the "new" Mass, which the Vatican mandated in 1969) or according to its "old" form (the so-called Tridentine Mass, which the Vatican wanted to abolish totally in 1969). The supporters of Latin start at the beginning. They note that Jesus, whose native language was Aramaic, saw nothing wrong with worship in Hebrew, a dead, priestly language in his lifetime. They point out that words in Latin were attached to the cross at the crucifixion. They bring our attention to the continuing presence of this "dead" language in modern English: in the thousands of words that come from Latin roots and in the very letters of the alphabet we use. (All the letters on this page come from the Latin alphabet or evolved from it.) They quote from sections of the Second Vatican Council's Constitution on the Sacred Liturgy, which command that the Latin language and music in Latin shall continue to be used in the liturgy, along with vernacular languages:

Article 36: Particular law remaining in force, the use of the Latin language is to be preserved in the Latin rites.

Article 54: Steps should be taken so that the faithful may also be able to say or sing together in Latin those parts of the Ordinary of the Mass which pertain to them.

Article 114: The treasure of sacred music [in Latin] is to be preserved and fostered with very great care.

Article 116: The Church acknowledges [Latin] Gregorian Chant as proper to the Roman Liturgy. Therefore, other things being equal, it should be given pride of place in liturgical services. [In Article 117 the council orders the publication of more chant books, including one with simpler music for smaller churches.]

The Council Fathers bolstered the position of Latin in the Decree on Priestly Formation (Article 13): Seminarians "should acquire a command of Latin which will enable them to understand and use the source material of so many sciences, and the documents of the Church as well. The study of the liturgical language proper to each rite is to be regarded as necessary."

Xavier Rynne — the pseudonym for Francis X. Murphy, a Redemptorist priest — "infiltrated" the council and wrote behind-the-scenes articles about the proceedings; this highly informative "mole"/snoop described the thinking of the Council Fathers this way:

> A large number, perhaps the majority, of western prelates were inclined to agree with the middle of the road position of Bishop Calewaert... [from Ghent, Belgium] who thought that it was best to retain Latin as the language of the principal parts of the mass in the Roman rite, at least in those countries where the Church was long established and people were used to it, reserving the vernacular for the catechetical or dialogue portion at the beginning of the mass, and for all other liturgical functions.[2]

Albert Gregory Cardinal Meyer, the much-loved archbishop of Chicago and one of the "presidents" of the council, clarified this matter for his perplexed seminarians, while the council was still in session. "I have good news," he announced to the seminarians. "English will be permitted in the liturgy." But he assured his startled audience that the Canon of the Mass (the Eucharistic Prayer) would never be permitted in the vernacular. *Never!*

All of the above documentation is on one side of the battle. On the other, we have what looks like a small but militant army of opponents who insist that the last vestiges of Latin must be purged from the liturgy for all time, because this is what Vatican II wanted, regardless of what the official documents say. Thus, we have the odd situation where the church's "official policy" on Latin seems to be going in opposite directions at the same time. The Latin Mass survives in one diocese but is systematically discouraged in another. An older, highly respected pastor will celebrate a well-attended Latin Mass in his church every week; but in the same diocese any other priest or seminarian who expresses the slightest interest in Latin will ruin his career.

Ostensibly, everyone is worried about some Catholic Traditionalists and followers of Archbishop Marcel Lefebvre (1905–91) — schismatics who still celebrate the so-called Tridentine Mass in Latin and refuse to accept either the "new" Mass rituals or even the edicts of Vatican II. According to a logic that is almost charming in its historical naiveté, a parish that has a Mass in Latin will give the impression that it agrees with separatists who claim that Vatican II was a hoax perpetrated by illegally elected popes. Catholics loyal to Vatican II and the pope, so the thinking goes, are loyal to the use of the vernacular; only disloyal Catholics are interested in Latin, even the approved Latin rites used by the pope himself in Rome. Another complication: some European supporters of the Latin liturgy are right-wing extremists and foaming anti-Semites. Many bishops and priests fear that, if they tolerate Latin, they might be associated, however remotely, with a form of religious fascism. It looks as if most of the clergy have decided that, all things considered, the best course of action is to suppress anything that even vaguely resembles the Latin Mass, since the use of Latin is a symbol of reactionary fanaticism and (do not chuckle) disloyalty to the pope.

This suppression of the Latin rites is accomplished by the subtle method of pretending that such things do not exist, and probably never did. An example of this deliberate amnesia is the *Notre Dame Study of Catholic Parish Life* — fifteen reports issued between 1984 and 1989, 142 pages of sociologically scientific data (surveys, charts, statistics) and on-site observations; it mentions the Latin Mass just twice, in passing and as ancient history, but the sections that report on liturgy do not allude to it at all. What an amazing omission! In all the detailed surveys for the study, the researchers from Notre Dame never dared to ask parishioners, "Would you like to have a Latin Mass in your parish? Would you like to hear or sing more Latin chant? How would you compare the present parish Mass with the Latin version which existed before the 1970s?" Instead, the liturgical use of Latin is treated the way an important but inconvenient figure (the "unperson") used to be treated in Soviet history books; it is simply erased from the memory; it never existed.

A book version of the *Notre Dame Study* published in 1988

(*The Emerging Parish* by Joseph Gremillion and Jim Castelli) makes up for this incredible omission and briefly mentions that all-Latin rites existed in the past, but the authors "lower their voice" when the subject comes up, as if they are referring to a shameful episode. In any case, the book does not even hint that the Latin Mass still survives anywhere. What could be called the "liturgical establishment" has a vested interest in making sure that the subject will never come up, except in a derogatory fashion. Whole departments of liturgical studies at Catholic universities, journals and publishing houses, diocesan commissions, and countless liturgical specialists justify their existence on the premise that the Church of Rome, which once committed a crime against humanity by worshiping in Latin, must now be redirected, as far away from the Latin Mass as possible — and they will do the redirecting. The existence of a Latin liturgy (of any sort, anywhere) threatens the credibility of the redirectors. Also, there is the embarrassing possibility that a portion of the Catholic population might actually develop an affection for the Latin Mass, no matter how modernized. So, the safest policy is to maintain that the ideals of the old ritual have simply evaporated without a trace.

WHO NEEDS IT?

The Catholic bishops of the United States never commissioned a survey to gauge the feelings of the laity on the matter of Latin. There have probably been only a few instances of a pastor asking parishioners how they felt about having at least an occasional Latin Mass. Latin was simply banned or left to linger in a few places. Perhaps the closest the church ever came to an official study of opinions on the matter was a survey conducted in 1980 by the Vatican.[3] In that year Cardinal Knox, prefect of the Vatican's Sacred Congregation for the Sacraments and Divine Worship, asked 2,317 bishops throughout the world to report on the liturgical use of Latin. There were 1,750 responses. The results of the survey, published in the congregation's journal *Notitiae*, showed that the number of Latin Masses had declined dramatically and Gregorian chant was on its way to extinction; in many dioceses the faithful were not even asking for a Latin Mass. Overjoyed with this information, the director of the U.S. bishops' committee on liturgical matters commented that the near extinction of Latin and chant "demonstrates the success of liturgical reform" in the church.[4] (In other words, success is measured by the amount of demolition.)

The Vatican's attempt to get at the facts about the Latin Mass by means of a survey was, to say the least, scientifically flawed. Note that Rome asked only bishops about the Latin Mass, the same bishops who forbid its use in the parishes and banish it to obscure chapels. There was virtually no publicity about Cardinal Knox's letter and no request for "input" from the laity. The bishops then concluded that the late, great Latin Mass was indeed dead and not popular. One imagines a scene: a family gathered around the hospital bed of a relative; with a slight twinge of sorrow they comment on the poor patient's failing condition — as one of them steps on the oxygen cord and another ties a knot in the I-V tubes.

If we want accurate information about the Catholic laity and the Latin Mass, we have to consult an objective Gallup poll that was commissioned by a breakaway Traditionalist parish in 1984. According to these statistics, 40 percent of the Catholics in the United States think that the Latin Mass ought to be available as an alternative to the newer English Mass. In addition, 53 percent said they would attend a Latin Mass if it were offered at a convenient time and place. A substantial 35 percent opposed bringing back the Mass in the form used before 1970 and 37 percent said they would not go to any Latin Mass. The rest had no opinion or were undecided. The number of Catholics who want the option of Latin worship is down from the 64 percent, which the Gallup poll recorded in 1978, but the newer statistics still translate into millions of people.[5] In 1990 another Gallup poll got a different set of reactions to slightly different questions; it seemed to indicate that 8 percent of American Catholics would always attend the old pre–Vatican II version of the Latin Mass (the so-called Tridentine Mass) if it were available; 17 percent would frequently attend, and 51 percent would occasionally go to the old Latin ritual; 23 percent said they would never participate in this old form of the Latin Mass. Surprisingly, the statistics for this particular poll did not show any sharp divisions among various demographic groups; for example, the percentages among the young and old were remarkably similar.[6]

Another study also seems to show that many of the Catholic laity (or at least those old enough to remember) still have feelings of affection for the Latin Mass. *Attitudes of Priests, Adults and College Students on Catholic Parish Life and Leadership* (1986), a survey designed by three researchers at Catholic University in Washington and supported by grants from the Lily Foundation, contains the following question: Should the church allow "periodic celebration of the Latin Mass if a parish desires?" Twenty-two percent of all priests surveyed said that the Latin Mass would "hurt" the parish, and 30 percent thought it would have no effect. (In other words, 52 percent of priests have chilly emotions about the Latin Mass, in any form.) But an amazing 67 percent of the adult laypeople questioned thought that the Latin Mass would "help" a parish that wanted it; a mere 4 percent thought that it would "hurt" the parish.[7]

The evidence, statistical and anecdotal, is very convincing. It shows that a significant number of Catholic laypeople in the United States would be quite happy to participate in a Latin liturgy, the new form, in their own parishes, at a sensible time, now and then (perhaps with some English mixed in). Nostalgia has something to do with this gentle longing for Latin, and some of the old chants may provide a welcome reminder that the community can be proud of its historical roots. (The sentiments go like this: "We special and distinctive Roman Catholics have a special and distinctive form of worship, which we use on occasion.") Certainly a lot of Catholics just want to be reassured that the Latin rite is still there, although they might not always want to attend it. But perhaps the main reason why the Catholic laity, in surprisingly large numbers, have not rejected Latin goes back to the matter of *protection*. In some remote corner of the Catholic laity's collective unconscious, Latin represents protection against the encroachments of the aggressively hospitable clergy, the liturgical explainers, the song leaders, and all those other smiling annoyances who pounce on some Catholic congregations every Sunday. Maybe older Catholics remember that the Latin Mass (with all its inadequacies) at least forced the various ministers in the sanctuary to concentrate on their role and gave them no opportunities to impress the congregation with their charming personalities; it seemed to keep musicians under control. In addition, Latin rituals invited everyone, protected from annoyances, to reach for an emotional and spiritual level above the commonplace.

But then there is another interpretation of the "protection" factor. It may be that many Catholic supporters of the Latin Mass really do not want to see its return so much as they want some form of worship — anything — that does not virtually require them to fall in love with someone else's personality or singing voice.

"WHAT'S LEFT" AND THE HORSE'S ASS

I listened carefully as a couple I know told me about the torture of attending Mass in their parish. The pastor, they said, was unbearable. He always began the liturgy with vacuous comments about the weather and parish activities. Sometimes, while reciting parts of the Mass, he would try to imitate the resonant tones of a John Gielgud or Lawrence Olivier delivering a Shakespearean soliloquy. Sometimes he would try to appear warm and loveable. Sometimes he would drive everybody crazy.

The pastor was not a wicked man, my friends insisted; he was close to retirement yet certainly not senile, but, they wondered, why was he acting like this? I suggested that perhaps he was just following orders from the diocese, just performing the little tricks that, according to modern liturgical thinking, would "build community" and turn liturgy into a homey, human experience. The problem was that every Sunday, for approximately fifty minutes, these little tricks had a way of forcing the worshiper to focus not on the warm experience but on the personality of this man and its dense banality. The only religious thought that ever crossed the worshiper's mind was that, while the pastor was saying Mass, all the angels and archangels and all the saints in heaven must surely be watching and weeping.

Stories like this make you realize why Roman Catholicism refused to release its grip on the Latin liturgy for so long. In its wisdom, accumulated over the centuries, the church realized that this ancient language acted as a kind of wallpaper that hid the cracks — and when one has a clergy limited to males and (for the most part) bachelors, one has cracks.

"Get rid of the Latin, the incense, the archaic art music. Get rid of it all."

I can remember angry talk like that back in the late 1960s and I even agreed with a lot of it. But then I saw what happened. When you get rid of Latin and all the "cultural baggage" that supposedly interferes with true worship, what is left? A man who is behind a table and doing a solo performance, interspersed with songs and group activity called participation.

A Protestant minister is hired and fired for many reasons, one of which is his or her ability to do a solo performance in front of a congregation. A Roman Catholic priest is ordained partly because he seems to be an exemplar of virtue; his ability to perform agreeably in front of a congregation does not enter into the picture. Exemplars of virtue do not always make good solo performers.

* * *

"Yes, it was all very unfortunate," my acquaintance said. The minister of her Protestant church just wasn't "working out" and he had to be fired.

The burnt-out Baptist minister, age fifty, may find himself searching for a new career. Years ago, the burnt-out Catholic pastor could go on and on in his job, even if he was brain-dead; and when he left the parish, it was feet first. The Latin Mass protected him and his job. (Latin also protected the congregation from him.) In those days — and may they never return — the laity, during Mass, could not really tell the difference between the decrepit bishop and the snappy young priest; both looked roughly the same (impressive) buried underneath the formalities of the Latin ritual. Both looked as if they could hold their jobs.

* * *

I listened as an acquaintance described the recent Holy Saturday liturgy in his parish. I thought my jaw would fall off my face. It seems the pastor at this large suburban parish had decided to scrap the entire Holy Saturday ceremony prescribed in the official books. To replace it, he and his parish musicians invented their own highly condensed ceremony, which (according to the description I was given) resembled a comic book version of the original. But the best was saved for last. Just as the liturgy was ending, people in the church began to notice something unusual in the back of the sanctuary — a pair of large rabbit ears wiggling from behind one of the decorations. Then, after a few seconds, the congregation realized that the ears belonged to someone dressed up like the Easter Bunny, who was playing peekaboo with them. Finally, the Holy Hare hopped out into full view, mingled with the departing congregation, and gave out candy.

A week later, the pastor, dispensing with his homily, grabbed a portable microphone and walked down to the congregation.

"What ya think of that Holy Saturday liturgy?" he asked a parishioner in the first pew.

"Well, uh . . . "

"It was *great*," the pastor interrupted enthusiastically, "and it only lasted forty-five minutes!"

Now, strange tales about liturgical aberrations in Catholic parishes no longer surprise me. I have heard it all. (I think I went numb after somebody told me about the parish where the opening song for Mass — the congregation holding hands — is sometimes "Getting to Know You" from *The King and I*.) But this particular parish, with the Holy Saturday travesty, really impressed me. This had style, nerve, *chutzpah*. It made me recall an old inspirational saying that I was taught in my youth and that still comforts me in trying moments. It goes like this: *There are more horses' asses than there are horses.*

The Catholic church knew all about the horse's ass problem centuries ago. The Latin ritual, like the sung rituals of the East, was the church's imperfect way of making sure that the congregation would not realize that there was, on some occasions, a horse's ass in the sanctuary, and Latin also limited the damage that the horse's ass could inflict on the prescribed ceremonies.

With Latin virtually gone, the Catholic church has lost its liturgical North Star — its "fixed point," something which permitted it to navigate safely. In that rare parish where the Latin ritual or a genuine sung Mass in the vernacular still provides a "fixed point" just once on a Sunday, the horse's ass (priest, cantor, musician) might be reined in slightly by shame; after all, that "great idea," that horse's ass liturgical or musical gimmick at the 9:00 A.M. Mass, might put everybody to shame if it has to be measured against the traditional "fixed point" at 11:00 A.M.

Liturgists are not unaware of the horse's ass problem. Some of them practically *beg* clergy and musicians to follow the prescribed rites (with practical adjustments), to trust the "spirit" of liturgical custom, to submit to the collective wisdom of the ages, to stay close to the appointed texts. Treat the prescribed rites as the "fixed point," these liturgists say, and Holy Saturday fiascoes will disappear.

Other liturgists listen to tales of worship imbecility and then, with humorless thoroughness, use the opportunity to deliver a prepared speech that sounds like this: Yes, there are liturgical misunderstandings, but they will miraculously go away — when the ethnic cultural customs of the local people become the "fixed point" and are skillfully inculturated with worship, when Spirit-guided communities devote hours to prayerful planning of worship, when the rubrics of the liturgy are purged of obsolete customs from the past, when the language of the texts is thoroughly modernized, when a true Liturgical Renewal (from the grassroots) is finally allowed to take place, when seminarians receive more poise training on how to be warm and endearing presiders, when we go beyond the archaic Roman Rite, when . . .

When and if.

In the meantime, until all the "whens" fall into place and there is perfection on earth, the horse's ass problem persists and it can be summarized thus: *The horse's ass, with unshakable confidence, believes that he or she is the North Star, the "fixed point" against which everything is measured.* The horse's ass cannot tolerate symbols of submission — and something like a Latin Mass is submission multiplied exponentially. All the Spirit-guided prayerful planning by a culturally homogeneous faith community, all the theologically modernized liturgical texts, all the training in ways to preside with poise, all the Masters Degrees in liturgy — all of it comes to nothing if, at the very end of the whole noisy parade, is the horse's ass . . . who knows better.

A gentleman once told me a story about his unforgettable high school English teacher back in the 1940s. Let us call the teacher Miss Bumbershoot.

A woman of candy-sweet disposition, stately proportions, and indefinite age, Miss Bumbershoot decided one day to teach her public school class a poem about winter and snow. To prepare for this, she put up, all around the room, dozens of magazine pictures and calendars with winter scenes. When the class assembled (in this gallery of winter images), she had the students close their eyes and listen to a scratchy recording of music that she thought sounded cold and icy. Then, with the music still going in the background, she told the students to open their eyes and read the poem in unison, slowly, while she walked up and down the aisles and, stopping occasionally, sprinkled little bits of white paper on a student's desk, in order to stimulate thoughts of snowflakes.

After the bell rang, the nice girls in the class came up to Miss Bumbershoot and complimented her on the beauty of her presentation. The boys, however, quickly dashed out to recess and, in a remote corner of the playground, threw themselves into such violent convulsions of laughter that an onlooker would have thought that they were all having a simultaneous attack of appendicitis.

In another part of the same town, I am sure there was a Catholic school for boys. Father (or Brother) Gruff must have presided over his no-nonsense, no-idleness class on English literature. The students in the class probably scanned every syllable of that same poem about winter, parsed and diagramed every sentence, memorized every stanza — and completely missed the beauty and the meaning behind the words. If there had been some girls in the class, they would have gone home and cried.

During the early centuries of Christianity, the church discovered, to its horror, that there was at least one Miss Bumbershoot and one Father Gruff in almost every community, and these two characters were a greater threat than the world, the flesh, and the devil. You see, this sweet lady and this loyal man say they only want to serve the church, to help, but what they really want is to take over, to control something that threatens their definition of sexual identity.

Miss Bumbershoot and Father Gruff — both thoroughbred horses' asses — always resented the Latin Mass because it limited their access to control and because it seemed to operate in a territory that was sexually "self-assured" and, oddly enough, both male and female. Sometimes the Latin ritual could be like a play by Shakespeare or a novel by Tolstoy; it was extraordinarily sensitive to the "masculine" and the "feminine." Sometimes it was like a symphony by Beethoven, with moments of "masculine strength" combined together with moments of "feminine grace" in the most beguiling way. (There was, for example, the all-male "cast," but they were in dresses; a man was in charge, but he was controlled by an exquisite ritualistic choreography, which suggested femininity.)

When the Latin Mass began to falter back in the 1960s, Miss

Bumbershoot and Father Gruff saw an opportunity and moved in for the kill.

Occasionally, I will listen to acquaintances complain about liturgical discomforts they have to endure in their parishes in different parts of the country, and then it will suddenly hit me: What they are complaining about is not necessarily something that can be improved (by, for example, training seminarians on how to sparkle with charm when they preside at Mass). Rather, the real source of the irritation and the anguish is the unstoppable Miss Bumbershoot and Father Gruff, who seem to be at each other's throats in a struggle for power in the parishes. Miss Bumbershoot is determined to prove that she can bring such happiness to a brutish world, especially if she can position the children in the sanctuary, as only she can, and have them do such darling things (like sing "Happy Birthday to You" at a Christmas Mass). Father Gruff, equally determined, shall prove in front of the entire congregation that he is *no sissy*. He is not going to be part of all that fairy art stuff that used to go with the Latin Mass. He is a regular guy.

All Christian churches have their nasty struggles between the macho men and the feminists. Roman Catholicism, to judge from what friends tell me, is also stuck with Miss Bumbershoot and Father Gruff. I wonder which one of them will eventually win.

Two major points concerning horses' asses are worth remembering: (1) Thick of skull, they are beyond help. Even the Holy Ghost gave up trying to crack their monumental egotism. (2) Everybody — in one way or another, in at least one respect — is a horse's ass. We are all twisted somewhere.

With Latin gone, and even the memory of its restraining majesty going fast, all that is left, in some places, is the horse's ass.

A LITTLE SPACE

In 1965 I visited a Jesuit friend of mine who was living in a Jesuit residence in a large city. When I got to the lobby of the building, a sign stopped me. All visitors, it sternly warned, must announce themselves at the receptionist's desk. At the bottom of the sign were the following Latin words in small letters: "Sacerdotes intereant ad libitum," which means, "[But] priests and bishops may come and go as they please," without bothering to announce themselves.

Latin once provided a hedge between clergy and the unen-lightened laity. It emphasized a "them" and "us." But is that necessarily a bad thing?

My wife told me about attending an Episcopalian service and hearing a bishop preach on this topic: "The laity should stay away from the clergy." All kinds of men and women, said the Protes-tant bishop, present themselves to the church as volunteers. They want to do this and that for the sake of religion, they want to change the world, they cannot get enough of the faith. But the closer they get to the clergy, the more disillusioned they become. They discover that their minister is only human, all too human. In the interest of promoting a happy community, the bishop po-litely urged that the laity should give the clergy some "space" to themselves, especially during worship.

At the conclusion of his sermon, the bishop went back to his chair, which was behind an ornamental choir screen and against the side of the sanctuary, where the congregation could not see him clearly.

Latin once allowed the Roman Catholic clergy a vast amount of private "space" where they could be safe from most of the laity. It provided them with a secret club-language for the exclu-sive band of brothers. ("All professions," George Bernard Shaw reminds us, "are conspiracies against the laity.") This sounds hor-ribly snobbish, but the exclusiveness was something that lured many young men into the seminary, with the energetic support of their mothers. Everything has now changed, of course. Most Catholic priests do not want to go about their liturgical business *exclusively*; they yearn to become blended and merged with the assembly, the "priests in the pews." (One of these days someone will suggest that a television screen should be in every pew of every Catholic church and the up-close picture on the screen, most of the time, should be that of the priest's sincere face.) But when the priest strains mightily to bring the worshiper into his "space," especially with the aid of a microphone, he forcibly intrudes him-self into the worshiper's "space." Too much of this pushing, this intruding, can come across as threatening.

Please note: I am not saying that priests must be educated and treated as if they were rare human orchids. I am not maintaining that they should wear cassocks on the public streets. I am not saying anything about "worker priest" experiments or excluding women from ordination. My only point here is that, in a public act of worship in a church, "space" symbolizes equality and democracy. Any attempt to make that space smaller — with cute jokes, holding hands, affected friendliness — can cause stress. It shatters the equality; it creates the impression that the purpose of liturgy is to provide an opportunity for worshipers (people of low status) to be welcomed by the priest (a person of high status) into his "space."

"Space" — researchers who study animal or human behavior take this concept very seriously.[8] Centuries ago, long before the scientific theories about personal space, the Roman Catholic church instinctively understood what individual "territory" meant: a sense of autonomy, security, and equality with everyone else. With all its faults, the Latin Mass used to be an extraordinarily *spacious* event (maybe too spacious); it allowed clergy and laity lots of territory; it minimized stress. But perhaps I am really talking about the "old" Mass in Latin, with the priest mumbling toward the back wall and, more important, the old assumption that hearing and understanding every last word of a liturgy was not crucial for salvation. Perhaps I am about to hit a raw nerve.

CRUSH THE INFAMOUS THING!

In 1984, Rome confused a confusing situation even more when it virtually admitted that its own survey of the bishops did not begin to reveal the depth of feeling for the pre–Vatican II Mass among the laity, especially in Europe. As a temporary measure *and* just for those Catholics who were having trouble adjusting to the new rites *and* only under certain conditions, the Vatican cautiously issued a decree, an Indult, allowing the return of the so-called Tridentine Mass, the "old" Latin Mass, which had been virtually banned in 1969; one of the stringent provisos attached to the Indult was that the local bishop could add even more stringent provisos as to where, when, and if the "old" liturgy could be celebrated.

Most Catholics shrugged their shoulders at the news, but

prominent liturgical specialists were outraged. The director of the liturgy committee of the Catholic bishops in the United States told the *Washington Post* that he learned about the Indult when he was reading the paper at breakfast. "I nearly choked over my coffee," he said. Another liturgist denounced the Indult as "the biggest act of betrayal in the Church since Judas."[9] Various stories in the LLA's *Newsletter* described how this outrage turned into panic when a very small number of Catholics in the United States began to ask for permission to have the "old" Mass.

• In one diocese, according to the LLA, a group of Catholics received permission for the old rite, with the restriction that the event would be secret and receive absolutely no publicity. Six hundred people showed up. Very quickly thereafter, permission for the "old" Mass was revoked and, for good measure, further celebration of the "new" Latin Mass in that parish was also discontinued.

• In another diocese, permission for the "old" Mass is granted, as long as nobody under the age of thirty will be allowed to set foot on the premises.

• Another diocese flatly refuses all requests for the Tridentine Mass because of the danger of opening up "old wounds" (?) and causing division in a parish.

• Any group foolish enough to ask for the "old" Mass in one Midwestern diocese will receive a cold form letter from the head of the liturgical commission; the request is condemned and the petitioners are reminded that the church cannot have all of these "splinter groups" going off by themselves.

• A few elderly and pious Catholics in New York State were graciously allowed to have one Tridentine Mass — and then, at the conclusion of this liturgy, the priest, who had been sent down by the chancery, gave the assembled faithful a vicious twenty-minute tongue-lashing for making such an idiotic request in the first place.

In every diocese, the word is out that any priest who is party to a request for the "old" Mass, Indult or no Indult, will be under suspicion for treason.

My own favorite reaction to the Vatican's permission to bring back the "old" Mass can be found in the pages of *Worship*. The editor of this journal, known for its openness and tolerance, spent one half of a commentary fuming about the return of the Tridentine Mass. People who ask for it, he declares, are trying to form a quasi-parish and "withdraw in effect from the worship and life of the local church." (This same journal, it should be noted, does not devote much space to complaints about "intentional communities," which, in effect, withdraw from the official church and its rites.) In our free country and in the church that now advertises its commitment to diversity, the editor of *Worship* would have this Indult, this permission for the old rites, this "unwarranted and very unwise concession" *quashed*, at once and without pity for the few dissidents who like it.

In the other half of this same commentary in *Worship*, the editor speaks kindly about the use of clowns and mimes during a liturgy. He is distressed because the American bishops, supposedly giving in to archconservatives here and in Rome, have politely suggested that these circus characters must absent themselves from the sanctuary during a ritual. Clowns and mimes, the editor maintains, are a legitimate form of expression and their decorative presence around the altar could do beautiful things to a liturgy, if they are just given some guidelines. The Tridentine Latin Mass, however, a form of liturgical expression that lasted four hundred years, *must be crushed.*[10]

What the hell is going on here? Why are so many of the Catholic clergy scared witless by the reappearance of the old rites? Why do so many of the influential liturgical specialists encourage liturgical dance, which sometimes looks like a Marx Brothers skit, but, at the same time, shake their fists at the handful of people who attend the old form of the Mass? It is true that in parts of Europe the "old" Latin Mass has sometimes become identified with anti-Semitism and hatred of postconciliar Catholicism, but extremism of that sort is rare on this side of the Atlantic. All of the available information shows that (at least in North America) the "illegal but now legal" Tridentine Mass causes a stir when it is first allowed in a community, then interest fades and it is usually attended just by a few.[11] The wisest policy would be to challenge the Lefebvrists and Traditionalists by allowing the "old" Mass publicly in various places, and then let it alone. But influential members of the clergy and the diocesan commissars for liturgy lose sleep at night over the prospect of the Tridentine Mass in their midst. They are petrified by the thought that the laity will once again see how the Latin and the uncompromising rigidity of the old rites "control" the priest and force him to act like a very humble servant.

A ghost is haunting Roman Catholicism, the ghost of its "old" Mass. That austere formality of the old Latin rituals sometimes used to encourage much more intense commitment and much more respect than the typical parish's breezy version of the "new" Mass, and the liturgical specialists know this. If at least one Tridentine Mass had been allowed to remain in most parishes (priest and people facing the same direction, participation of the "interior" sort, maybe no music at all), perhaps a third of the Catholic population would have gravitated to it every Sunday. These old rites, especially the quiet Low Mass, would have remained modestly popular, not because of defiance or rabid conservatism but because of those principles of "space" and "protection" (in this case self-protection). I explain what I mean in the following paragraphs.

A thriving Episcopalian church I know (a Low Church establishment with absolutely no "smells and bells") has three services every Sunday. At one service the choir provides vigorous support for congregational singing and occasionally sings some impressive music. At another there are hymns accompanied just by the organ. Any visitor who would happen to wander into one of these services would recognize immediately that the quality of the music in the church is above average and that the community feeling is in great shape. But then there is another service on Sunday, at 8:00 A.M. No music is used at all. None. From beginning to end, the ceremony remains subdued, quietly formal; some of it is not very audible. Every Sunday, approximately one third of this church's worshipers attend it. For their own protection, they avoid the fine music and the rousing liturgical hoopla; they deliberately choose the broad "space" of the quiet ceremony. A Catholic liturgist (with credentials more academic than pastoral) would scorn this "escape" from reality, this retreat into the "private." But these good Episcopalians know they will just burn out if they submit themselves to heavy doses of worship thrills every single week. They recognize that they cannot appreciate the liturgical and musical "peaks" that the church provides, unless they spend some Sundays in the quiet "valleys."

Roman Catholicism needs to have its own liturgical "valley," but the vernacular Mass (according to the *Novus Ordo*, or Rite of Paul VI) is usually turned into a very noisy, talky event. The ambitious singing, which seems to be a method for improving the worshiper's cardiovascular system, the pushy priests, who are determined to make you love their personalities, the avalanche of spoken words, all of them blasted through amplification — it is hard to turn that kind of communication overkill into something subdued and quietly formal. Roman Catholicism once had a tranquil "valley" in the Tridentine Low Mass. But today the liturgical authorities routinely condemn the old rites for being totally at odds with the values emphasized by Vatican II; they never seem to realize that the quiet Low Mass, in one form or another, goes back to the Middle Ages; it survived because people *wanted* it. Maybe some of them still want the broad "space" that it once gave them; maybe they are longing not for Latin but for the *low stress* of the old Low Mass.

Another unsolicited opinion: The Tridentine version of the Latin Mass should be conspicuously and "legally" celebrated in at least one church in every diocese. This would prevent it from being turned into a symbol of defiance. But if the Tridentine Mass is treated with official contempt or not allowed, the result will be more harm than good.

A LOSING BATTLE

Lately, the *Newsletter* of the Latin Liturgy Association has been describing a situation that looks more like a slaughter than a battle over ideas. Latin is being beaten back into a very tight corner. The LLA's reporting about this slaughter usually falls into three categories:

• *Suppression of Competition.* In a big Midwestern city, the regular Latin Mass attracts a large congregation to a Dominican church in the downtown area. The local head of the Dominican Order, the provincial, fires the pastor and stops the Latin Mass (the "legal" rite); hundreds of people protest but to no avail; the provincial says he will not have this church used "as a haven for people who are discontented with their parishes." (The Catholic church is terrified by the thought of parishes competing for customers.)

• *The Disappearance of an Asset.* A mysterious letter arrives at the offices of the archdiocese of Detroit; it is written in a strange tongue that nobody can decipher; it goes through various offices until an older priest recognizes the language: Latin. The letter, from a missionary in a developing nation, is a plea for funds; the missionary explains that his command of English is not good, but he is sure that everybody in the chancery would understand the church's universal language. (Latin used to be an invaluable asset for international communication and for worship with an international or multiethnic congregation.)

• *The Latinless Clergy.* Two Jesuit seminarians in St. Louis, unlike their colleagues, want to study Latin above the elementary level, but their own order is no help to them; they have to enroll in nonsectarian Washington University; in their Latin class, students from nearby Protestant seminaries outnumber them.

In 1985 the LLA took a survey of all the Roman Catholic seminaries in the United States and asked questions about the place of Latin and Gregorian chant in the education of seminarians.[12] Most of the seminaries ignored the request for information, but from the sampling received two clear facts have emerged: (1) The majority of men studying for the priesthood in the United States probably will never know enough Latin to translate the Ave Maria. (2) All but a few of these seminarians have been scrupulously shielded from any real exposure to Gregorian chant. Both of these developments violate the letter and the spirit of Vatican II's Constitution on the Sacred Liturgy.

Now, to be sure, the heavens will not fall if some newly ordained priests cannot translate a sentence in Latin (especially men who have a delayed vocation or are working in countries that do not have a culture that derives from Western Europe). And, also to be sure, keeping a seminarian innocently ignorant of Gregorian chant is a felony but not a matter of central importance. The real crisis here is something that can be summed up in an old saying, rephrased: *Unfamiliarity breeds contempt.* The seminarians who are assured that they never have to learn a word of Latin will eventually surround that deficiency in their education with all kinds of rationalizations, most of which will be hostile. They will conclude that worship in Latin is and always was an abomination. They will have to disparage anything that even suggests the "ambiance" of the Latin Mass, in order to justify a conspicuous hole in their education.

The clergy in Roman Catholicism's Eastern Rites remain loyal to the successor of St. Peter, the bishop of Rome, without the historical link of the Latin language; but they have a long history of worshiping in a liturgical "style" that has the same intentions as the Latin Mass. The Latinless priest, however, may have been trained to distance himself not only from Latin but from the whole idea of worship as practiced by the historic "Catholic" churches. He has been subtly encouraged to renounce his church's past. It is only a matter of time before he and his Latinless colleagues join together and remove themselves from the whole structure, the whole "package," and start an "American National Church" that has never been touched by Latin. The United States, which produced interesting variations on Protestantism (Seventh-Day Adventists, Jehovah's Witnesses, Christian Scientists, Mormons), will someday produce significant breakaway Catholic denominations that will point to the Roman church's former use of Latin as one justification for separating from it.

BEYOND WORDS

At some of the most intense parts of the liturgy in English, the assembly runs out of words, as it were. Normal vocabulary becomes inadequate. The faithful struggle to express the inexpressible and they find that they have to enter into another form of consciousness. It is no accident that at these climactic points in the Eucharist the congregation leaves the normal, everyday vernacular and uses words derived from Hebrew: Alleluia, Hosanna, and Amen. Very few Catholics could make any sense out of the original Hebrew letters, and yet these foreign expressions belong in the vernacular Mass.

Ever since Pentecost, Christianity has been "running out of words." It has always found that normal, spoken vocabulary can be frustratingly inadequate when the believer confronts what the Old Testament calls the "terrible," mighty God, whose sanctuary on earth is "dreadful." This inability of spoken vernacular words to express what is beyond words — the "terrible" or the awesome — explains why so many Catholics support two things that release them from everyday language: the Charismatic movement and the optional Latin Mass.

In 1983 I attended an international symposium entitled "Gregorian Chant in Liturgy and Education." This conference, at

Catholic University in Washington, was scheduled to begin with
a sung Pontifical Latin Mass (according to the new ritual) in the
National Shrine of the Immaculate Conception. The brochure for
this symposium informed me that all the music at the opening
liturgy would consist of Latin chant sung either by a choir or the
entire assembly, without any harmony or accompaniment. (The
organ would be played only before and after the actual Mass.)
Aware of the astringent seriousness of the music, I decided to put
on the most sensible suit I owned but . . . I should have worn sports
clothes. The event was an organized riot.

At the center, the ritual itself burned with uncommon heat.
(Were these people "speaking in tongues," in a collective way?)
There was a crowd in the sanctuary — the celebrant, a beautifully
robed cardinal, acolytes, singers, and an abbess (who chanted one
of the readings) — but they were almost completely "hidden," as
were their personalities, in all the stately confusion: the elaborate
rubrics, the formalities, the "unreal" chanting. Gathered in front
of or around this central heat, people in the congregation seemed
to be in various kinds of states (mumbling in fervor, singing in
the strange language, lost in reverie, curious, beaming with pride,
and, yes, even bored). A kind of reverent but "happy party" atmosphere prevailed in the pews. Stunned tourists, who had wandered
in just for a peek, stayed until the end. The ushers chatted with
worshipers who were standing in the rear. Little children bounced
around. The whole thing was "madness" and yet solemn, "crazy"
and yet majestically serious. Participation was not just "full"; it
was combustive, even when the congregation watched and listened. The sustained lunacy of the ceremony reminded everyone
that they were in the presence of the "awesome" God and were
also surrendering to Him, by leaping into the absurd.

At this point the reader is probably expecting me to say that
this Latin Mass stimulated my sense of the sacred and mystery,
but that would be only partially true. What it really awakened in
me was my sense of the carnival. The historic sung Catholic rituals — Latin, Byzantine, Orthodox, and so forth — have always
been heavily disguised displays of religious frenzy; the liturgical
ceremony safely channels all the energy and enthusiasm so that
they will not cause damage. These ceremonial attempts to go
beyond the earthbound logic of everyday prose are a form of reg-
ulated Charismatic or Pentecostal worship and a way of dealing

with an unruly crowd. Unfortunately, this insight is all too often forgotten today. Maybe the forgetting began in the nineteenth century when High Church Anglicans and some Roman Catholics introduced the new and corrupting theory that such rituals are not carnivals but really a dignified form of prayer, conducted with aplomb, in front of a dignified congregation.

The novelist and newspaper reporter Joe Flaherty put it perfectly. "When the Latin mass and grand opera were reduced to English," he commented in 1976, "both our sins and our passions seemed smaller. . . . If the romantic soul is to operate, a dash of voodoo is needed."[13] When the Catholic church just about banished Latin, it also banished its zany romantic soul, its passions (and most definitely the sense of sin). Maybe if the huge gap that was left after the removal of Latin had been filled with hymns "sung like Methodists" or spectacular sermons or Charismatic boisterousness, maybe if more English rites were "elevated" in some kind of chant, there would be a new form of passion, but this is not the common experience, at least not everywhere. The typical parish Mass has become a rather prim talk-event, without passion, without awareness of the "awesome" God. There might be deafening noise and rush-hour commotion in the sanctuary, historicism in the form of some old music might even make an appearance, but there is rarely a "dash of voodoo."

"Voodoo!" Many of the decision-makers in Catholicism are deeply embarrassed by such a comparison. The Mass is *not* mysterious or transcendent or an example of "voodoo," they insist. The Eucharist, the "source and summit" of the Catholic religion, is a very scientific matter and should be scientifically presented to the faithful, perhaps in a manner that suggests something from a textbook on physics. The modern Catholic is supposed to put aside outmoded notions of the mysterious, get down to reality, and remember that Christ is present in . . .

"Present in" — this is where the trouble begins. We have to review a little history at this point.

*   *   *

During the era of the Latin liturgy, Catholics believed that in the Mass Christ was mysteriously present ("body and blood") in the form of the consecrated bread and wine. With this change, this transformation of mere earthly food into his own presence, Christ continued his loving Sacrifice, the Sacrifice of the Cross.

The Second Vatican Council, without wavering from this dogmatic position in the slightest, increased the church's awareness of Christ's presence in his church. In the Constitution on the Sacred Liturgy (Article 7), the Council Fathers reminded the faithful that Christ promised to be in the midst of two or three who were gathered in his name (Matt. 18:20). Christ is, therefore, "always present in His Church, especially in her liturgical celebrations. . . . He is present in his word, since it is He Himself who speaks when the holy Scriptures are read in the church." He is present in the priest who administers the sacraments in his name and is in the midst of the faithful at a liturgy. But the Fathers of Vatican II carefully add that Christ is *especially* present in the Eucharistic species (*"maxime sub speciebus eucharisticis"*).

In the Western church (i.e., where the Latin Mass had prevailed), the concept of "the presence of Christ" evolved into something very narrow and concentrated; the faithful tended to see his presence as a sudden arrival only after the words of consecration in the Mass and a presence only in the Eucharistic species. In the Eastern churches, there was a more balanced concept of a "presence." The structure of the Byzantine rites helped to make people aware of an unfolding liturgical continuity and continuous sacred presence. Vatican II's broadening of the concept of Christ's "presence" — long overdue — was really a return to an older, traditional way of thinking about the Mass, a theology that had survived in the Eastern churches.

One occasionally comes across a somewhat radical specialist in theology or liturgy who seems to be totally bored by any traditional Eastern and Western way of affirming Christ's presence in the liturgy. The bored specialists put the issue this way: The Eastern churches may go in the right liturgical "direction" but they focus too much on the *divinity* of the Christ who is present; these Eastern expressions of Christianity ignore the *humanity* of the Christ who is the head of our redeemed human race. The Western church, according to these same theologians and liturgists, had almost completely lost any sense of liturgical "direction." Congregations were encouraged (supposedly) to treat the Eucharistic liturgy as if it were a reverence session during which Christ, present only in the Eucharistic species, was adored by a silent audience. The excessive emphasis on the Sacrifice of Christ, with courtly ceremonial and especially with the use of Latin (supposedly) distorted the true meaning of the Mass — which should be a dynamic affirmation of a new life in Christ, a family meal that bonds together those who are renewed by his presence among them. These specialists (and not a few amateurs) all seem to agree that the old liturgical ceremonies, East and West, are too royalist and make Christ into a distant king; for this reason, the old rites should be modified, perhaps even abandoned. (A correspondent tells me about a priest who demands that the church stop the ritualistic foolishness that distorts the true purpose of the Mass, and this would mean getting rid of the outmoded adoration, the Roman formalism, and, most of all, the medieval "cookie worship.")

Whether radical or cautiously middle-of-the-road, reforming theologians and liturgists have always had the best of intentions. They wanted the pendulum to swing: away from passivity and fear, to joyous affirmation; they wanted adoration to be moved away from an almost total focus on the Eucharistic species and, instead, actively directed, with thanksgiving, through Christ to God the Father. They wanted the Eucharist to be the center of a lively and honest Christianity, not just an excuse for beautiful historic pageantry. Perhaps most of all they wanted to get away from the strident preaching and the teaching that were still continuing the battles of the Counter Reformation, still denouncing the Protestant proposition that communion was only a memorial meal that had nothing to do with sacrifice. (I can remember the priests who used to shout the phrase "Holy Sacrifice of the Mass" again and again in a sermon, as if this expression formed one indivisible word. They were not going to abandon the central dogmas of the church; they were not going to slide into comfortable Protestant compromises; they were not going to let themselves become distracted by liturgical irrelevances, which included things like congregational participation. The Mass was a Holy Sacrifice and nothing else.)

And so, with the help of Vatican II, the pendulum did swing. Or did it swing out of control? Is there any pendulum left in some places?

"Presence of Christ" — this is a bit of an embarrassment for some Catholics if the place of the "presence" is the Eucharistic species. Many feminists become tense because this Eucharistic "presence" has long been associated with special powers given only to ordained men. Many theologians and liturgists fret about an exaggerated emphasis on the adoration of a divine Christ in a Eucharistic "presence"; this, they fear, will make the people in the congregation forget that they are one with the human Christ who has ennobled the human race. Christianity is not about the adoration of a "presence" but about action, they insist.

One way out of all the embarrassments is to convince Catholics that this "presence" has now been spread out and equalized: Christ is present in bread and wine, but also (to the same "degree") in the priest, in the words of scripture, in our neighbor next to us, and even in the world. It is all the same. And this Christ who is present everywhere in the church shares our humanity. In the liturgy the faithful are declaring, as one distinguished liturgist put it, "that we are one with the humanity of Christ." He goes on to say, "Our affirmation of our shared humanity with Christ must then find expression in all sorts of social movements concerned with the freedom and dignity of the human person, including the struggle for civil rights, women's equality, and peace."[14]

The thinking here is as old as the New Testament. It is really nothing new to say that Christ, according to orthodox Christian thinking, was a real human being or that Christians must show their love of God by showing their love of and concern for their neighbors. What is new here is the emphasis. A pre–Vatican II church emphasized that the Eucharist, the Mass, was a gift to the human race; the liturgy and art that surrounded it were symbols of gratitude for this unending gift. A postconciliar church, in some places, seems to be emphasizing that human beings are the gift — with extraordinary powers to become the "presence of Christ" when they gather together. If the Mass has any purpose, it is really adoration: an opportunity for gifted human beings to worship their perfect and sinless unification with the human Christ. If the "presence of Christ" has any meaning, it is primarily as a new life dedicated to approved social causes — which is much more nourishing than any "presence of Christ" as bread and wine.

That is what the "new emphasis" often sounds like, and it helps to explain the constant tone of self-congratulation that runs through many modernized postconciliar liturgies.

"Presence of Christ" — What does it mean? With all of their imperfections, the Latin Mass and the continuously sung rites of the Eastern churches, more or less, have always made the worshiper aware of Christ's presence — the awesome and divine Christ of the Incarnation, the Transfiguration, Calvary, the Resurrection, the Ascension, and the mystery of the unending Eucharist. Anyone who believes in such things (which are at the center of cosmic history) must shudder at their implications. Spoken, everyday words cannot always begin to express the surrender of belief in this "awesome" God. A "dash of voodoo" is the only way to show gratitude for this astonishing revelation that God has entered into and shared our human destiny. Anything less would be, for a start, impolite.

"Presence of Christ" — What does it mean today? Do some modern Catholics really believe that Christ is divine and "awesome"? Walk into a few churches or chapels and the strongest impression you will have is that the truly "awesome" thing about the Mass is the presence of the gathering priest and the gathered faithful. If Christ's "presence" is acknowledged, it is in his role as genial teacher, social reformer, champion of equality, and invited guest. Like all good guests, he does not make much of a fuss or draw too much attention to himself.

Latin is largely avoided today in Catholic parishes and chapels not because of progress or the church's new image of itself or the need for greater participation but because so many of Catholicism's influential leaders (clergy and laity) no longer believe in an "awesome" God who has entered into history in an "awesome" way. This fact became vivid to me as I watched a video for Catholic youngsters preparing to make their Confirmation. The format of the video was a little like a television talk show combined with the glitter of a game show. Multicolored lights, cute banter, and almost frantic movement enlivened this flashy presentation — on the meaning of prayer. All that was missing was a spinning wheel and prizes. "What do you think prayer is, Sally?" asked the show's host as he thrust a microphone into Sally's face. The frightened teenager managed to produce a few titters but no coherent answer. The show's host then moved on to the next teenager (contestant?). "What do you think prayer is, Freddie?" the game-show host again asked and again received a particularly shallow answer, which nevertheless managed to make the audience laugh. Finally, after all this questioning — and getting nowhere — the host provided the right answer. Prayer, he said, is just a personal, *casual* conversation with God, your best friend.

Now this is a breakthrough! Prayer at last simplified and made easy! Prayer that you too can offer, casually, in your spare time! It's really a shame that Francis of Assisi, John of the Cross, Teresa of Avila, and all those other saints never had microwave ovens and no-iron shirts, never knew about this modern, labor-saving definition of prayer. They could have spared themselves such needless sweat. God, who is not the least bit "awesome," is really just the believer's best friend, who can be treated in a personal, casual way. Since God is no Big Deal, prayer is no Big Deal. The only theological mystery that remains, concerning prayer, is whether or not our best friend, while listening to prayer, chews gum.

Interruption from an angry reader: "You evil people and your Latin Mass and your beautiful Gregorian chant in Latin and all that. Can't you see that it's escapist nonsense? It promotes the illusion that Christ/God is *out there*, something remote, and not part of our lives. Well, I tell you that God is here — now, today — alive in our own time. Service to others is what Christianity is all about. The arcane, the unintelligible, and the exotic — phony metaphors for God — distract us from social movements, from reality, from the starving peasants in Guatemala, from the beggars dying in the streets of India. . . . "

Two quite different reactions come to mind: (1) "Oh, feel the lash of righteousness!" and (2) "Oh, get off it!"

For hundreds and hundreds of years, Catholics attended the Latin Mass. They heard the charming, sweet Gregorian chant in Latin; maybe they even sang it. Then many of these same people went out into the world and did something. Some struggled to live Christian lives and raise families. Some left home forever, in order to bring the faith to the pagans. Some started labor unions and marched in picket lines. Some educated ungrateful children in the parochial schools or cared for the poor and the sick. The families, churches, seminaries, hospitals, schools, orphanages, missions, and charities were all made possible because of incalculable personal sacrifices. Maybe such things were not considered "social justice," but they were examples of doing good, and these heroic doers of good felt a "presence" of Christ in their lives, especially when they attended the Latin Mass.[15]

Let us marvel at the bravura performance (the very convincing performance) of the arrogant ones who announce to us that before Vatican II Catholics were lost in a haze of escapism during a liturgy, that they were passive, and that they exiled their Latin-speaking Christ to a remote place "out there." And let us marvel even more at a form of arrogance beyond the accepted definition of the word when a few liturgists, together with composers and performers of "contemporary" songs for the church, announce that they have come to replace centuries of error with a new, socially conscious, and relevant form of worship that, at long last, represents the true essence of an active Christianity. Yes indeed: *Oh, get off it!*

A clarification: I am not implying that Latin liturgies and Gregorian chant in Latin will automatically produce a vibrant Christianity and a commitment to social justice, just as they did in days of old. I am not denying the efficacy of "casual" prayer nor am I advocating a return to archaic ceremonies in church. I am only pointing out that this is not a simple matter. Hearing or singing liturgical texts, in the vernacular, about social justice will not automatically motivate someone to work for equality or help the poor. A Latin Mass in one parish — celebrated fervently and with conviction — could be associated with as much social justice, hospitality, and service to the poor as the most up-to-date "contemporary" liturgical environment (with up-to-date, relevant words) in another parish down the street. Human beings are not predictable; they are not puppets.

*   *   *

Roman Catholics are deluged with words. Every time a Catholic turns around there is another article, book, speech with words about a new and broader interpretation of the Mass and the church — words upon words of explanations and predictions of what the faith is going to do for the faithful, for the world.

In church, at a liturgy, Catholics are up to their necks in an ocean of more words. "Congregational participation" has become something very wordy ("talky"); "worship" becomes the hearing and recitation of spoken words — not as prayer, but as a task for the higher functions of the brain. To put it another way, modern "participation" is supposed to take place in the cranium, where the received words are deposited and processed. Somebody says, "Christ is present," and the worshiper is supposed to absorb this information as information. At least the Latin Mass, even with its manifold faults, had a way of suggesting that "the presence of Christ" was not just information but an "assurance" that was important, big, exalted, overpowering, and utterly in-expressible in human sounds called everyday spoken words; you felt that you had to react to this profound "presence" *by doing something.* Another way of putting it: during the Latin Mass, "congregational participation" *sometimes* reached human beings (and helped them to "do good") not through their craniums but through another part of human anatomy — their gut instincts.

The modern theologians and liturgists deserve all kinds of credit for their efforts, especially for reminding Catholics that worship is more than beauty and historicism, but they still have a lot to learn from the Latin Mass — about words, about gut instincts.

RITE I

When the Catholic church began to modernize its rituals and in-sert more vernacular texts into the Mass back in the late 1960s, a few parishes continued to schedule some Masses that were kept entirely in Latin. Then (according to stories I have heard), a most remarkable thing happened — a significant number of parish-ioners were avoiding the English/Latin liturgies and going out of their way to attend the all-Latin Masses (with no "participation") in other parishes. Pastors began to notice a drop in the Sunday collections and they complained to their bishops that the parishes with the Latin Masses were draining away business. The bishops responded by virtually eliminating all Latin Masses. There would be no options, no capitalist free enterprise, no competition.

When the Protestant Episcopal Church modernized its ser-vices in the 1970s, it gave parishes the option of using a Rite I, with the old "thee" and "thou," or a Rite II, with modernized Eng-lish. When other Protestant denominations brought their own services up to date, they sometimes offered a few options for choosing modern or more traditional English, and they also left the old-fashioned thee-and-thou language of their classic hymns substantially intact. The Roman Catholic church in the United States, ever fearful of competition among parishes, took a differ-ent approach; it drastically eliminated real options for the faithful. There is no choice of a "Rite I" or "Rite II" for most Catholics. The Latin Mass, even with readings and hymns in English, is certainly the church's "Rite I," but it is celebrated on a regular basis at only about 240 churches and chapels in the United States; Latin also comes back from time to time at a few other places, but this is out of a total of approximately 18,500 churches. A Solemn Mass chanted in English certainly qualifies as a successor to the Latin liturgy, especially if amplification is restrained, but this kind of chanted Mass in English is as hard to find as one in Latin.

A few years ago I attended the funeral Mass of a friend in an impoverished inner-city parish. About two minutes into the service I realized something that mildly jolted me: this was Rite I½. The priest, a Jesuit friend of mine, was chanting various parts of the Mass in English, without amplification; the congregation joined in all the sung dialogues with him. I had never heard anything like this before in a parish church. (Chanting in English, with tiny exceptions, is virtually unknown in most American Catholic parishes.)

This entire funeral liturgy (Rite I½) was exceedingly plain, with the congregation singing hymns from a missalette, but it brought us to the gates of heaven. In the middle of such human poverty and despair, which we never forgot for a moment, the chanting (derived from the Latin Gregorian model) conveyed a strong sense of hope. The congregation's exact understanding of the syntax and grammar of the sentences that came out of the priest's mouth did not suggest this hope, this awareness of something profound and deeply comforting; rather, it was that eternal, timeless "groaning" of the chant that had this deeply moving effect. "Groaning," Latin or English, can be powerful stuff. (Oddly enough, this power decreases as the volume is increased through amplification.) Chanting/"groaning" seems to come from nature, from the sound of the wind or the waves or something deep within the earth. It sounds like New Age music.

"*Groaning?* What is this person talking about?"

Let me explain to the reader by using an old educational device: the pop quiz, actually three of them:

1. Near the beginning of Mass, a priest behind the altar adjusts his microphone, lifts his hands upward, and recites the opening prayer, the Collect. Just to make sure that you miss nothing, he speaks slowly and has the amplification turned up so far that it causes nerve damage. Now, as soon as he finishes, give the con-

gregation a pop quiz. Ask everyone to paraphrase what was just recited.

2. Another congregation, another Collect, but this time chanted in Latin, without that damnable irritation called amplification. Another pop quiz.

3. A third congregation and a third Collect; this one is chanted in English, without amplification. The final pop quiz.

How would these three congregations score on the quizzes? It depends on what result you want to measure. The second and third congregations probably "got the most" out of the opening prayer. Maybe they did not follow the exact meaning of every sentence, but that neutral "groaning" allowed them to participate actively by filling in the verbal ambiguity with their own inner words. The first congregation would probably do the worst recalling the prayer. Even though all of those recited English words had been riveted into skulls by means of amplification, only a few people would remember a disconnected noun or verb and even fewer would receive spiritual nourishment from passively listening to recited sentences.

Many Catholics who can remember the old Solemn High Mass in Latin know intuitively what this primal "groaning" means. Episcopalian priests who have converted to Roman Catholicism get my point. So does a Hindu who knows a mantra. This "groaning" can be the "fluent croaking" of a priest that James Joyce described in *Ulysses*. It can be beautiful or a little grating or in any language but, whatever the form, it often has the ability to stun, to shock us with its defiant display of confidence. (Of course, a more unpleasant kind of shock comes from listening to the tone-deaf attempt to sing. These poor individuals are sometimes helped by turning off the amplification; when that does not work, everyone grants them a permanent dispensation to recite instead of chant.)

If this timeless "groaning" of a chanted text can sometimes be so convincing, why is it virtually outlawed in most Catholic churches? The explanations I have heard go something like this: "Well, most priests have wretched voices. . . . They feel self-conscious about singing when they have to face a congregation. . . . Chant is grand opera; we're beyond that now. . . . People threw out their old LPs when compact disks became available; they threw out the Latin High Mass to make way for something better. . . . People today want progress; they don't want any chanting, which suggests the technologically backward *style* of the Latin Mass," and so forth.

Feeble excuses. How can people reject what they have never been allowed to know?

*   *   *

I was told recently about a man who was angrily fired from his job as a music teacher in a seminary. The reason? He had taught the seminarians a few snippets of Gregorian chant in Latin and, even worse, how to chant the Mass in English. (He used music that was in standard song books and in the official *Sacramentary* that the presider uses at the altar.) This man, who is quite liberal and impatient with traditionalism, had dared to teach the seminarians another option: a form of liturgical music that slightly recalls the old sung Latin Mass; he had dared to introduce the option of Rite I½. For that transgression, he had to go.

Last I heard, these seminarians are now told that any kind of chanting by the priest is an inconsequential decoration and probably a distraction from the true meaning of Christianity. But some instruction is available, by appointment, for anyone who still wants to learn how to sing a fragment or two. (The local cardinal-archbishop, by the way, is known as the conservative's conservative.)

WHOSE VERNACULAR IS THIS, ANYWAY?

Some Catholics of my vintage may remember a mild disagreement that broke out in the Catholic church shortly before the Second Vatican Council. The issue was this: Should American Catholics end a prayer by saying *Ae-men* or *Ah-men?* Red-blooded, John-Wayne-loving Americans were supposed to twang a forceful and Americanized *Ae-men*. Those who favored things European (and Latin, in particular) insisted on the more Roman *Ah-men*.

This difference of opinion may look trivial, but it provided an early warning that a rebellion was brewing among some of the troops. Without the council, the monopoly of Latin would not have lasted much longer than it did. One way or another, the whole Latin phenomenon was either going to be violently attacked by the *Ae-men* faction or peacefully dismantled.

The Latin monopoly really should have faded centuries ago. If a "normal" history had been allowed to take its course (and when is history ever "normal"?), the use of vernacular languages and Latin in the liturgy might have evolved into some kind of happy arrangement. Both would have flourished. But the church did not enjoy the luxury of a "normal" history. Challenged by Protestantism, secularism, nationalism, communism, and all the rest, Rome was determined to show the world an impregnable fortress. Latin provided many of the bricks in that fortress.

And then there has always been another persistent danger: the very volatile issue of *whose* vernacular would replace Latin. A language map of Europe has always looked like a tossed salad. There was a time, before the modern system of communications and transportation brought people closer together (and weakened regional differences), when the pieces in this language salad were sometimes very small indeed. Dialects changed from one valley to the next in some areas; sometimes the language changed from one village to the next. The Italians would have hooted a new priest out of the church if he prayed aloud with words from the wrong kind of dialect. The Flemish-speakers in Belgium would have set fire to the church if the priest tried to conduct services in French. This language mess was, for centuries, complicated even further by the politics of appointing bishops. Under pressure from, let us say, a German-speaking emperor in Vienna, the church sometimes had to appoint a royalist, German-speaking bishop as the head of a diocese where most of the population spoke Hungarian or Czech or Polish. When all of these issues were taken into consideration, praying in Latin was seen partly as an astute compromise and partly as a way to avoid open warfare.

Latin still provides a shrewd way to steer clear of language battles. When a parish in New York City finds that it has more immigrant groups than it can count, when French-speaking and English-speaking Canadians get together, when there is an international congregation, and so forth, Latin makes good sense. But this kind of language compromise is sometimes not even considered. There are *Ae-men* militants everywhere, and they are determined to prove that God, who is one of their own, understands only their talking. (I am told that Latin is barely used even at Lourdes. Pilgrims are expected to sort themselves out by language groups and worship separately.)

* * *

In the past hundred years or so it has probably happened at least twice a month to every pope: At about three in the morning the pope cries out in his sleep. His valet, hurriedly putting on a bathrobe, dashes down the hallway to the pope's room. He finds the pontiff sitting up in bed and sweating in terror.

"The same nightmare, Holiness?" asks the valet.

"Yes, yes, the same one," responds the pope, "the threat of tribalism."

Religion is a strong force in the world, but tribalism (sometimes manifested as nationalism and ethnic chauvinism) is even stronger and exceedingly dangerous. It could shatter Catholicism into innumerable shards. Latin was once a linguistic weapon that defended the church against the threat of tribalism. This ancient language had a way of conveying a blunt message to the warring tribes of Europe and their descendants elsewhere: "Look, you hotheads, Christianity and its message are bigger than your ethnic pride. Christ is not some kind of local deity, a private mascot. Cool it, at least when you're in church."

* * *

Listen to the birds singing in springtime. It sounds beautiful, but it is really quite savage. Sometimes the function of the chirping and sweet singing is not to express beauty and happiness but to establish territory. The bird's song is a way of shouting, "This is my territory, not yours. Get out!"

Vernacular singing in Catholic parishes, without the balance of some Latin, has become a way of establishing territory. When the insistence on the use of the vernacular becomes almost fanatical, this is a sign that the externals of the ceremony have been turned into a way of establishing turf, not devotion. The vernacular (without the moderation of some Latin) proclaims, "This is our territory, not yours. Get out!"

A FEMININE DECLENSION

The telephone rang. A friend of mine, an organist, received a call from a colleague on a Friday afternoon. It seems that the colleague was the local organizer of a Catholic conference on something or other; he needed a musician who could provide "a little music" for the opening liturgical celebration — Evening Prayer — at this gathering. Could my friend help?

"What kind of music do you need?" my friend asked.

"Just some simple hymns that everybody knows. Something ecumenical, because people from different religions have been invited."

"When is this Evening Prayer going to be held?"

"Tonight, in about four hours."

Being an obliging sort person, my friend put on his coat, got in his car, and immediately drove to the conference. There was no time to lose. As soon as he arrived, he went looking for the members of the Liturgy Committee, who were not easy to locate. When he finally got a couple of them together, he showed them the missalette that was in the pews of the Catholic chapel where Evening Prayer would take place and he mentioned about a dozen possible songs.

His recommendations were received in silence, an eerie silence. Then a member of the Liturgy Committee — a woman — responded with disgust in her voice. The first song, she said, had the word "Lord" in it; the second referred to God as "Him"; the third, with its emphasis on a mighty and muscular Christianity, was an example of patriarchy, and so forth. Did he not realize that the committee had labored on the text of this liturgy for months; did he not see that all references to a male divinity had been skillfully avoided in this service. People like him, with their sexist bigotry and their "art music" composed by some DWEM (Dead White European Male), had ruined the liturgy for centuries.

The planning session continued. My friend looked at the clock. Finally, after a long and exhausting discussion, the committee came to a decision. The congregation could safely sing "Be Not Afraid" and "Dona Nobis Pacem" ("Grant Us Peace"), the round. Both songs steer clear of the "He" problem in reference to God. The first is what I call a "Voice of God" song; the congregation, in languid and almost tired tones, sings God's own words. (The dreamy, casual "Voice of God" song, without the addition of phrases like, "The Lord said," is a radical break with Jewish and Christian tradition.) The second song used a Latin text.

For me, this story confirms a crank theory that I have long believed (and we are all entitled to at least one crank theory). I phrase the theory thus: Many centuries ago, the Catholic church — the institution, the organization run by males — became "gender sensitive." Church leaders realized that all of those liturgical texts with "male words" would antagonize women and also give the false impression that God is masculine. To get around this problem, church leaders began to chant the liturgy. This process — removing the words one step from everyday talk — seemed to take the gender associations out of the liturgical words. By going a step further — by using Latin — the whole ceremony was effectively "de-gendered." The sung Latin allowed women in the congregation to construct their own meanings and symbols for the rituals; once they realized they had the power to "shape" the ceremonies any way they wanted, women could, without hesitation, enter into the spirit of the ritual (conducted by men). At the same time, men could also "shape" their own interpretations of the Latin liturgy. An exclusive language (Latin) turned out to be an extremely useful way to insure inclusive worship.

On second thought, maybe this is not such a crank theory.

* * *

On August 26, 1991, Sister Mary Collins, O.S.B., chair of the Religion and Religious Education Department at Catholic University of America, gave a speech at the annual assembly of the Leadership Conference of Women Religious. Her address, "Is the Eucharist Still a Source of Meaning for Women?"[16] analyzes the spiritual unhappiness (sometimes the misery) of some Catholic women in and out of religious orders. Her main point: "The crux of the troubled relationship American women religious have with the Roman Catholic Church...is centered in contemporary Catholic eucharistic praxis."

Sister Mary Collins — who just "tells it like it is" — maintains that a number of women in religious orders "identify eucharistic liturgy as part of the system of power and privilege they reject." The bishops and priests

who want women to celebrate with them the mystery of Christ as the bond of unity, the world's peace and its salvation also claim to find in the eucharist a warrant for legitimating male dominance in the community and their own clerical hold on institutional power. Such theological claims about male superiority and clerical power have begun to hang over eucharistic assemblies like storm systems. . . . The gains women and men have made in ecclesial collaboration at the level of ministry have only made ritual separation more poisonous.

Sister Mary Collins also observes that there is an "emergent resistance among some women religious to joining in celebrations of the eucharist of the Roman rite." They resent going to Mass in their convent if the presider is an appointed priest with whom the community has "little or no rapport." They devise substitute liturgies that women control. Sister Mary Collins sympathizes with these complaints; she knows all about disappointment with the church. In her opinion, this "present disillusionment is grace offered to women and through women to the whole church." But she also makes the point that all of the unhappiness needs to be put in proper perspective:

Ordinary women and the poor have often worn the clerical construction of reality lightly. Poor women, outcast women, spiritually gifted women and prayerful women have always known a God whose mystery is not exhausted in the authoritative patriarchal, clerical rendering of Jesus' revelation. . . .

To insist upon construing eucharist solely as a symbol of male power is to squander a known source of spiritual vitality in the Catholic Community.

She despairs about the present. She looks to the future.

Right in the middle of reading this speech by Sister Mary Collins, a vivid scene entered my memory — Mass in a convent chapel, long ago.

In the early 1950s, when I was a boy, I was taken to a liturgy in the chapel of a motherhouse of the Sisters of Mercy. "Chapel" is not quite the appropriate word, since this structure was a church of grand proportions and larger than many parish churches. Along the sides of the chapel/church were wooden stalls that faced the center of the building (not the sanctuary). In these stalls were rows of sisters, all in identical habits and facing us, the visitors, in the pews. I remember a line of burning candles, which were attached to the carvings on the stalls, one candle between each of the sisters in the top row. I remember all of the nuns chanting the High Mass with gentleness and yet with a powerfully confident volume. In a way, it was all rather simple and uneventful, but the impact on us visitors was — what? Healing and yet disturbing... routine and yet astonishing. Whatever the case, a memory to cherish.

Now please, women religious, do not throw this book across the room. Some of you lead extremely busy lives; you have to go out into the world and work three jobs just to support yourself, a retired sister, and a novice. Nobody is suggesting that you should go back to veils and bulky habits. Nobody is suggesting that you would be so much happier if you would just retreat to the safety of the cloister, sing pretty music in Latin, and mind your own business. I am, however, going to recommend that we all take a closer look at that Latin High Mass for a moment.

Father K (sweet old man, in bad health) was the celebrant. He was at the center of things; he was "controlling everything" — or was he? The tight rubrics and Latin language of the Tridentine Mass wiped out his personality. The layers of vestments seemed to obliterate his sex. We seldom saw his face. Sometimes the congregation was not even aware that he was in the sanctuary. His liturgical job was nobody's definition of "power and privilege" (the phrase that Sister Mary Collins uses). In fact, with all the bowing and genuflections and minute regulations for his movements, the job was rather demeaning.

At various points in the Mass Father K entered into a musical dialogue with the community of sisters; priest and women religious chanted back and forth — as equals. (No microphones in those days.) The Gregorian melodies that the sisters chanted did not seem to be the property of elitists or conservatives; they belonged to everybody, even to the visitors in the pews.

For *that time* and *that place*, this Solemn Mass was an example of Catholicism's unrivaled shrewdness. The church had cleverly managed to minimize the dangers of the "battle of the sexes" by humbling the priest and by defusing any resentments about male "power and privilege." Perhaps a sociologist in that congregation would have concluded that this ritual was like an ingeniously constructed "game" (in the most sublime sense of that word), which nobody wins, but nobody loses either.

The rock concert, the Las Vegas nightclub extravaganza, the second act of *Aida* at the Metropolitan Opera, modern liturgical dance around the altar — all of these things can have an impact on us, but nothing quite like that High Mass in the convent chapel. Perhaps the "extra ingredient" that made that liturgy so memorable (and left such a lasting impression on my family) was the overwhelming sense of "giving up" power. It was like a theatrical show with a large cast of temperamental actors, and every one of them refuses to accept the role of star, except perhaps during the sermon. It was a social and sexual truce, a mutual surrender (to a new life in Christ).

Where are the snows of yesteryear? They were very beautiful indeed, but they have disappeared. There is no sense in trying to wish them back. Life is change, and the snows of tomorrow will be just as impressive. And yet, there is so much to be learned from yesteryear, from that archaic, outdated, "irrelevant" High Mass long ago. I am not referring primarily to the old language or the old music at that liturgy but to the old virtue of humility — that deep sense of common purpose and service to something bigger than yourself or your sex. Beginning in the late 1960s, what really vanished in many churches and chapels was not Latin but this "group humility," something more beautiful than any snows of any year. The disappearance of humility and surrender came first; the disappearance of Latin followed as a consequence.

Today, in some convent chapel somewhere, the sisters go to Mass. There they encounter a priest who faces them constantly. He does not surrender to the appointed texts of the ritual; he "improves" them with his own embellishments. He smiles, sincerely. He turns on his rapport, his warmth, his postconciliar desire to *include* them — and it all comes across as flirting. He speaks into a microphone that transforms him into the biggest thing in the room. He has good intentions, but all of his nice personal touches only seem to glorify his "power and privilege." The man is not a presider; he is a provocation. In this skirmish in the "battle of the sexes," he has all of the weapons.

At one point in her speech, Sister Mary Collins refers briefly to the few communities of nuns who have maintained their monastic identity and still assemble in the chapel to sing the Divine Office at various times of the day (Matins, Lauds, Vespers, and so forth). These traditional prayer services (in Latin or English, probably sung in some kind of chant) help these communities with their "self-definition," according to Sister Mary Collins.

They also provide "some buffer against wholly clericalized public prayer."

This is an old story. Religious communities of women were practicing "womanspirit" centuries before feminists gave it a name. In the Divine Office and the Latin High Mass, some women religious used to find their own self-definition and their own liturgical life. For a long list of reasons, it is impractical to "go back," to restore a monastic liturgical ideal for all women religious; nevertheless, it would be very useful to extract "wisdom" from those old rituals — a "wisdom" that keeps men in their place.

I saw this "wisdom" in a television program on Mother Teresa of Calcutta. In one scene, Mother Teresa and her followers were sitting on the floor of a bare room and praying quietly; they seemed to be using standard, familiar forms of prayer. There was no elaborate chant or Latin, but the simplicity and "standardization" of this small prayer service was another version of the old monastic Divine Office. Without gimmicks, ludicrous dancing, or special feminist texts, this prayer service seemed to bond these women together in an extraordinarily powerful way.

*   *   *

Should women be ordained as priests? We follow the reasoning that justifies the ordination of women — and then we hear about a particularly macabre example of worship conducted by and for women only.[17] It completely destroys their credibility.

We listen to those who find evidence in history for the ordination of women, but we are soon distracted by some radical feminist who denounces the men priests and their selfish hold on power — and it is obvious that what is fueling her anger is not a desire for Christian unity or equality but for power. She wants a piece of the action. She wants to be a modern presider, to feel the surge of power and the glow of prestige given to men who sit on thrones behind altars. She wants to be a part of the problem.

We listen to celibates go on and on about the injustice of not ordaining women — and we get the impression that they really mean *celibate* women. When will it occur to them that they should at least make a passing reference to the question of ordaining married women and more married men?

Would a woman priest ever say a Latin Mass? Would a woman bishop ever allow such a thing in her diocese?

TE IGITUR

Stage I: It is the early Middle Ages. The priest has come to that part of the Mass called the Eucharistic Prayer, in this case the Roman Canon. As is the custom, he goes to an area behind an ornamental screen or curtains, where the congregation cannot clearly see him, and then he chants these words:

Te igitur, clementissime Pater, per Jesum Christum Filium tuum Dominum nostrum, supplices rogamus ac petimus, uti accepta habeas, et benedicas, haec dona, haec munera, haec sancta sacrificia illibata...

Stage II: It is the early 1960s. The priest quietly recites these same words of the Roman Canon, perhaps while the choir sings a Sanctus that splits the air with exhilarating harmonies. Some people in the congregation sense that an important moment has arrived; others, consulting their missals, are a little more focused and know that a rough translation of the priest's prayer goes something like this:

Most merciful Father, we therefore humbly ask and beseech, through Jesus Christ, Thy Son, Our Lord, that Thou shouldst accept and bless these gifts, these presents, these holy and unspotted sacrifices...

Stage III: The time is the present. The congregation listens as the priest, his voice hugely magnified through electronic amplification, reads the official English language version of the same Canon, as prepared by the International Committee on English in the Liturgy (ICEL):

> We come to you, Father,
> with praise and thanksgiving,
> through Jesus Christ your Son.
> Through him
> we ask you to accept and bless
> these gifts which we offer in sacrifice.

Observe the evolution here. In the original Latin (Stages I and II), God the Father is addressed in submissive and deferential language. The echoing repetitions (ask...beseech, accept... bless, gifts... presents... sacrifices) seem perfectly fitting; the extra-ordinary religious act called the Mass required extra-ordinary language. In Stage III, however, the official English translation reads like a recipe from a cookbook. Not one word in it suggests humility, respect, awe, or the extra-ordinary, and this is because of a deliberate policy. The ICEL, which was given the task of preparing the official English texts for worship, frequently went out of its way to make sure that the congregation would always receive the place of honor, while God would be spoken to in language that sounds like an efficient memo. Note that "we" is the first word in the ICEL's translation of the old Roman Canon; in the original Latin, and any sensitive English translation, God the Father comes first. (Stage IV is on its way; the ICEL has promised to release an improved version of these texts for the Mass.)

In Stages I and II the congregation could stare right through the priest and almost remain unaware of his presence, because this man was only one part of a complicated "event" that involved the whole community. Mr. Smith thinking pious thoughts, Mrs. Jones carefully following every word of the liturgy with her missal, Miss White saying the rosary, and the priest taking care of the official supplications to God the Father — these were all considered to be important contributions to the liturgical "event," although the priest's job was the most important. Everybody's contribution was valid.

In Stage III, with microphones, there is a new and drastically simplified flow chart. The ceremony is structured in a way that forces everything — prayers, pieties, thoughts — to flow through the priest to God or from the priest to the congregation. The celebrant's amplified words take over completely (except for those moments when a reader or song leader controls the sound system). The flow chart demands that the worshiper's first duty is absolute and undivided attention to the few individuals at the top of it. This arrangement can provide opportunities for structured *participation* (such as the movement of vocal cords in song) but not necessarily for that supreme form of participation called *involvement*. A sincerely committed, prayerful involvement in worship — something that always begins as a personal and private matter — is deliberately suppressed in an environment dominated by people behind microphones; the flow chart seems to suggest that the worshiper's involvement must flow in one and only one direction: to the person controlling the sound system at a particular moment.

The secret source of power behind the structures of the "old" Latin Mass and even the "new" one (without heavy amplification) is that they both welcome involvement, because the flow chart is much more confused. The worshiper can, as it were, go "around" the priest and musicians. The ritual gently guides the "imagination" here and there but basically leaves it alone. This absence of any straining for the worshiper's attention is what makes the Latin ritual (properly conducted) so appealing. A vernacular liturgy, to be sure, can also have this same appeal, this same impact — but not in places where the congregation senses that it has to perform in front of the individuals at the top of the flow chart (participation), without being allowed a moment to think about their own personal commitment (involvement).

FOR FURTHER MEDITATION AND GROUP DISCUSSION

1. Day's First Law of Liturgical Dynamics: *The bigger their ego, the more they hate the Latin Mass.*

Those outspoken, enraged Catholics who oppose any type of Latin liturgy all have one thing in common — an ego the size of a major basilica. Their pronouncements sound so correct, so dramatic, but a closer look at the individuals issuing these denunciations will reveal that their principal concern is themselves. Too many priests, bishops, leaders of song, guitarists, and neighborhood liturgy planners seem to think that liturgy is a vaudeville act, starring them. What angers them about the Latin liturgy is its tendency to "cramp their style," to submerge their egos in an inclusive public event. Oh, does that cause irritation!

Day's Second Law of Liturgical Dynamics is not quite ready to be formulated, but its general outline is this: Most Catholics, the ones who keep their egos within manageable proportions, are quite broad-minded about a Latin Mass that is an option among options. Or maybe they are just indifferent.

2. "You watch: Roman Catholic worship is going to become more and more like the rituals of the Byzantines."

I heard that many times in the late 1960s, during and after Vatican II. The Roman Rite, we were told, would soon resemble the ceremonies of the Eastern Rites and the Orthodox churches — continuous chanting, more litanies, more antiphons sung by the congregation, the vernacular, and so forth.

Some liturgical specialists, green with envy, explained that the Eastern churches (the Greeks, Russians, Ukrainians, and all the rest) were the ones that had really preserved the ideals of true liturgy. According to these same specialists, the Latin church had wandered in a liturgical desert for centuries; the quietly mumbled prayers and all the useless complications of "art music" in the Roman Rite were signs of a corruption that would now be rooted out. Yes, everything was going to change now. Rome had come to its senses and would move closer to the East. Do not mourn for the Latin liturgy, we were told; instead, rejoice at the return to authentic principles of worship, as preserved across the centuries in the East.

I'm still waiting for this shift eastward. There are, to be sure, a few monasteries that practice a Byzantinized Roman Rite, but nearly all of the other churches and chapels have moved farther and farther away from the rituals of the Eastern brethren. When it comes to liturgy, the Latin Rite Roman Catholic parish and, let us say, a Ukrainian Rite Roman Catholic parish down the street are moving farther apart; often they look like two different, incompatible religions.

Sometimes you come across a Latin Rite church or chapel where the people in charge have decided to "go back to their liturgical roots," back to the pure and uncorrupted traditions. But well-intentioned people like this frequently become confused about the whole process of "restoration" and start to imitate Anglicanism.

3. In 1969 I visited Oxford, England, and happened to walk into the University Church of St. Mary the Virgin. A brochure that I found in the back of this church, an Anglo-Catholic Protestant establishment, informed me that a series of preachers would deliver the sermons during the Hilary Term. After each service there was to be a discussion of the sermon in the Seminar Room of All Souls College. According to this brochure, one change in the normal routine would occur on January 19. On that date the Rev.

P. Curtis, M.A., chaplain of Giggleswick School, would preach: "Sermon in Latin. (No Discussion.)"

4. Back in the 1960s I met a young man who was studying to become an Episcopalian priest. His fellow seminarians, he told me, sometimes skipped chapel services and sometimes went outside the seminary for worship, but there was one occasion when chapel attendance was slightly higher than normal; that was when the lector had to begin his reading with words from 1 Corinthians that went something like this: "I hear there are fornicators among you."

"How do you deliver that line?" my acquaintance asked me. Does the reader take off his glasses, tilt his head, and say, "I *hear* . . . " Does he frown? In any case, the solution to the reading of the line always caused merriment among the seminarians.

After I heard this story, I contemplated: In another part of town, the deacon at a Roman Catholic service will proclaim the same text but he will not have to worry about the right way to deliver his lines. He just chants (in a neutral, objective voice), "Omnino auditur inter vos fornicatio."

We come to you, Father — How is the Catholic priest supposed to say that line or any public prayer? Does he produce deep, rounded tones? Does he turn the words into a sincere speech and pronounce every word, "as if he really means it"? Does he try "method acting" and give the impression that he is spontaneously making up his lines as he goes along? Or does he read or chant the words in a neutral, objective tone of voice? The last solution is an old tradition familiar to Orthodox Jews, Orthodox Christians, and Catholics who remember the Latin Mass. It allows people to give shape to their own parallel but wordless prayer.

5. Monsignor Majestic tries to affect what is called a "stained-glass voice" during Mass. He does not realize that his rich and dramatic diction, enunciated into a microphone, tilts everything in his favor.

Monsignor: a-MAY . . . THE LORD . . . BE . . . a-WITH a-YOU.

Congregation: Andalsowithyou.

Compare that with the Latin formula, chanted:

Celebrant: Dominus vobiscum [which weighs three pounds and two ounces in importance].

Congregation: Et cum spiritu tuo [which also weighs three pounds and two ounces in importance].

That kind of "balance" can also exist in a vernacular liturgy, but you must go back to the Latin model, preferably the sung version, to see how it is done. (Do not, of course, go back to that rapid style of recitation and singing that sounded like machine-gun fire.)

6. You can't go home again . . . but, if you don't go home again, you will become lonely and rootless.

7. Away with the convenient old "liberal" and "conservative" labels! They are useless when it comes to the Latin Mass. Some bedrock conservative bishops virtually forbid any kind of Latin Mass in their dioceses. Some Catholics thumb their noses at the church on a variety of issues and then tell you that they go out of their way to attend a Latin Mass. It's a crazy world.

8. The Latin Mass did not last for so many centuries because it was some dear old thing, a lovely antique to be preserved. It was not what a steam railroad is today: a charming piece of history, a nostalgia trip. Rather, the Latin Mass was pure "counter-culture" and almost an act of rebellion against business-as-usual, against commonplace morality.

A Latin Mass used to be a form of existentialist tension, in which the worshiper was caught in the paradox of anguish and assurance, the unknowable and the familiar, the enigmatic and the logical — but that is what the spiritual life is all about.

The Latin Mass is not now and never was "charming." Without causing stress, it disturbs the worshiper, it challenges.

9. I can remember the time, back in my youth, when good Catholic boys who sensed at least the hint of a calling to the priesthood would have "pretend altars" in their bedrooms. (My friend J, who lived his short adult life as a wonderful priest, was rumored to have had a bureau with so many kneeling angels, statues, and candles on top that it looked like the high altar in a cathedral.) These boys, in the privacy of their rooms, would go through the motions of the Latin Mass, as well as they understood them.

"How disgraceful! The deplorable escapism, the romantic nonsense!" Well, maybe, and it certainly encouraged the notion that the Mass was a private monopoly of the priest. But, in any case, we can be sure that not many boys today will put a chair behind their bureaus and pretend to be presiders.

10. Sometimes I get the impression that in just about any area of the United States where there are ten or more parishioners of Irish descent, the local church will have, on St. Patrick's Day, a Gaelic Mass. At this same church the assistant pastor who even mentions the possibility of a Latin Mass would probably be defrocked, on the spot, for spreading heresy, for suggesting prayers in a "foreign" language. But on March 17 the Mass in this church will be in the Irish, a tongue incomprehensible to 99.99 percent of the assembled faithful.

The music at this Gaelic Mass is hastily concocted stuff and unbearable. Is the music perhaps the reason why the face of St. Patrick — in the stained glass or the statue over in the corner — winces in pain? Or maybe the saint and founder of Irish Christianity is in discomfort because he told the Irish to worship in Latin, not Gaelic.

During the centuries of British colonial rule in Ireland, the Latin Mass, celebrated in secret, was a powerful unifying symbol among the persecuted Irish. But how quickly symbols and history have been forgotten. It now looks as if the Gaelic Mass, something St. Patrick did not want, might eventually become the symbol of the Catholic Irish — their struggles and their Christianity, at home and abroad. Latin, which came from someplace else, might be expelled as if it were a foreign bacteria, like the British. (St. Patrick, a foreigner in Ireland, brought his Latin Mass from someplace else.) The liturgy of Irish Catholics and their American cousins would have to be strictly Irish. Themselves alone.

The American Irish are not the only ones to rewrite the place of Latin in their history. Down the road, in the Polish parish, the Polish language has displaced historic Latin for special occasions. Catholics from a French background use the French Mass to remind themselves of their historic identity (and they ignore the French contribution to the repertory of Gregorian chant). Even the Italians (*Marrone! Vergogna!*) boast about their Italian Mass in the parish on special feasts. Have they never heard of Pre-Italian, Latin?

11. Crusty old Professor X — Jewish, cynical, and one of the nicest persons I have ever known — had a low opinion of my Catholic education at the hands of the Jesuits. "A waste of time," he pronounced it. But the old curmudgeon sat up and paid attention the time I described my training in Latin. That impressed him.

"Hmmm. Just like the Jews and Hebrew," he commented. From that day on I received from him a measure of respect that he had never bestowed on me before.

Let us be honest. Latin, like Hebrew, is loaded with mystique. It gave the Catholic clergy and Catholic worship the respect and even power that come with mystique. The distinctions between classical Latin and church Latin do not enter into the picture. Latin, no matter what form, commands respect.

The fact is, the Catholic church survived — got through some very hard times — partly because of its mystique. Sanctity, good example, prayer, commitment to the poor, and divine assistance will bring their own kind of mystique, but still there is that extra edge, that compelling impressiveness that is bestowed upon a clergyman when he uses Latin — or Hebrew or seventeenth-century English or chanted modern English.

You have to feel sorry for the young Latinless priests coming out of the seminaries these days. These fellows are being sent out into the hostile world without much mystique to help them. A good command of basic Latin would have made them more...interesting.

12. A friend of mine was born and raised in Connecticut. English, of course, became his native language, but he also learned to speak Slovak from his immigrant grandparents.

In the early 1960s my friend, while traveling in Europe, visited his grandparents' ancestral village. Relatives and old family friends welcomed him. There was much to talk about — but something was wrong. Communication was strained. After a few hours of conversation, one of his relatives politely informed him that his Slovak was, well, funny. He was using quaint old phrases and vocabulary that went back to the days when that part of the world belonged to the Austro-Hungarian Empire. The language had changed.

The philosopher Heraclitus maintained that everything is change; everything is in a state of flux; permanence is an illusion; you cannot step into the same river twice.

You certainly cannot step into the same linguistic river twice. Language is in a constant state of transition to another transition.

Good luck to the innocent liturgists and clergy who are working diligently to achieve this perfect "contemporary" language, this "modern English of our time." Many of them will live to see the day when their efforts look so dated, even funny.

The scholars who translated the King James Bible used a lively modern style of English — just for their dedicatory preface. Their actual translation of the Bible is in an invented, artificial language that is close to poetry. The language of the preface went out of style fast; the language of the Bible text, however, survived a lot longer.

The use of some Latin in a liturgy is a symbol of enduring values amid the rushing flow of constant change. All human things change; sometimes they must be changed. But the Latin liturgy — subtly and psychologically — suggests that some spiritual things will endure.

13. A "practicing" Christian is someone who also practices an unconscious form of dishonesty called "holding back a little something." The Christian, even an exemplary one, can go to church regularly, keep the commandments, give to the poor, rejoice in being born again, love the unloveable neighbor, and still, in one corner of the mind, "hold back a little something." Maybe the "something" is the sin of pride; maybe it is intolerance or a less-than-total acceptance of a theological matter. "Holding back a little something" is not necessarily hypocritical; it is merely human. Healthy and happy Christians recognize their "holding back" and pray for a release from this human weakness. They realize that a total and perfect practice of Christianity is an impossibility and absolutely unattainable, but a glorious goal. Nietzsche was right: the last real Christian was the one who died on the Cross.

A "practicing" Catholic is someone who learns to practice "holding back a little something" with cunning, with creative virtuosity, even brilliance, as if it were one of the fine arts. There are Catholics who accept every word of every sentence in Canon Law, but they have never quite understood the gentle spirit of the

New Testament. And there are those terribly modern Catholics who advertise their shared humanity with Christ, their renewed postconciliar spirituality, their total surrender to joy in the Resurrection, but they have no use for Canon Law and that whole side of the Catholic "package."

The great majority of Catholics maneuver somewhere between the extremes; they "hold back" here and there; they cope. Again, this is not a case of scandalous hypocrisy — just the reality of human imperfection. Any parish priest who has been mellowed by years of pastoral experience discovered long ago that all those "imperfect" people listening to his homily will fade in and out while he is talking. He knows that the waters of baptism failed to cover maybe a toe on one parishioner or even a whole foot on another. He knows he lives in the imperfect world.

Lately, many Catholics have been holding back more than a "little something." They may recite the Creed and say that they believe in "one holy catholic and apostolic Church," but then, mentally, they add long footnotes: about artificial birth control, the ordination of women, and so forth. They do not acquiesce totally.

Because of an unfortunate accident of history, the Latin Mass has been dragged into the whole business of "holding back a little something." It has become a symbol of *the conservative backlash*. Mention the Latin Mass — or even things that "go with it," such as traditional music — and many Catholics start ranting: about reactionaries who want to put nuns back into starched habits and sensible oxford shoes; about religious Stalinism; about Vatican cardinals, with jeweled fingers, and their determination to silence nonconformists. In other words, "Latin Mass" *equals* the revenge of the reactionaries, the crackdown on the lazy practice of "holding back a little something."

This kind of panic is unwarranted. If we are talking about the liturgy according to the new rite (the *Novus Ordo*), the "Latin Mass types" are people from across the entire spectrum. Many conservatives will share the same pews with many liberals. If we are talking about the return to the so-called Tridentine Latin Mass, then the situation in the pews becomes more complex. The person on one side of you is a true Christian, a living saint; the person on the other side is a Nazi.

14. Years ago Catholic parishes used to have names like "Blessed Sacrament" and "Most Precious Blood." Someday I expect to see, on the lawn of a new suburban parish, a sign that reads, "The Faith Community of the Bread and the Cup (Catholic)." You will seldom hear a word of Latin in a place like that.

15. Any Catholic who can remember the days before Vatican II can also remember horror stories about the Catholic clergy's occasional heartless insensitivity. (The situation might have involved a woman being told that, in spite of her drunken, abusive husband and life-threatening pregnancies, she should learn to suffer in silence. Divorce was a disgrace and artificial birth control out of the question.)

Part of the reason for this tendency to reduce the human condition, at its most wretched, to cold abstractions could be blamed on the theological and pastoral training of seminarians, which was sometimes conducted in Latin. The lectures in Latin had a way of reducing life's pain and complexities to formulas that were detached from reality.

16. For anyone with an obsessive or compulsive personality, the old Latin rituals were almost an addictive form of comfort because they were so predictable, so unyielding. When the old rituals were replaced by looser ones, a few of these people went through severe anguish; they never recovered. But many others — and this can happen with the obsessive personality — switched overnight. One Sunday they were ferociously defending the Latin Mass against the slightest accommodation to the vernacular; the next Sunday they were demanding the abolition of the sung Ave Maria because it was in Latin.

17. A wiseguy like me has everything figured out, including the Latin Mass.

I once heard the secretary of the Latin Liturgy Association give a speech. He said that he and other members of the association felt very strongly about the Latin Mass and wanted to promote it not primarily for historical or cultural reasons but "for the love of God."

When I heard that sentence, spoken with the plainest simplicity, all my wiseguy pretensions and pomposities collapsed.

18. A few readers and reviewers will, no doubt, spread the malicious nonsense that the author "only wants to bring back the Latin Mass." The author will respond to such aggravated obtuseness by recommending that these individuals read this chapter again, line by line, perhaps with the aid of a ruler. Maybe this way they will discover that this author's thesis (if one even exists) is contradictory, nebulous, and evasive. Perhaps the author's true sentiments, unclear even to him, can be really summed up thus: *Long live the vernacular! Long live Latin!*

Chapter Three

PRIDE, COVETOUSNESS, LUST
...AND MUSEUMS
Edifice Wrecked

A STRETCH OF URBAN HIGHWAY, the wind blowing bits of trash down a deserted street, aging tenement buildings, parking lots, a big hospital — Boston's South End, a bleak landscape.

Then you turn a corner and are stunned by an unexpected surprise: Immaculate Conception Church, one of the city's architectural treasures and property of the Jesuits. What is it doing here?

Completed in 1861, this splendid building — massive, ornate, yet somehow chastely simple — had long been a symbol of the Catholic church's presence in that city. It was one way that a largely immigrant community could proclaim to its hostile neighbors, "We have arrived, we are here to stay, and we are capable of great accomplishments." To get this message across, the Jesuits hired the best architects and artists; they used the best materials. In the rear gallery of the church is arguably the finest nineteenth-century pipe organ (with a French Romantic accent) in the United States.

By the middle of the twentieth century the Church of the Immaculate Conception, affectionately known as The Immaculate, would fall on hard times. The neighborhood deteriorated. The "core" of the church's community had been the students who attended the Jesuits' college and high school, which were both right next door; but the college departed for the suburbs in 1913, the high school in 1957. With the schools gone, there was no real parish left and no endowment. By the 1980s the worshipers had dwindled to perhaps a few hundred loyal friends of the church and people from a nearby hospital. Far away from the usual tourist routes and far from the business district, the building became a sad architectural orphan. The great upper church was locked up for months at a time and only opened for an occasional liturgy or concert. Most services were held in the basement church.

Architectural treasures do not take care of themselves. Repairing a leaky old roof of a building like this could bankrupt a millionaire. Heating bills in New England can be enormous. Everyone knew that the situation at Immaculate Conception Church was desperate. Something had to be done.

In 1985 a new rector took charge of the church. Without telling anyone, he and his associates decided that the upper church had outlived its usefulness and would no longer be a place of worship. Demolishing the building was not an easy option, because the city's Landmarks Commission protected its exterior. The interior, however, had no such protection. The rector (most certainly with the cooperation of his superiors) decided on a way to transform the useless interior into something practical. He secretly had architects prepare plans to chop up the nave of the church and convert it into two floors of offices for the Jesuits. The richly decorated ceiling would be preserved as an atrium at the center of the offices; the organ would be removed.

When news of this drastic plan leaked out, the staff at the church calmed the fears of the community and implied that the interior would remain unchanged. The assurances quickly became meaningless when the rector held an auction to sell off statues, etched glass globes, and other items that were part of the church's interior. Then in early October 1986, neighbors began to hear strange noises coming from the church. Piles of rubbish appeared on the sidewalk; it soon became apparent that wreckers were at work — in violation of the law, since no wrecking permit had been issued. A building inspector from the city arrived, but the Jesuits would not allow him inside the church. The following morning an assistant commissioner showed up and was also barred from entering. When he threatened to close down all the buildings that the Jesuits owned on the block, he was allowed to enter.

The interior of the church was a pitiful sight. The pews had been ripped out of the floors, Stations of the Cross were smashed, the walls had been sprayed with paint. Looking at this destruction was a little like looking at an old lady who had just been mugged and beaten up.

The savagery of the wreckers inspired an admiration of sorts; an angry mob could not have done this much damage. But it is important to remember that these same wreckers (as professionals) must have followed the specific instructions of the person who had hired them. ("Demolish that; smash that; pulverize that thing with a sledge hammer, but spare that," and so forth.) The person who gave the orders must have been a priest and a Jesuit.

Another kind of wreckage extended well beyond the church building. The sense of trust and loyalty, which helped to build that church, was also in ruins. Who would ever give a nickel donation to a parish staff like that?

Public reaction to the trashing of the church was swift and angry. Boston's Brahmins emitted reserved expressions of shock. (But their ancestors would have been quite happy to see the church burn to the ground.) Art historians declared this Pearl Harbor attack to be an act of war against the city's cultural heritage. The community of laypeople who regularly came to the church felt betrayed. "IMMACULATE DECEPTION" screamed a headline in the *Boston Herald*.

The rector and his assistants responded to the criticism with defiance. This was the Jesuits' church — or, more precisely, their former high school/college chapel. It was not a parish church; therefore, no parishioners had a stake in the building. It belonged to the Jesuits, not to the archdiocese. (There was speculation that not even the local cardinal-archbishop had been consulted about the demolition.) The rector could not understand the point of all the complaints. He had, after all, planned to preserve the exterior and the ornate ceiling of the interior — a sensitive reuse of an obsolete building. Wasn't this the sort of thing that the preservationists wanted?

The Landmarks Commission, not sure that this was what historic preservation was all about, put a stop to further wrecking, temporarily.

I watched the television coverage, which included interviews and background reports. I read the newspapers. I listened to some of the testimony before the Landmarks Commission. I was still confused. Trying to figure out the logic behind this whole situation was like trying to put together an insane jigsaw puzzle.

Some puzzle pieces that would not fit: The upkeep of the building was a burden, but why was there no effort to raise funds? Why were all offers of help rebuffed? (One Jesuit told me that a few of his colleagues in the area were very eager to preserve Immaculate Conception Church and they had all kinds of ideas for injecting new life into it.) The parish staff claimed that there was no money to keep the upper church open and make necessary repairs. But why was there lots of money to hire wreckers, architects, construction workers, and lawyers? Somebody could write an inspiring article about how the Jesuits in the United States, since Vatican II, have made every effort to preserve and enhance the architectural beauty of their churches and chapels. But why was there a different policy in Boston?

The contradictions were giving me a headache. Nothing seemed to make sense until I began to connect assorted phrases spoken by some Catholics who defended the gutting of the church. (A few were interviewed on television.) A coherent philosophy emerged and it goes something like this: "The people who attend Immaculate Conception Church would be better off using the basement of that building, where the simplified architecture is more in accord with the principles established by the Second Vatican Council. The upstairs church, really obsolete now, is a museum stuffed with *things*. Christians must not become attached to *things*, to worldly goods. Art and other treasures of this world belong in museums, not churches. People who concern themselves with art and concert music in church have forgotten the meaning of the Gospel; they want to divert funds from the poor and spend them on the modern equivalent of the Golden Calf. We must always remember that Jesus Christ was not the founder of a museum. He founded a *church*." And office buildings.

*　*　*

In the Gospels, the poor are blessed. The rich have trouble getting into heaven. Does it follow that "poor" church art is also blessed, while "rich" art for the church ("museum art") will lead few people to heaven? Did the Second Vatican Council really declare buildings like Immaculate Conception Church to be out of favor?

The New Testament provides no clear answers on this matter. Jesus taught his disciples about the virtues of poverty and the dangers of wealth, but he had no objection when a woman "wasted" expensive ointment by pouring it on him (Matt. 26, John 12). He was a dinner guest in the houses of the rich and the prominent. After his triumphal entry into Jerusalem, Jesus taught in the Temple. His followers were quite impressed by the lavishness of this complex of buildings (Matt. 24, Mark 13, Luke 21). Was Jesus also impressed? The Gospels only record him as saying that all of the Temple's beauty would soon be destroyed; they contain no statements in favor of or against the precious stones and ornaments on the walls of this structure, the majestic columns, or the ornate rituals.

The walls of the Temple in Jerusalem enclosed vast spaces that were open to the sky. Jewish visitors from all over the Mediterranean world — people who did not speak the local Aramaic — crowded into these spaces. This unusual set of circumstances called for unusual music, something that Jesus and his followers never heard in their synagogues back home: liturgical singing accompanied by musical instruments. The last psalm, in the Revised Standard Version, exclaims, Praise the Lord "with trumpet . . . lute and harp . . . timbrel and dance . . . strings and pipe . . . cymbals." This "symphonic" music — elaborate and "rich" but perfectly natural for the huge dimensions of the Temple and for the heterogeneous congregation — does not receive a sentence of praise or criticism in the New Testament.

If the New Testament contains no definitive answers on the matter of liturgical art (or on the merits of a virtuous artistic "poverty" versus pernicious "richness"), the Second Vatican Council's pronouncements are even less helpful in providing a clear set of directions, although they do describe ideals that, to any artist, must sound almost exciting. The section on religious art in the council's Constitution on the Sacred Liturgy begins by emphasizing, right away, the incalculable importance of sacred art by relating it to nothing less than "God's boundless beauty." Furthermore, to the extent that sacred works of art turn our thoughts "to God persuasively and devoutly, they are dedicated to God and to the cause of His greater honor and glory" (Article 122). The Council Fathers refrain (quite wisely) from offering any specific descriptions of what this art should look like and they do not set down any regulations about the correct layout of a church. But when the Constitution on the Sacred Liturgy does come close to what looks like specific instructions for the artist, the result is genuinely helpful — and, at the same time, not a little confusing.

For example: Art that is truly sacred (and this also applies to vestments and church ornaments) should exhibit "nobilem... pulchritudinem quam meram sumptuositatem," which has been translated two ways: (1) "noble beauty rather than mere extravagance" or (2) "noble beauty rather than mere sumptuous display" (Article 124). But these very words were written, debated, and promulgated under the beautifully detailed ceiling of St. Peter's Basilica and within a few steps of the tombs of various popes — art that will fit any definition of extravagance and sumptuous display.

New churches are supposed to be designed with the active participation of the faithful in mind (Article 124). Does this mean that older churches hinder the full participation of the faithful? Should they be gutted and rebuilt? The constitution evades the issue.

Another confusion: The Council Fathers speak with pride about the "treasury of art" created for the church's use over the years. It must be carefully preserved (Article 123). Sacred furnishings and works of value are not to be disposed of or dispersed, "for they are ornaments of the house of God" (Article 126). But soon after the Council Fathers voted in favor of these words, many of them went home and ordered that their cathedrals and chapels be stripped of these same "ornaments of the house of God," because they were confident that this was what the Constitution on the Sacred Liturgy wanted them to do.

The Council Fathers made sure that their wishes on sacred art would be broad and positive. They knew that standards of artistic taste could never be legislated. Rather than get into a debate about aesthetics, they forwarded all the problems concerning taste and policy to the local authorities, who would have to make sense out of these broad ideals in the Constitution on the Sacred Liturgy. What the bishops did not realize was that they were also forwarding a great deal of this artistic power into the hands of people who had another agenda: a systematic rearrangement, perhaps even a dismantling, piece by piece, of all the doctrinal propositions that had supported the theology of the Catholic Mass for centuries. Whoever controlled the art and architecture controlled the theology.

* * *

"Take and eat. This is my body. Drink. This is my blood." The God-man, not symbolized *by* but actually present *as* a form of human food, the God-man broken and consumed — judged by the terms of scientific logic this central aspect of the Catholic Eucharist is preposterous. Judged as an act of continuing love and sacrifice, this is staggering. The Eucharist, the Mystery of Faith, is no small matter. Where to put the emphasis on this mystery may go through all kinds of changes — on this theological insight or that one — but at the very core of the Catholic Mass is the belief (a belief that requires not an acceptance but a passion) that Christ is in the midst of the faithful gathered in his name.

In past centuries, Roman Catholic and Orthodox Christians built their churches to be places where heaven and earth touched in this Mystery of Faith. They did not always need gold, marble, and great art to convey this message; they only required a special place where people assembled for a special act.

Up until, let us say, 1945, American Catholics had no trouble deciding what this special place should look like. A church should recall a great European monument, preferably medieval, or it should look like that grand Baroque pile of masonry that dominated the village square back in the Old Country. A lot of strikingly beautiful churches were built following this principle of "recollection," and also a lot of half-baked imitations.

There was also another set of highly influential values about the "look" of a church, values that were subconscious and never mentioned: *The church building should remind worshipers of the taste of simple working-class people who were unburdened by knowledge about rich art for the rich.* Where this subconscious set of values predominated, the church interior was made to look like an enlarged version of Aunt Maggie's parlor.

* * *

Everybody loved Aunt Maggie and she dearly loved her parlor: that riot of lace doilies, cute bric-a-brac figurines, flamboyant lamps, fringe, and downright incomprehensible wallpaper. What she did with her own home was, of course, her own business — and nobody was going to point out to her that not one item in the parlor seemed to come from human hands (except the doilies).

Everything in sight, including the portraits of the Sacred Heart and John F. Kennedy on the wall, came from factories that cranked out, day after day and by the millions, these decorative equivalents of stale store-bought white bread. If someone ever gave her a piece of hand-crafted art (especially folk art), she would have thrown it in the trash.

When Aunt Maggie's son became pastor of a church, he remembered his mother's fondness for lace, for factory-made cuteness and kitsch every time he had to make an artistic decision about his church, and he made these decisions quickly. At the next parish over, another pastor would almost be in pain from the artistic decisions he had to make. He believed that all the noble ideals of church art — uplifting, the best that a particular group or era can offer, universal, tasteful, theologically "correct" — would somehow inspire his flock to contemplate things more exalted than their parlors. He thought long and hard about every candlestick he purchased. He wanted to do the right thing. He got the best advice. . . . He also got the reputation for being an elitist and snob — the only kind of people who take an interest in the arts.

THEY TRIED VERY HARD

In 1927, fourteen men gathered at Portsmouth Priory in Rhode Island for a spiritual retreat but also for an opportunity to discuss the deplorable state of ecclesiastical art. They were disturbed by the routine, pseudo-this, pseudo-that Catholic churches being built in the United States and elsewhere in the world. They yearned for the unification of spiritual and artistic values — the kind of symbiotic relationship between church and craftsman that had enriched ecclesiastical art in the past.

With the encouragement of the Benedictine monks at Portsmouth Priory (today an abbey), the group met again, expanded its membership, and in 1928 incorporated as the Liturgical Arts Society. The mission of this organization was to improve the aesthetic qualities of American Catholic churches and to make Catholics aware of better alternatives to the pretentious vulgarity that was corrupting so much ecclesiastical art at that time. But the Liturgical Arts Society's crusade for good taste was not just a matter of artistic prettiness — whether, for example, mauve looked better than beige. Rather, the society seemed to preach that a deeper understanding of spirituality, neoscholastic philosophy, Gregorian chant, and liturgy would lead to an artistic "correctness." With a little guidance, good taste would come directly out of good theology.

The Liturgical Arts Society worked very hard at its program of reeducating the Catholic population. It introduced clients and craftsmen to one another, sponsored lectures, and published *Liturgical Arts*, a quarterly journal, which was so carefully put together that it was a work of art. *Liturgical Arts* always had favorable things to say about traditional, historic styles — at their best — but, as it evolved, it began to put more effort into the promotion of modern art for modern churches.

In her admirable book *Art, Architecture, and Liturgical Reform: The Liturgical Arts Society (1928–1972)* (New York, 1990), Susan J. White points out that the original fourteen men who met at Portsmouth Priory in 1927 had a lot in common:

> With few exceptions, they were Roman Catholic laymen from wealthy families, fledgling architects, draftsmen, and artists, and graduates of prestigious East Coast universities: Harvard, Yale, Princeton, Columbia. . . .
>
> As a group they mirrored the conflicting strains of the Roman Catholicism of the period between the wars, the longing for a positive identity and status in a society dominated by Anglo-Saxon Protestantism and, at the same time, the fear of succumbing entirely to the forces at work in the present age. . . . Those individuals who felt that the Church could not come to terms with the modern world without losing its essential identity soon discontinued their association with the Liturgical Arts Society, while those more optimistic about the relationship came to dominate it.

The founders of the Liturgical Arts Society — those who stayed with it, as well as those who eventually withdrew their membership over the issue of modernistic art in church — may have had much in common with one another, but they were, in a sense, "odd men out" in the American Catholic church of the 1920s and even later. What caused their isolation was a kind of class/cultural antagonism built into the demography of the church at that time. "Real American Catholics," perhaps the majority, were supposed to find a symbol of their orthodoxy and identity in the factory-made, plaster-of-Paris statue — perhaps one with genuine glass eyeballs, tinted skin, and saccharine smile.[1] This kind of art (often the art of the wax museum) was popular and thought to be an authentic expression of the faith in solid form; it certainly required very little "imagination" and it offered immediate personal gratification for many. "Real American Catholics" suspected heresy when someone from the upper class, or from a non-Catholic educational experience, began to talk about religious art that was better than a plaster statue. (The Liturgical Arts Society received regular and severe criticism for showing signs of latent Anglicanism.)

One could argue that the Liturgical Arts Society was a noble failure. Systematically ignored except in a few isolated pockets, this dedicated, idealistic organization banged its collective head against a sensitively designed brick wall. For every new church inspired by the principles of the Liturgical Arts Society, a hundred others were built by factory formula — joyless barns without character, without any sign that human craftsmen had labored (with love and even passion) to shape them. There were even a few instances of churches being decorated with help from the society and later drastically redecorated (or, if you like, vandalized) when a new pastor took charge; the original artworks were pushed aside to make room for a whole gang of factory-made statues. In spite of all its outstanding qualities, *Liturgical Arts* never had more than about twenty-five hundred subscribers. Perhaps the Liturgical Arts Society really died in the 1940s; the organization was able to survive only as long as it did because Maurice Lavanoux, one of its founders, virtually "donated" his life to it and ran the whole operation. When Lavanoux retired, the society folded. There was no great outpouring of regret; nobody started another organization to succeed it.

One could also argue that the Liturgical Arts Society, in an indirect way, was somewhat successful, and that things would have been much worse without its discreet influence. About a third of the subscribers to *Liturgical Arts* were members of the clergy, and many of them were probably important decision-makers in the Catholic church. The society, whose office was located in New York City, had cordial relations with the local bishop (Cardinals Hayes, Spellman, and Cooke); a few other bishops were very supportive. It is true that most bishops kept their distance and seemed to be indifferent to the society, but they were probably being discreet about doing anything that would look like an official endorsement of a particular set of artistic values. Maybe the society's moment of vindication came during the Second Vatican Council when Lavanoux was named as a "technical adviser" for a subcommittee that was working on the question of sacred art; perhaps some of his suggestions found their way into the council's Constitution on the Sacred Liturgy.

No matter how we interpret the history of the Liturgical Arts Society — as an irrelevant happening on the sidelines or as an important influence — it is nevertheless a cautionary tale with this very strict warning: *If you are going to devote time and energy to the cause of "good taste" in the Catholic church (for sacred art or music or anything else), be prepared for grief.*

THE SHAPE OF THINGS TO COME

The Constitution on the Sacred Liturgy, the Instruction of the Congregation of Rites for the Proper Implementation of the Constitution on the Sacred Liturgy, the detailed General Instruction of the *Roman Missal,* countless proclamations from the Vatican, opinions from theologians, liturgists, artists, and architects, elucidations of elucidations, an entire freight train filled with words, and so many of them could relate to the proper shape of the post–Vatican II church ... Could anybody ever absorb all of these words and transform them into a real building?

In the United States, the Bishops' Committee on the Liturgy and the National Conference of Catholic Bishops have tried to be helpful by summarizing the gist of postconciliar artistic ideals in a booklet entitled *Environment and Art in Catholic Worship* (Washington, D.C., 1977). Anyone who wants to build a Catholic church in the United States — or demolish the interior of an older church — will have to read this booklet.

Without any restrained language or apologies, *Environment and Art in Catholic Worship* makes it clear that a church must be beautiful; architectural and artistic beauty are what Vatican II wanted. "Admittedly difficult to define, the beautiful is related to the sense of the numinous, the holy." God is holiness itself, this booklet reminds us. "Because the assembly gathers in the presence of God to celebrate his saving deeds, liturgy's climate is one of awe, mystery, wonder, reverence, thanksgiving and praise."

This was old news back in the Middle Ages, when artisans were putting together the stained-glass windows of Chartres Cathedral. In many ways, *Environment and Art in Catholic Worship* is only reemphasizing traditional values that Roman Catholicism had always preached (but not always practiced in the United States, especially after the 1940s). And yet while this booklet, published by the American Catholic bishops, reaffirms traditional ideals about the beauty of the house of worship, it also subtly suggests that a primary purpose of this beauty is not to praise God or stimulate piety but to promote *hospitality*, a feeling of togetherness. The ideal church building, which is supposed to provide the ideal space for the ideal liturgy, should help people in the assembly to be "comfortable with one another, either knowing or being introduced to one another." Furthermore, "the faithful should be able to have visual contact, being attentive to one another as they celebrate the liturgy."

"...comfortable with one another...attentive to one another...." Those little phrases (so odd, when you think about them) sound like something from the bylaws of a country club. What are they doing here?

This calls for a long digression:

* * *

"Vatican II has met! It has decreed so many exciting things. What does it all mean? What do we do?"

"It means that we are all the People of God and that means we should build round churches with the altar right in the center. ...No, on second thought, it means everybody should sing four Protestant hymns at Mass....No, make that four songs by Ray Repp...the St. Louis Jesuits...well, yes, some classical music is permitted...but definitely move the altar closer to the congregation and put the musicians where everybody can see them and put the baptismal area at the entrance of the church building or maybe start all over again and construct a completely new building or...Have you tried liturgical dance? Baptism by total immersion?...You know, burlap banners are fun and..."

All during this frantic presentation of ideas we see, over in the corner, a group of people sitting there quietly, all of them with slanted and amused smiles on their faces. They listen to the suggestions and the theories, but they are not impressed; only they really know what Vatican II was all about — and that is, the breaking down of parishes into small communities of friends. The Latin Mass, religious art, liturgical music, banners, and all the rest are such trivialities, they do not even deserve to be discussed. These possessors of the truth — believers in what I call Catholic Communalism — are convinced that Vatican II created a new image of the church, and this new image comes alive not in a remodeled church building with new art and new music but in small groups of people; parishes with small interconnecting communities of believers are the real postconciliar church.

Communalism in Roman Catholicism is nothing new. Catholics have always formed friendships, clubs, societies, sodalities, and even religious orders, in order to bring themselves in contact with other like-minded believers. But that has not always been easy. Catholics have a tendency to think of themselves as (1) self-employed spiritual individualists — each believer working out a unique relationship with God — but, at the same time, as (2) small atoms in a mega-structure, a great Communion of Saints. Forming smaller structures could appear to be somehow unnatural in the ecology of the whole system.

In the United States, the mega-church has frequently tried to serve the needs of the faithful in the mega-parish, an immense assemblage of real estate and bricks. In the most complete version of the mega-parish, the church building can hold hundreds, maybe thousands; next to it stands a school, a rectory, and a convent. The mega-parish was (and still is) the dominant image of American Catholicism in action — a smokestack industry, with the parish Mass as mass production. On a financial basis, the mega-parish seems to work. On a personal basis, a lot of people can be neglected.

The neglected people have found hope in the idea of the small faith community — the religious cell with Communalist Catholics who get together and, in one way or another, bring the faith into their lives. But just what kind of cell the Communalists have in mind is not a settled issue. Opinions range from the small community as "just another parish activity," like the bowling league, to plans for a top-to-bottom revolution, with small, separate groups replacing the parish.

Father Arthur Baranowski, who has written books on the formation of small faith communities, is one of the better-known advocates of Catholic Communalism; his views could be classified as "moderate" and "middle-of-the-road."[2] In an interview he explained that small faith groups are just "communities of people who meet each week or every other week." They talk about values, "about how God speaks to people," ordinary people.[3]

Father Baranowski does not think that these communities should be simply parish groups that develop personal and spiritual growth. Rather, he insists that they are the most effective means for restructuring the parish. The only way the church will ever reach people and help them "assess society" is on a personal level; the most effective way to do this is through small groups. Father Baranowski is not talking about turning everyone into a shouting, rolling-in-the-aisle true-believer. He is even uneasy about someone who barges into a group and says, "Let's share the faith." That sort of zeal, he suggests, only makes ordinary people nervous. His vision of the small faith community is something a little less extroverted, but highly effective.

Father Baranowski described the liturgy in a parish that had completely restructured itself into a network of small communities, which are like small churches. Visitors to the liturgy immediately sense an atmosphere that is "friendly" and "different." This is because the people in the congregation notice and greet one another. Maybe a quarter of the congregation had already heard and discussed the scriptures before coming to Mass. These people at the friendly liturgy were not

> high-powered, born-again types who want to convert everybody. They weren't like the people who participate in weekend renewals and come back and hug everyone and the lamppost. Most people are afraid of that and avoid people like that. But these parishioners were ordinary, low-key people — people who had never talked about God in their lives.

It was these ordinary people, Father Baranowski explains, who had made the experience of this liturgy "friendly" and "different." They impressed the visitor, and this wonderful liturgical atmosphere "wasn't totally dependent on the musicians or the priest."

Catholic Communalism may have started out as a reaction to the impersonal processing of the mega-parish, but, as Father Baranowski correctly observes, the phenomenon has other causes: "People need support, and the world we live in doesn't supply it. . . . People are dying of loneliness. . . . There's a crying need for belonging — for people we can be safe with, who know us and something of our struggles." He is quite correct.

Catholic Communalism is another manifestation of the group therapy phenomenon. Like Alcoholics Anonymous, support groups of every conceivable variety, encounter groups, manhood retreats, and all the other forms of group therapy, it is a symptom of a society with lonely and troubled people who are trying to get through the ordeal of life or to put together the pieces of a broken life. Group therapy (and this includes Catholic Communalism) can help and heal; sometimes it can be as important and valuable as any wonder drug to come out of modern medicine.

Catholic Communalism has certainly not "taken over." It has only just begun, and yet its goals have become so impressive and its ideals so luminous that its indirect influence is enormous. In fact, it has reached such a high spiritual plateau that it is immune from scrutiny or even critical analysis. Catholic Communalism may be exactly what is needed at this point in history (and even crucial for the church's survival in Latin America and places where there is a severe shortage of priests), but like all things human it is not perfect. A few questions need to be asked about its imperfections. For this purpose, I offer the following stream-of-consciousness meditation on Communalism and its extremely imperfect fit into the fundamental structure of the Catholic church:

. . . Small groups of people tend to select their own kind and to expel outsiders, especially people who are not compatible. . . .

. . . What is the status of a parishioner who is not part of a small faith group? Second class? . . .

. . . Roman Catholicism is a "universal" (catholic) church. It can boast that the doors of its churches are open to anyone, not just insiders bonded together through friendship. . . .

. . . The traditional rituals of Roman Catholicism are also "catholic." Their structure is broad and inclusive. They have been "designed" so that they will not look, in any way, like a club meeting. The rituals could, of course, accommodate a specific ethnic group or even a club in the congregation, but, at the same time, they give the impression that someone sitting alone in the back is also included (the person saying privately, "Lord, be merciful to me a sinner")....

... Small faith groups do not just happen, like fields of lovely wildflowers. They are developed, managed, moderated, guided, orchestrated, and even dissolved by a skillful pastor or facilitator — and there is not an abundant supply of such politically smooth operators....

... Groups or any organization of any type will always develop rivalries, power disputes, antagonisms. Some people will begin to think of their group as the true church (and far superior to the official corporation). The pastor with exceptional political skills might be able to "finesse" all the problems, but even he will occasionally close his eyes and think of all those small faith groups out there as a scene from *The Sorcerer's Apprentice* (immortalized by Mickey Mouse in the movie *Fantasia*), where all the brooms keep multiplying and get out of control....

... In Catholic Communalism, liturgical *Gemütlichkeit* — communal warmth, friendliness, welcoming hospitality, I-know-you smiles — can easily be mistaken for the source and summit of the faith. Anything that does not "produce" feelings of cozy friendliness can be interpreted as irrelevant. Even "incompatible" people in the parish can begin to look irrelevant....

... The temptation is that many Communalists will want Catholic liturgy in a church to reproduce, on a larger scale, the intimacy and solidarity of the small group in the living room. But the combination of the ancient ritual (priest in flowing robes, ancient prayer formulas) and the ambiance of a friendly family get-together does not work in a public setting....

... In brief asides here and there, some Catholics display an impatient contempt for the traditional art and music of the church. "Good liturgy" in the good environment is supposed to be beautiful people; beautiful sculpture or music has nothing to do with the matter. These impatient Catholics, influenced by Communalist ideals, see no need to pay the slightest attention to artistic distractions. They think of themselves as builders of the new church; they have left the past and are preparing for the glorious world of tomorrow, the Future Kingdom church of small groups that have no need of elitist art and music. (Utopia is always more beautiful and alluring than anything that has ever existed.) ...

... In the nineteenth century, reformers of the liturgy looked to the Middle Ages for inspiration — that era of knights and ladies, yeoman farmers and honest craftsmen. After Vatican II, the liturgical reformers found their inspiration in perhaps the sixth century A.D., when all was perfect and everybody participated in worship. More recently, the trend has been to long for the upper rooms and catacombs, the small communities of early Christians huddled together. They didn't need fancy art or music back then, just each other. ...

* * *

Roman Catholicism is an accommodating religion. It has shown an uncanny ability to take something new or "incorrect" or even threatening and absorb it. The pagan philosophies of Plato and Aristotle were adapted to serve the needs of Catholic theologians. In books on the history of art, architecture, or music, we read about the church bravely welcoming some new, radical style. (At one time, Gothic, Renaissance, and Baroque architecture were exciting novelties.) Is there a pagan feast that is still popular? Transform it into a Christian Holy Day. Does the Infant Jesus of Prague make some theologians and historians nauseous? No problem. Find a corner of the church for this popular devotion. And there is also some room for Marxism (moderated as liberation theology), for Charismatics, for liturgical dancers, for yet another Marian apparition.

The editors of *Environment and Art in Catholic Worship* (with the blessing of the bishops) seem to be accommodating Communalism; following ancient custom, they are trying to find room for something new, for the ideals of the Future Kingdom community, the parish as a utopian gathering of compatible types. But in this accommodating process, the editors are forced to contradict themselves; they have to promote something that is impossible to build. In one sentence, the editors of this booklet are putting forth orthodox dogma: liturgy's "climate" (and this includes the building) combines "awe, mystery, wonder, reverence, thanksgiving and praise." All is directed to God. But then, in another sentence, people in the congregation are supposed to be looking at and "attentive to one another as they celebrate the liturgy." All is directed to the congregation. The church building must affirm architectural and artistic values that are centuries old and traditional, for such things are related to "the numinous, the holy." But, at the same time, the numinous and holy church building is supposed to be a kind of picture frame that surrounds the *social* beauty of beautiful people.

The editors of *Environment and Art in Catholic Worship* emphasize the value of good art and architecture for the church building; they mention good acoustics (for good singing). All of this artistic goodness, in the service of religion, will help to provide an appropriate environment for good liturgy and warm communal feelings. But the arts really do not cooperate. They demand attention; they sometimes have a way of asserting the importance of realities and values that are greater than the individual's own self-infatuation. A striking religious painting, an icon, a noble hymn accompanied by a pipe organ — all of these things help to distract a community away from its self-congratulation and socializing; in a somewhat impolite, decisive, and even scary manner, the arts can point people toward their religious "job" on earth. For this reason, it is impossible to design a church that exploits the power of the fine arts and, at the same time, is supposed to be the spiritual equivalent of a large communal hot tub.

* * *

Because the assembly is of such paramount importance to Catholic worship, it follows (according to current thinking) that anything that distracts this gathering from itself must be ripped out of the liturgical environment. Flimsy artifacts or maudlin statues might qualify as unwelcome distractions that should be removed — but could the Mystery of Faith, the sacrament of the Body and Blood of Christ, also be considered an annoying distraction? The authors of *Environment and Art in Catholic Worship* are extraordinarily reluctant to reduce the importance of the gathered faithful by bringing up such large, intimidating concepts as "Blessed Sacrament" or "Real Presence." Instead, nonthreatening words like "bread" and "cup" are used (in the vicinity of the words "symbol" or "symbolic"). The great Mystery of Faith is the warm and symbolic sharing of bread by people comfortable with one another. The only time this booklet gets near the phrase "body and blood" is in a sentence that emphasizes the primacy of modern art: "Because it [liturgy] is the action of a contemporary assembly, it has to clothe its basically traditional structures with the living flesh and blood of our times and our arts."

Environment and Art in Catholic Worship has high aspirations for the assembled and undistracted faithful — extremely high. During a liturgy, a Catholic assembly is supposed to seek "its own expression in an atmosphere which is beautiful, amidst actions which probe the entire human experience. This is what is most basic and most noble. It is what the assembly seeks in order to express the heart of the Church's liturgy." Such lofty sentiments! If we only knew what they meant! What is this "heart" of liturgy? (The text does not say; the paragraph ends there.) Is it perhaps this "entire human experience"? Is it the mutually comfortable assembly seeking its own group expression in a beautiful atmosphere?

The Second Vatican Council's Constitution on the Sacred Liturgy unambiguously announces that "our Savior instituted the Eucharistic Sacrifice of His Body and Blood. He did this in order to perpetuate the sacrifice of the Cross throughout the centuries" (Article 47). If anything, the Good Friday "aspect" of the Mass has always been at its heart. But "sacrifice" is such a diverting concept and it interferes with the whole idea of people gathering together to feel comfortable with one another and seek their own expression in a beautiful atmosphere. Perhaps this is why the issue of "sacrifice" is entirely suppressed in *Environment and Art in Catholic Worship*. It is not even mentioned, for the sake of balance, in connection with other "aspects" of the Mass: Holy Thursday (meal) and Easter (the Mystical Body of the Risen Christ). The closest that this booklet ever comes to the concept of "Eucharistic Sacrifice" is a quick reference to "living sacrifice," a phrase from the Third Eucharistic Prayer of the Mass — but in this context it is the assembly that is the sacrificial victim, not Christ: "To gather intentionally in God's presence is to gather our total selves, our complete persons — a 'living sacrifice.' "

* * *

The photographs at the end of *Environment and Art in Catholic Worship* include examples of what the editors consider to be good liturgical environments. The postconciliar designs all seem pleasant enough, as photographs. Some "before and after" photographs show genuine improvements. (One "before" picture of a modern sanctuary built just before Vatican II illustrates the loss of nerve, the utter artistic cowardice, that characterized so many of these ecclesiastical garages of the 1950s and early '60s.) One set of "before and after" photographs is supposed to demonstrate that fancy old churches can be renovated for modern use without turning them over to the wreckers. Everything in this photographic essay looks fairly harmless, until you "add them up" and discover a surprising new trend: the glorification of the priest's throne. At the very center (the heart?) of so many newer or renovated liturgical environments — especially those stark, science-fiction architectural spaces — is the Royal Seat, sometimes the most formidable artistic "statement" in the whole church. (In a few cases that I have seen, one can almost imagine Ming the Merciless slouching on his throne and commanding, "Bring Flash Gordon to me!")

A presider has to have a seat where he can preside. This chair, according to *Environment and Art in Catholic Worship*, "should not suggest either domination or remoteness," but it is easy to find churches where this place for sitting loudly proclaims both. It is also easy to conclude that the hidden motivation behind the design of so many newer churches and the ruthless modernization of older ones is the proper placement of that seat of power — where no architectural or artistic feature will compete with it.

Liturgical Renewal started out with such fervent hopes. The church's rites (plus its music and architecture) would be renovated; the faithful would "see" their role more clearly and be spiritually transformed. Then, somewhere along the road to this renewal, detour signs were put up; a new road was taken and at the end of it is — the priest's throne. Whatever Liturgical Renewal was, whatever exalted hopes that a Virgil Michel or Karl Rahner may have had for it, this whole historical and theological phenomenon became absolutely meaningless with the installation of the conspicuously placed chair for the presider in so many Catholic churches. Whether it is just a small wooden piece of furniture or something more substantial, the *artistic* power of that seat, as the visual climax of the whole building (maybe with the altar somewhere as a little hyphen), can be overwhelming. Some photographs in *Environment and Art in Catholic Worship* strongly suggest that this chair is the reason for the entire building.

The people who put up the detour signs (and, in effect, took Liturgical Renewal far from its original destination) believe that human beings are deeply moved, in church, by experiencing the sincerity of someone else's personality. Art does not help to direct people to the spiritual life, nor does music. Rather, it is the personality of the priest — centrally placed, preferably with dramatic shafts of natural or artificial light bringing out his radiance — that will set the assembly ablaze with fervor; and if the congregation needs even more fervor, help is available from the personalities of the musicians, also up front and almost centrally placed. Churches must be designed or redesigned so that the worshiper can constantly gaze upon the wonder of someone's personality. In former times, the Catholic church developed the custom of putting the consecrated host in a beautiful golden monstrance so that the faithful might contemplate the mystery of the Eucharist and show their gratitude for it. The postconciliar church frequently puts the priest in a kind of grand architectural monstrance, with the presider's seat at its center, so that the faithful might, without distractions, experience the joy of marveling at one man's personality.

*   *   *

After Christians emerged from the catacombs and worshiped in public, they had to concern themselves with the architectural layout of a building for public worship. They also had to come up with various solutions to the problem of fitting the priest into the whole design. Sometimes, for the Eucharistic part of the liturgy, they put their presiding priests behind a rood screen or iconostasis or even curtains; the congregation could not see a priest clearly during this part of the rite. Sometimes the priest said Mass under a large canopy, a baldacchino, which seemed to squash his personality under its weight. Sometimes priest and people faced the same direction during Mass (and this is now misunderstood as "the priest with his back to the people"). What all of these historic Catholic "solutions" have in common is anxiety: an intense worry that the priest's personality would become the main ingredient of the whole ritual. The architectural traditions of Catholic Christianity (East and West) — with their artistic "assertiveness" — made it difficult for the priest to shine forth as the only object in the worshiper's field of vision; all the competition from the art made it difficult for the priest to abuse power by turning ritual into a one-man show.

*   *   *

The editors of *Environment and Art in Catholic Worship* make a passing reference to the "architectural floor plans" of ancient churches, which were great gathering spaces for a communal act of worship. The implication is that the illustrations and comments in this booklet are merely a continuation of ancient traditions that Roman Catholicism had neglected over the centuries. Supposedly, the church is really just going back to the best kind of worship space that it once knew. But this nostalgic longing for the ideal churches of long ago is highly selective. Some things are blocked out of the memory. For example: Those early churches did not have pews; the congregation stood, knelt, and wandered around the place; many came late and left early; everything was rather "fluid." The entire ceremony was sung, perhaps in Greek (not always the mother-tongue of the congregation) or, later, in Latin (when it was no longer the vernacular). There was only one Eucharist in the building on a Sunday. The practice of having the priest go to a closed-off space for the Eucharistic prayers started very early in Christianity's history as a public church.

The editors of *Environment and Art in Catholic Worship* cannot honestly explain the illustrations and many of the ideas in this booklet as a "restoration," a "going back," a return to wonderful ancient church designs that were, unfortunately, forgotten over the years. There is no archeological or historical justification for the kind of sanctuary design that puts such exaggerated emphasis on the priest as the central architectural feature of an entire building. That "postconciliar look" in so many churches — kingly seat and altar, perhaps both of them alone and forbidding objects (isolated upon a cold plane), both positioned so that the priest's personality will constantly be at the very center of the viewer's attention — does not belong to any Christian tradition. It is a modern invention, the result of a modern overconfidence in the power of personal magnetism. If some beautiful old church has been handed over to the demolition crews, if useful religious music from the past (especially the sung Mass) has been abandoned, it is partly because such things tend to diminish the importance of personal magnetism.

The "postconciliar look" in some churches (i.e., the church interior as throne room) would not be such a destructive force if the priest entered with a little more reserve, took care of preliminary rites at the entrance of the sanctuary, and then proceeded to his chair for the readings. (He should also save the Rotary-Club-banquet introductory pleasantries for the homily.) But this rarely happens. Instead, the priest enters to music that seems to be the fanfare for his arrival, he mounts his throne, and then, from that high position, literally "talks down" to the congregation.

* * *

In pre–Vatican II days the floor plans of Catholic churches and chapels used to be designed in the shape of a triangle — figuratively speaking. Whether the worshipers were in a church that was round or square or in the shape of a cross, they had the feeling that they were inside a large triangle that was flat on the earth and pointed in a certain direction. The priest was also inside this triangle, but at its tip. He faced a shelf altar or, as was the case in some churches in Rome, he faced the congregation; sometimes he was distant, at the back of the apse; sometimes he was closer. Whatever the case, there was a strong feeling that he and the congregation were part of a great wedge whose perspective and lines pointed toward something beyond the vanishing point. Not every "triangular" church worked ideally as a place for worship but, in the best cases, the building helped to accomplish one task that is essential for liturgy: its artistic features somehow encouraged people to put their autonomy aside, to "empty themselves," so that they could be one with — united with — the sacramental action. The priest, just one of many within the triangle, led the congregation "forward."

The new postconciliar church building or the renovated one still keeps the pattern of the triangle, but in too many cases the priest has moved to a place outside of this geometric form; in fact, the triangle now points to him. This becomes obvious when the priest is a well-liked person and most everybody has come because of him. The congregation spends most of the time contemplating the man rather than the message. This new arrangement — the wedge of people pointed to a man who is outside of the formation — approaches obscenity when the presiding priest tries to be a welcoming, convivial cheerleader of liveliness.

With prayer and luck, the priest, during the next stage of Liturgical Renewal, will once again join everyone else in the triangle. But this return to the egalitarian (yet confining) triangle will not be easy. Because of the influence of *Environment and Art in Catho-*

lic Worship and similar pronouncements, those new postconciliar churches and the renovated older ones are deliberately designed so that the priest is cut off from the assembly and placed in a stage setting where he must "act" — like a television announcer or a stand-up comic or a program host or a king. The lighting, the architectural lines, and especially the excessive amplification all tend to make his personality the object of the congregation's attention. The congregation reasons: Why should we put our autonomy aside, why should we "empty ourselves" for this act of worship when the man up front (and outside of the triangle) is not doing that sort of thing?

THE COMPLEX EDIFICE

Parts of it are quite beautiful, impressive, strong; but then you turn your head just slightly and encounter something that enhances your comprehension of the word "ghastly." This combination of the magnificent and the sentimental, the profound and the banal, on such a massive scale, might cause, in any sensitive beholder, at least an occasional twinge of discomfort.

The building I have in mind is the National Shrine of the Immaculate Conception on the campus of Catholic University in Washington, D.C. The Catholic population of the United States built this structure with their donations, their hard-earned money. Anyone who would like to gain insights into American Catholicism should take a leisurely stroll through the great spaces of this edifice. (There are only about ten churches in the world that are larger.)

The alert visitor's first impression will probably be that the Shrine, in many ways, is not a single architectural "statement" with separate artistic elements harmoniously united. It is really a very extensive collection of Marian iconography from around the world, combined with a series of visual history lessons about the role of Mary in some countries, combined with a house of worship, combined with a gift shop and cafeteria in the basement. To complicate matters even more, the building sometimes gives the impression that a dozen or more religions — with different, competing messages — have invaded and seized various portions of the premises. For example, a dominating (and fiercely masculine) mosaic of Christ at the top of the apse reminds visitors that he is the center of the faith, but the innumerable representations of Mary, wherever one looks, can suggest that she (the gentle feminine) is more important; she is worshiped. A glorious ceiling mosaic by Millard Sheets, "The Triumph of the Lamb," and the kitsch trinkets for sale in the basement gift shop do not seem to come from the same faith.

If the National Shrine looks as if it is slightly "unsettled" and full of contradictions, the reason is that the religion "behind" this edifice is itself far from unified. The building proves that Roman Catholicism in the United States is not a great monolith but really a coalition of different ethnic groups, cults, and social classes that somehow manage to coexist.

The idea of building a large shrine in the nation's capital goes back to 1846 when the bishops of the United States were trying to decide on a patron saint for the republic. They knew that the English could claim St. George as their heavenly patron and symbol, that Ireland honored St. Patrick, and that other nations boasted about their special relationship with particular saints. But who would be the patron saint of the nation that had not yet produced any beatified saints? Eventually, the bishops decided to claim the Virgin Mary, conceived without Original Sin, as the nation's patroness; the building of a pilgrimage church in her honor seemed only fitting.

In 1914 the rector of Catholic University received permission to build this edifice on that campus; the respected firm of Maginnis and Walsh was selected to design the structure. With Charles Donagh Maginnis (1867–1955),[4] a superb architect, involved in the project, the result was sure to be a subtle combination of flair and serenity. But what would the style be? Gothic was out of the question. (It would invite comparisons with the Episcopalians' National Cathedral on the other side of town.)

Maginnis, the chief supervising architect (and, incidentally, the first president of the Liturgical Arts Society), made detailed drawings for an imposing structure whose style might be called Americanized Roman Baroque or perhaps just Beaux Arts. The Shrine was going to be another example of classical poise and grandeur in a city famous for its monuments in the classical tradition. The cornerstone was laid in 1920 and work proceeded on the crypt, the largest in the world. Unfortunately, the Great Depression stalled the whole project and work stopped in 1932, although planning continued.

For Maginnis, the National Shrine project, with which he was associated (sometimes more, sometimes less) for almost forty years, was a steady source of irritation; he frequently complained to his family about what was happening to his plans for the building. One of his daughters wrote to me that he "moaned and groaned, especially at dinner, over the insults, of open season on saints, ethnics, and factions, but maybe most of all, over the vicissitudes of infrastructure politics."[5] Bit by bit, his artistically unified structure had to be changed (or perhaps disfigured), in order to comply with one immovable reality: getting money from a very diverse and opinionated Catholic population.

The National Shrine of the Immaculate Conception may have been the dream of the bishops, but the religious orders, various Catholic organizations, and the laity had the money. To make the dream a reality, funds had to be solicited from that disorderly coalition called "Roman Catholicism in the United States" for a coalition building — something so thoroughly "popular" that it would bring in the donations. There was no aristocracy or cultural elite to set the standards of taste and pay the bill. There was no pope or king or millionaire who would allow Maginnis to create a consistent "work of art." The only realistic way to raise funds was to provide "a little something" for everybody, even if, as a result, restrained beauty had to share space with a bit of vulgarity and show-biz glitz. Religious profundity expressed with the finest artistic craftsmanship would have attracted a few pennies in donations, but the multitude would put up millions of dollars to have what amounts to a little ceramic figurine, with philodendron in the back, enlarged and rendered in polished marble. And then, to keep everybody proud and happy, the ethnic groups would get their showcases here and there; popular saints and devotions also needed space. Economic reality dictated that the building would have to become a mall of National Shrines for a wide assortment of ethnic groups and interests. If Maginnis and the architects who succeeded him — backed by the bishops — had resolutely held to the idea that this church should be an elegant, tightly unified edifice, with a minimum of clashing "messages," it would still be just a sketch on paper.

During the decades when the National Shrine was only a set of plans or an unfinished building, the whole idea of what architecture should be changed radically. By the 1930s some leading architects and schools of architecture were loudly condemning the "dishonesty" of modern people building in old-fashioned styles. Respect for the Baroque and the Beaux Arts was disappearing rapidly. Also disappearing were the craftsmen who could produce the harmoniously consistent designs that Maginnis had originally envisioned. All of these developments meant that the directors of the Shrine had to find a way to deal with an unexpected turn of events: the "defeat" of architecture inspired by classicism and the "victory" of modern architecture as a kind of bearer of scientific truth and honesty. A decision was made to keep the general outline of the church that Maginnis had proposed but to embellish it in an approximation of a "Byzantine" style — which could be given a modern look.

Construction work on the Shrine resumed in 1954. (Maginnis, who died in 1955, would not be responsible for most of the major decisions about decorations.) The massive nave was finally opened for worshipers in 1959, although much work needed to be done on the bare brick walls. In the following years, the building would gradually be embellished in a style that could be described as Rampant Eclecticism, the old and the new pulled together in a tense alliance. The Byzantine is there, with Romanesque and Italian Renaissance elements, in order to recall timeless traditions, but the modern era boldly announces its presence — not the severe modernism of the International Style, not the smooth elegance of Art Deco, but rather the kind of taste found in swank Miami Beach hotels built during the 1950s (e.g., the Fountainbleu and Eden Roc by Morris Lapidus).[6]

* * *

From the day the upper church opened, armchair critics have scorned the National Shrine, privately. (Adjectives I have heard: garish, tasteless, vulgar, bombastic.) Although one of the most ambitious building projects of this century, important books on architecture have ignored its existence. Nothing in the building has been singled out as a significant contribution to the art of our time. Certainly, there are imposing features of the structure but, as one guide book puts it, "some of the lesser chapels (not that any of them are small) focus on doll-like figures verging on the cloying and mawkish, reminiscent of Hallmark in their pastel sentimentality."[7]

Perfectionists grumble. Their objections to the Shrine are many: The building is on a North-South axis; for symbolic and traditional reasons, the large, historically important churches have always been built on an East-West axis. The multiplication of Marian images all over the place — Our Lady of Lourdes, Guadalupe, Bistricia, Brezja, Siluva, Czestochowa, and so forth — is overkill. This is a case where less would have been more. The chapels donated by the various ethnic groups create an especially discordant mess; this jumble of competing spaces has transformed a Marian shrine into an Immigration Monument. Some of the stained-glass windows are undistinguished; they only increase the redundancy of Marian images.

The perfectionists then go on to make the inescapable comparison, which goes something like this: "Why couldn't this place be something like the National Cathedral, the Protestant Episcopal edifice in the same city. Unified, dignified, restrained, supremely tasteful, the National Cathedral has a serenity and a religious feeling that one does not easily find in all the razzmatazz of the Shrine." To add a dash of salt in the wounds they mention that the principal architect of the National Cathedral, Philip Frohman, lived and died a Roman Catholic. To rub it in, they remind everyone that most of the stonemasons who worked on the Episcopalian National Cathedral were Italians and presumably Roman Catholic.

In the future, when the Shrine has more of the mosaics that will pull the separate elements together, the critics may discover that they have been wrong. The building might be seen as a highly successful example of "popular" art, architecture calculated to appeal to a wide spectrum of humanity with a wide assortment of "attractions." Perhaps this building will one day be celebrated as "fun," populist art, an ecclesiastical Disneyland.

* * *

Jesus Christ is the sole mediator between God and the human race. That is orthodox Catholic theology and always has been. But if this is so, why is the Virgin Mary represented by hundreds of different works of art in the National Shrine of the Immaculate Conception? What are all of these statues and paintings of saints doing in Catholic churches? The art could be justified as a pious

reminder, but so much of it is about visions and "miraculous occurrences" that seem to have no place in the great message of the
New Testament.

A helpful insight, which explains what is going on, can be
found in, of all places, Edward Gibbon's *Decline and Fall of the
Roman Empire* (published between 1776 and 1788), chapter 2,
where the author discusses the bewildering number of cults that
found their way into ancient Roman civilization:

> The various modes of worship, which prevailed in the Roman
> world, were all considered by the people as equally true; by the
> philosopher, as equally false; and by the magistrate, as equally
> useful.

There are millions of Catholics who believe that the Virgin
Mary appeared in Guadalupe, Paris, LaSalette, Lourdes, Pont-
main, Knock, Fatima, Medjugorje, Queens (New York), suburban
New Jersey (on a lawn), and hundreds of other locations. They believe that all the messages she is supposed to have given are true.
And all the stories about saints are also equally true. Saints really
did fly through the air or levitate.

The atheistic philosopher is not impressed. The stories about
Marian apparitions are all rubbish — fictions, hallucinations for
the kind of credulous people who believe in space aliens.

The Catholic church acts as a magistrate in such matters.
Throughout history, the men who run the church — men with
power in society — have usually been unsympathetic when children and women — the powerless in society — came to them with
stories about private revelations from heavenly sources. (For example, the Catholic bishops of Yugoslavia, before that country
fell apart, discouraged the belief that Mary appeared at Medjugorje.) It is also true that visions, secrets, and revelations from
the Virgin Mary and that stories from the lives of the saints are
not part of Catholic dogma; no Catholic is ever required to believe any of it. (The bishops at Vatican II, in spite of intense pleas
from some of the clergy and laity, refused to issue a syllable of endorsement for either Lourdes or Fatima.) But people want signs
and wonders. What does one do when the "private revelation"
gains a popularity that is unstoppable? If there does not seem to be
anything theologically pernicious involved and if genuine piety is
excited, the church acquiesces; the new Marian apparition or de-

votion receives official recognition; any miracles are a welcome, if unexplainable blessing. God works in mysterious ways, not just through treatises on correct theology.

Older Catholic churches, like the National Shrine, are visual examples of Catholicism trying — no, struggling — to negotiate some compromise between orthodox theology and the popular longing for miraculous reassurances. I think it is safe to say that, in the past, the ugliest and most grotesque churches were often the ones where the "private devotion" to "miraculous occurrences" seemed to take over; some of the most beautiful churches were the ones that maintained, as their central focus, the theology of the Mass.

* * *

On a busy Sunday morning, the crowded nave of the National Shrine "makes sense"; it comes alive. This great space (like St. Peter's in Rome) functions as Catholicism's version of the Temple in Jerusalem; it is the perfect gathering place for that diverse coalition called Roman Catholicism: the rich and the poor, all the ethnic groups, foreign visitors, plus the tourists in Bermuda shorts. The preaching is outstanding, and the music is several notches above excellent. Somehow, everything comes together for this act of faith that glows in the center of the building — and, at the same time, around the periphery or in the basement, out of sight, are the popular side shows: the visual references to miraculous medals, appearances, water, images, and so forth. Somehow the conflict between the center and the periphery works out nicely.

But does everybody think that the National Shrine really "works"? Today the pamphlets, articles, and books that talk about "liturgical space" usually contain a moment of lamentation about those old "impersonal" churches that hinder liturgical progress — and the National Shrine happens to be a titanic example of everything that is supposedly "wrong" about the design of a church (too big, too many altars, too many artistic distractions, priest too far away, and so forth).[8] Measured against the standards described in *Environment and Art in Catholic Worship*, the Shrine is an enormous blunder — the "National Crime," as one priest in Washington puts it.

The directors of the National Shrine (in effect, the bishops) have responded energetically to the challenge of making the nave of that vast building "postconciliar" — which sometimes means shortening the "distance" between sanctuary and people. One way to close the "distance" is with a sound system that allows thousands of worshipers to hear every word of the ceremony. About a dozen different sound systems have been installed over the years and then ripped out because of deficiencies. (Last I heard, a technician has been hired to regulate individual microphones — turn them on or off, decrease or increase their volume — and this works reasonably well.) There is talk about moving the altar and baldacchino down closer to the congregation. I would not be surprised if somebody has suggested wall-to-wall carpets or wrecking the interior, filling it up with offices, and sending people to the crypt church, which is more postconciliar in its design. One of these days, demolishing the whole building and selling the rubble to help the poor will seem like an attractive idea (even though this church welcomes the poor and provides them with the same spiritual comfort it offers to everyone else).

Most Catholics go to the National Shrine and are refreshed by something they encounter there. Without shame, without guilt, they accept the pleasures that the building has to offer and they are appropriately reminded of spiritual matters. They are not bothered in the least by problems of "distance" or inhospitable spaces. They can accept all of the building's imperfections and preconciliar features because they sense one fact that gets lost in all of the idealistic rhetoric about providing the perfect liturgical space: that is, the fine arts are good. The Second Vatican Council reminded the church that the "fine arts are considered to rank among the noblest expressions of human genius." Art with a religious theme and "sacred art," the Council Fathers emphasize, "are related to God's boundless beauty, for this is the reality which these human efforts are trying to express in some way."[9]

L'EGLISE MODERNE

The fine arts as "good" and "related to God's boundless beauty" — it is important to remember that when Vatican II proclaimed those ideals, someone could spend months going from one modern art gallery to another and only rarely come across a first-class painting or sculpture with a Christian significance. At that time many new Christian churches may have had a modern design, but relatively few were considered worth discussing in books and articles on modern art. The truth was, the best modern artists did not find much in Christianity to inspire them. Christianity in general and Catholicism in particular found even less in the modern visual arts that was either good or an expression of "God's boundless beauty."

The story of how Catholicism, before Vatican II, eventually began to search for a rapprochement with the "modern artists" of the twentieth century could be told from different perspectives, but perhaps the most interesting and instructive episode in this whole story involves an obscure church in France.

* * *

France, predicted the critic Charles Augustin Sainte-Beuve (1804–69), would remain a Catholic country long after it had ceased to be Christian. In the first half of the twentieth century some wondered if France, well beyond Christianity, was, with unseemly haste, ceasing to be even nominally associated with Catholicism.

On the surface, the church in France looked as strong as ever. Pilgrims flocked to Lourdes and other shrines. Respected theologians and writers proclaimed a vibrant faith. But, still, there were millions of "lost souls" in the nation: those who had drifted away from a church that appeared to be an outdated institution just for aristocrats and peasants. As far as many in the working class were concerned, the communist gospel of equality and social justice was much more appealing than the vicious reactionary intolerance preached by the right wing of France's Catholic church.

The French Dominicans made it their mission to win back these "lost" Catholics. The members of this religious order would show that the church understood the problems of modern people in a modern world. One part of this effort to bring the faith to the alienated and forgotten was the support that the Dominicans gave to the idea of *prêtres-ouvriers,* worker-priests who would share the lives of common people — by living in ordinary housing (instead of monasteries and rectories) and by working alongside of laborers in factories and mines. Another part of this effort to revitalize the faith was in the area of modern art. The Dominicans soon became identified with the daring proposition that the church should show how relevant and *engagé* it was by welcoming boldly modernistic art into its churches.

Abstract theory about religious art became concrete fact in the church of Notre-Dame-de-Toute-Grâce in Assy, a Dominican parish in a remote, mountainous part of France. The Assy region was isolated and had few inhabitants until the 1920s, when tuberculosis patients began to come in great numbers in the hope that the mountain air would help to cure their disease. In 1937 the bishop of nearby Annecy established a new parish in Assy and assigned it to the Dominicans, who would have to build a new church.

The parish of Assy was destined to an existence of quiet obscurity as a church mostly for people from tuberculosis sanatoria, but that changed in 1939 when its Dominican pastor, Jean Devémy, happened to see a stained-glass window by Georges Rouault at an art exhibit. He was so impressed by it that he asked Rouault to provide a window for the new Assy church that would soon be built. (Rouault, then nearing seventy and perhaps the greatest "Catholic artist" of the twentieth century, had never before been asked to design anything for a Catholic church.) Rouault accepted the challenge. The expectation was that the figure of a suffering Christ would have a special meaning for the tuberculosis patients who would see it; the modernistic design would cause little commotion in a newly developed part of France that was not encumbered by provincial bias or traditions.

Work on the church stopped during World War II. When peace came, another Dominican, Marie-Alain Couturier, took over the task of finding decorations for the church at Assy. He was a sophisticated, sociable, well-respected priest who seemed to "know everybody" in France's artistic elite. Using his considerable charm, he managed to persuade some very important figures in twentieth-century art — Pierre Bonnard, Georges Braque, Marc Chagall, Fernand Léger, Jacques Lipchitz, and Henri Matisse — as well as some lesser-known artists, to create artifacts for the church at Assy; he also persuaded Rouault to design more windows for it. The church, with all its decorations in a modern style, was completed and consecrated in 1950.

William S. Rubin covers this whole complicated story in his book *Modern Sacred Art and the Church of Assy* (New York, 1961). It should come as no surprise that a large part of Rubin's study deals with the public reaction to the church, which he describes as "quick and violent."

First of all there was the matter of the artists. Chagall and Lipchitz were Jewish. Some of the others were fallen-away Catholics with communist sympathies. Rouault may have been a devout, even mystical Catholic but his windows seemed to deform the beauty of the faith. Then there was the bronze crucifix by Madame Germaine Richier. To some, the figure of Christ on it looked like a gnarled piece of metal; it was thunderously denounced as an "insult" and "sacrilege." (Perhaps most of the outrage was caused not by the actual work of art but by the idea of a woman designing a crucifix that was placed on the main altar of a church.) French Catholicism's vocal and uncompromising reactionaries condemned the entire Assy project as a plot by Jewish merchants, freemasons, communists, and Protestants to destroy the faith by means of art. The building was nothing less than the heresy of Modernism in an artistic form.

The Vatican soon entered the controversy. After some behind-the-scene pressure from Rome and letters of protest from some indignant French Catholics, the bishop of Annecy ordered the crucifix by Richier to be removed from the altar of the Assy church. But this was only the beginning of a campaign to root out heresy among the Dominicans. Respected members of this order were either demoted or removed from their teaching positions. French Dominicans were required to have all their writings submitted to a special censorship before publication. There were even rumors that Rome would disband the entire order in France.

In 1955 Pius XII issued an encyclical on music and devoted a few introductory sentences to "the artist" in general. "Now we are aware of the fact" the pope wrote, "that during recent years some artists, gravely offending against Christian piety, have dared to bring into churches works devoid of any religious inspiration and completely at variance with the right rules of art." For Pius XII it was self-evident that "the artist who does not profess the truths of the faith or who strays far from God in his attitude or conduct" simply cannot produce real religious art. Such an artist lacks, as it were, "that inward eye with which he might see what God's majesty and His worship demand." It is only the artist who is "firm in his faith and leads a life worthy of a Christian" who can create art or music worthy of the church.[10]

Roma locuta est, causa finita — Rome has spoken, the matter
is finished. But Rome, which may have had all the *theoretical* answers, could not provide any *practical* ones. In 1950 the Vatican
could not boast about its encouragement of great contemporary
artists who combined exceptional talent with exemplary piety and
the gift of that "inward eye." For all its talk, Rome had nothing to
show, no convincing modern alternatives.

Rubin points out that in 1950 (the year the Assy church was
finished) the Vatican organized an exhibit of sacred art as one part
of the Holy Year festivities in Rome. The first-place prize for excellence at this exhibit was awarded to Nenno Barabino for his
"madonna and child" painting — one of those dear sentimental
things that are the artistic equivalent of a cupcake.

There is much to think about here. For example: In all the
furor that surrounded the Assy church during its first years,
there were no protests from the parishioners; they rather liked
the place.... Pius XII honored Rouault by making him a papal
knight. Rouault's only liturgical art at the time was in the Assy
church.... On television I have seen Pope Paul VI and Pope John
Paul II carrying a bishop's crosier (a long staff) with a modernistic
figure of the Crucified Christ on top; that crucifix looks very much
like a small version of the one designed by Germaine Richier
for the church at Assy.... The men who were made cardinals by
Pius XII erected a statue to his memory in St. Peter's Basilica in
Rome; its style is assertively modernistic.... The church at Assy
is not entirely successful as a work of art. Rubin reports that the
viewer is struck "by a feeling of isolation of parts, resulting to some
extent from the absence of a continuous iconographic scheme" in
the church. "This sense of disjunction is reinforced by the marked
difference in style from one work to the next."[11] ... The angry
denunciations of the art in the Assy church did nothing to promote good religious art, but they did create a chill. Most churches
built in the 1950s and early '60s were examples of "playing it
safe": with incompetent approximations of tradition or with a
mild modernism that Rubin aptly describes as "polite decadence."

The church at Assy set no real precedents; it provided no
helpful examples for other churches to follow, but this is under-
standable. The "Modern Era," which has produced some brilliant
specimens of architecture and even some outstanding churches,
has not quite developed a "vernacular" ecclesiastical architecture

that combines a reasonable price with strong stylistic assertiveness. The problem is our modern idealization of individuality. Modern art is supposed to be the triumphant statement of the individual, who produces unique, "signature" creations. That kind of originality makes the world an interesting place but it does not allow for any "vernacular" compromise.

FOR FURTHER MEDITATION AND GROUP DISCUSSION

1. In 1987 the Landmarks Commission of Boston ruled that parts of the interior of Immaculate Conception Church were significant works of art and could not be changed without the commission's approval. Permission to subdivide the church into offices was denied.

The Jesuits took the matter to court. Telling a church what to do with its worship space, they argued, was interference with freedom of religion. Some leaders of other religious denominations agreed; the American Jewish Congress filed a legal brief in support of the Jesuits. On December 31, 1990, the highest court in the Commonwealth of Massachusetts ruled that no government agency could regulate the design of a church's interior; the people of Boston would have to "accept the possible loss of historically significant elements of the interior" as the price for freedom of religion. The Constitution guarantees the right of people to worship office space any way they want.[12]

2. We can be sure of this: The grandeur, the pomp, the "noblest expressions of human genius" (the words of Vatican II), the gold and the mosaics, the fine arts in the service of faith — all of it will pass away, like all human things. The New Testament is very clear about this. It is good to keep this in mind, always.

Nevertheless, it is still annoying to realize that so many things will pass away not because of age, natural disaster, or war but because of one generation's pigheaded sense of its own superiority.

3. This is what I am sometimes told: "Look at all those religious orders that threw themselves into the cause of good art and music in the church, back before Vatican II. They all are close

to extinction. But those Catholics who kept their Infant Jesus of
Prague statues and spurned all this concern about correct artistic
beauty — they are still going strong. They kept the faith."

4. In 1969, when I visited Venice with some friends, we wandered around the city and stepped into an old church. I was soon
attracted to some paintings (in frames) on the wall of a side chapel.
Why, I asked myself, were they hung one on top of another, like
something in an art gallery. A pleasant old priest, who was a member of the parish staff, walked by and we started a conversation
with him about the paintings.

"That thing way up there on the top," he said, "that's probably
from the workshop of Tintoretto." The sunlight from a window
was baking the canvas. "The one over there might be a copy of a
Giorgione." The surface was warped but still full of color.

The priest belonged to what I call the Italian School of Church
Art Appreciation. Its way of looking at religious art goes something like this: "These beautiful things in church belong to us,
they are part of our lives, they represent one way to express our religious fervor; we like them. Now that's enough of that; let's pray
and then go have dinner."

The attitudes of this Italian School — which you might find
in France or Austria or wherever — blend piety with casual fa-
miliarity (carelessness?) and pride in ownership. The statues and
paintings are part of the landscape, things that God put there for
us to enjoy, or ignore.

The members of the New American School of Church Art Appreciation look at a piece of good art in church (or encounter fine
church music) and get an allergic reaction, which is described in
these terms: "That tinsel is foreign; it belongs to the foreign elite,
those decadent people who make fun of our simple but honest
ways."

The followers of the New American School scarcely see any
difference between committing a particularly heinous sin and the
taking of pleasure in artistic beauty. They tend to think of the
church community as a kind of health club of the spirit. There,
among the like-minded and the self-selected, the faithful perform
liturgical aerobics; they meet the challenges of social issues; they
cleanse their arteries; they perfect themselves. Religious art —
even something plain and austere — invites contemplation, get-

ting out of the preoccupation with yourself. Contemplation — condemned as idleness, distraction, privacy, and inactivity — does not belong in the dynamic health-club Future-Kingdom church of the New American School. Contemplation, which easily slips into prayer, clogs the spiritual arteries.

Supposedly there is tension in Catholicism today between the old-timers, who mistakenly believe that "the beautiful church building is the church of Christ," and the post–Vatican II faithful, who realize that "the people are the church." But this evaluation of the situation misses the point. The tension is really between the "Italian" and the "New American" ways of looking at life. The "Italians" acknowledge that religious art (and this includes music) might be a symbol of a spiritual experience but it can also be, like a nice glass of red wine, just another enjoyable gift of God, a reminder of God's goodness and glory. The "Americans" are deeply suspicious of enjoyment that is not measurable, functional, and clearly useful for self-improvement. There are good people on both sides of the issue.

By the way: I have known various citizens of the United States who did quite a lot of hectic foreign travel as students — but with strict limits on the countries they would visit. Off they went to the remote corners of Britain, Scandinavia, Germany, and Eastern Europe (when it was in the hands of the communists), yet they would not set foot on Italian soil — or Spain or sometimes even France. The problem? These places were too Mediterranean, too garlicky. If you talked to these people about their travel limitations, they would eventually get around to their fear of the lack of control in these Mediterranean cultures where people accept artistic sensuality without shame.

5. Of course, what "Italian-Americans" do to artistic sensuality is sometimes altogether different.

In 1981 I went to a viewing for one of my Italian relatives in an "Italian-American" neighborhood. The first thing I saw in the vestibule of the funeral home was a copy of Leonardo da Vinci's Last Supper. Once I got inside, I immediately came across the same image but "translated" into carved wood. Nearby was a bas-relief version of the Last Supper in copper and also an ivory-colored, almost three-dimensional version in plaster. Holy cards featured — of course — the Last Supper. When I got to the deceased, there it was again on the kneeler and (in bronze) on the casket handles. I lost count, but I must have seen at least six variations on Leonardo da Vinci's Last Supper between the front door and the casket.

I am not laughing. I am not sneering.

Sometimes, the Catholic laity (and the clergy) tend to see religious art as an abstraction. The Last Supper becomes just a familiar collection of lines and planes in a rectangular space which symbolizes —

It is hard to say what: maybe pride in ethnic accomplishments, maybe a generic religiosity. In any case, the actual Last Supper and its place in Catholic belief get lost in the abstraction process and especially in the constant repetition.

This same tendency to lose or pervert the meaning of symbols comes out very strongly at Christmas time. In some communities, a few fiercely determined Catholics wage a campaign to set up a Nativity scene — a religious symbol, religious art — on public property, preferably on the grounds of the city hall. The reasoning sounds reasonable: "Put Christ back into an increasingly secularized Christmas" and "This country was founded on Judeo-Christian principles."

A quick reading of a few history books and even the daily newspapers will provide abundant information about the violence that occurs when one religion tries to put its mark on the state. A quick look at the Declaration of Independence and the Constitution will show that neither mentions Christianity. There may be Judeo-Christian principles subtly woven into the legal heritage of the nation, but nothing about the necessity of displaying a manger scene in front of city hall.

One thing we can be sure of is that the Nativity scene on public property has very little to do with putting the religious values back into Christmas or with Judeo-Christian principles or even with the Incarnation. The Christmas creche is a Roman Catholic artistic invention and its presence in front of city hall proclaims Catholic ascendency in that town. Even though there might be a Jewish menorah a few steps away from the three Wise Men, even though there might be sincere talk about reminding everyone about the true meaning of Christmas, the manger scene on public property is, above all, a display of political clout. In front of the city hall, that beautiful scene is reduced (like da Vinci's

Last Supper) to an abstraction: lines and planes in a rectangular space. The purpose of the abstraction is to ward off evil. Like a cross held in front of a vampire, the abstraction will frighten off evil — in this case, the atheists, the drug-pushers, the sexually depraved, and the businessmen who have destroyed the true meaning of Christmas. The abstraction is turned into a lucky charm, a rabbit's foot.

In the past, the Nativity scene, as an artistic creation, was a beautiful reminder. There was one in the church (maybe hand-carved by local artisans) and a little one in the home, with the most important one in your heart. The modern Nativity scene — in plastic, almost life-sized, with a light bulb inside each figure, in front of the church, on the front lawn — has to shout for attention in a very noisy world. It may have color, sentimentality, and a message, but the art that was originally there is totally gone.

6. What did I think of the architectural plans for the new church? Wonderful, impressive, I said, but where will the musicians go?

There would be no special place for them, I was informed. Since the choir is part of the assembly, the singers would sit in the pews with everybody else. This new church would have no elitist separation for musicians.

That used to be the most progressive postconciliar teaching on where to put musicians in a new or renovated church. A newer theory seems to be that musicians should go right in the center of things, right behind the altar — or maybe slightly to one side of the priest.

This may be the "look" of many new Catholic churches in the future. You walk into the building and your attention is immediately pulled to the musicians. (They might be "classical" but more likely they specialize in music of the "folk/contemporary" variety.)

7. Some Catholics were profoundly disturbed when the tabernacle in their parish church was moved from the main altar to a place on the side. They may have heard reasoned explanations about the custom of storing the Sacrament in a side chapel being much older than the custom of placing a tabernacle on the main altar, but this still does not calm them down.

A colleague told me about one parish that moved its tabernacle to the side of the sanctuary and placed it on a pedestal, upon which is an inscription that reads, "Bread of life." On the other side of the sanctuary is another, parallel pedestal and on top of it is a Bible; the inscription on this pedestal reads, "Word of life."

The theologian comes along, observes the pedestals, and finds ingenious things to say about the "Table of the Bread" being parallel to the "Table of the Word." The ordinary Catholic comes along, sees the parallel shrines with the parallel inscriptions *as an artistic statement* and concludes that there is not a bit of difference between the Sacrament on one side and the fat edition of the Bible on the other.

8. I was flipping through a Catholic magazine (in 1973, if I remember correctly) when I came across an article about a parish that had constructed a new church building in the post–Vatican II architectural style of the future. Pay attention, the reader was advised. This is what the future parish church will be like, and it works!

The building looked like another dull cardboard box to me, except that the whole area behind the altar — from end to end — was covered with mirrors. The congregation, lined up in pews, stared straight ahead at a reflection of itself in a wall of mirrors. According to the author of the article, these mirrors behind the altar were supposed to remind the people in the pews that they were important, they were the church.

9. In 1966 a friend of mine, a Jesuit seminarian at the time, invited me to visit him. While he was showing me around the seminary, he whispered, with a grin, "Want to see some real junk?"

He brought me to the chapel's sacristy and opened up a small walk-in vault in the wall.

"See what I mean," he said. "Real junk."

I gasped. There in front of me was a glittering hoard of gold and gems: chalices, monstrances, patens — all gold, some encrusted with jewels.

It took a few more seconds to see what he meant by "junk." The designs of these sacred vessels were all rather uninspired, even clumsy. I remember one chalice that had diamonds arranged in the shape of a cross at its base. Emeralds and rubies on other sacred items looked as if they had been stuck on with glue, as an afterthought.

According to my friend, Catholics had specified in their wills that their heirs were to purchase chalices or monstrances and, in some cases, encrust these objects with gems from the family's jewelry. These sacred vessels were to be given to the Jesuits. My friend further explained that this golden "junk" could not be sold or even hocked, under the terms of the bequest and church law (at that time). The seminary needed an endowment to help pay the oil bills, to educate the students, to support missionaries. But what did the Catholic laity give them? Gold and jewelry — most of which never left the vault.

Some years later I asked my friend what had happened to the "junk" in the vault? He said he thought that all of it had been cleaned out by thieves one night. Nothing was insured.

10. In his *Attack upon Christendom*, Søren Kierkegaard observes: "Long robes, splendid churches, etc., all this hangs together, and it is the human falsification of the Christianity of the New Testament, a falsification which shamelessly takes advantage of the fact that unfortunately the human mass only too easily lets itself be deluded by sense impressions, and therefore (exactly in opposition to the New Testament) is prone to judge true Christianity by sense impressions."[13]

Elsewhere, Kierkegaard reminds us that Christ was crucified on a wooden cross between two thieves, not on a silver crucifix between two silver candlesticks.

It is a shame that Kierkegaard never got as far south as France or Italy, never learned to relax in the sensual Mediterranean world, where Christianity first developed.

Everything we know — our feelings, our emotions, and even our spiritual values — have all started as sense impressions. Our whole conscious life has been built on what our senses have taught us. The sense impressions of a beautiful church can "teach" just as effectively as a book. Of course, there is a danger: when the sense impressions cease to have any religious value and just remain sense impressions.

11. Two acquaintances of mine were very puzzled by the plans to modernize the cathedral church that used to be their parish before they moved. They asked me what I thought.

The cathedral, a massive neo-Gothic extravaganza, needed repairs and a more "postconciliar look," my acquaintances reported. The cathedral staff, working with a church decorator, came up

with Plan A: a spaceship modern interior so artistically bare that
it looked as if it had been sterilized for surgery. The stained-glass
windows would all be replaced by clear glass; the old altar, with
its background of carved marble angels and turrets, would be removed; a continuous mural along the walls of the building, with
depictions of angels and religious symbols, would be obliterated,
except for one token angel. The altar would stand alone and bare,
at the crossing, the architectural center of the building, and behind it, at the focal point of the worshiper's attention, would be
the priest's chair.

The parishioners and the people of the diocese, who had to pay
for this Star Wars throne room, were not impressed. In fact, some
of them screamed bloody murder.

Well, Plan B was presented: Keep the windows, but get rid of
the wedding-cake altar.

At a meeting on the remodeling plans, a few of the older parishioners vigorously defended the old altar. A couple of them were
related to the workmen who had carved it. Keep the beautiful old
thing, they pleaded.

The designer in charge of the remodeling plans was also at
the meeting. He shot back at the old-altar defenders: "You're so
dumb! Can't you people see that the thing you want to save is just
a decorative retable, not an altar!"

Plan C: New designer; keep the windows and the old altar (just
as a decoration), but definitely paint over the mural with all the
angels.

Plan D: No money. Patch up.

12. I wanted to buy a new tie.

"Need some help?" asked the salesman (a semi-retired gentleman I know).

"Yes," I replied, "I was thinking of something in a solid color,"
and then I showed him a few possibilities I had picked out. (Solid-
color ties were in style then.)

He grabbed them out of my hand and put them back on the
rack. He looked angry.

"I was a soldier in World War II and afterward," he said angrily,
"and all during that time I could only wear a solid-color tie. When
I got out of the army, I swore I would never wear a solid-color tie
for the rest of my life."

I bought something with blue and white stripes and left the store fast.

We never know what traumas, prejudices, and notions people bring with them when they encounter art, or a man's tie.

We never know what some Catholics bring with them when they form opinions about art, architecture, or music for the church; sometimes they give the impression that what they really have in mind is "getting even" with the institution that had controlled them in pre–Vatican II days. The priest who was not allowed to eat or drink anything from midnight until he said Mass on Sunday (maybe at noon) and who had to endure the boot-camp life of the seminary, the nun who had to remain meekly submissive during her dealings with the nincompoop pastor or bishop, the layman who followed the church's teachings on sex and thinks he missed a lot of action — my goodness, the anger that exploded in the late 1960s! Has it stopped?

Art and music are two places where the anger and resentments can come out and take the form of demolition.

13. It was a very hot day. I drove my car up to the toll booth on a highway. The man in the booth stuck his arm out, accepted my money, and handed me the change.

The transaction took only a few seconds, but it gave me time to observe a dramatic artwork, a large tattoo on the biceps of this man's left arm. It was a picture of the Sacred Heart (in red and blue), framed by a Gothic arch. Underneath the picture were the words "Agnus Dei" (Lamb of God).

The People of God are the church. Right? Inculturation means bringing liturgy and church art down to the level of those people — their culture, what is meaningful to them. Right? We don't force the canons of European High Art on believers. If the People of God want tattoo art and tattoo music in church, we give it to them. Right?

14. There are homeless people roaming the streets, unemployed people who need work, the poor all over the world — and the local cathedral needs some *very expensive* repairs and improvements. All things rot, even cathedrals. (The laws of thermodynamics do not make an exception for religious or charitable institutions.) What do you do?

A news item showed a monumental old Catholic church with an unusual addition to its interior. Midway between the floor and the vaulted ceiling was a huge net. (It looked like something for a trapeze act at the circus.) The purpose of the net was to protect worshipers from falling plaster decorations. It seems that the roof leaked and the ceiling needed some fixing but the parish community, a fraction of its size when the church was new, could not afford the repairs. What do you do?

Should a decaying church be sold? This can be risky. The building could always fall into the hands of somebody who will use it for vulgar or even blasphemous purposes. (One Episcopalian church in Manhattan was sold and eventually became a kind of disco club whose "theme" is mockery of the building's religious associations.)

Should the building be demolished? This is the quick, hard-nosed, bottom-line solution, a favorite of administrators. In some cases, there is no other choice. In a few cases, however, it makes sense to lease the building to a board of trustees and have them take care of it — but the American Catholic hierarchy has a long history of distrusting the laity in the matter of controlling property.

Should everything possible be done to maintain a beautiful but ailing church? If the building has some architectural, artistic, historic, or even neighborhood significance, yes, absolutely — and for psychological reasons more than anything else. If the building goes, a sense of trust also goes. Money to build Catholic churches and to put art inside of them came from people who trusted their pastor and bishop (or mother superior). Maintaining at least some significant buildings in poor neighborhoods and in the downtown area is a psychological sign of commitment and trust; indirectly, it "pays for itself."

15. Shortly after the death of Francis Cardinal Spellman in 1967, a friend of mine said he had a scandalous secret to tell me about the late archbishop of New York.

According to my friend, after Cardinal Spellman died he went directly to heaven and was about to enter when an angel, who was on night duty at the time, stopped him. "State your name and occupation," said the angel. "Francis Spellman, religious leader," answered the archbishop. The angel looked at the Rolodex and checked the file cabinet but found nothing. "Wait here," he said sternly. His Eminence waited, for what seemed like an eternity, until St. Peter came rushing out. "We've found them!" announced St. Peter waving a file folder in his hand. "We've found your papers, and we're so sorry for the mix-up. You see, we had you filed under real estate."

One of the "well-known facts" in modern society is that the Catholic church has more money than it can spend. Just look at the real estate. And there must be sacks filled with gold doubloons in caverns beneath the Vatican. (In my youth, I was assured that "the cardinal uses a desk made entirely out of crystal and gold . . . the archdiocese of New York has a seat on the New York Stock Exchange . . . the Jesuits control the world market in copper, or maybe it's sugar.") Some Catholics still like to tell these blatantly preposterous stories about the church's wealth — almost with a touch of respect, since the "information" seems to prove that the people who run their church are uncommonly shrewd managers. ("Say what you want about those guys, but they certainly know how to run a business.")

After Vatican II, when parishes and dioceses began to give out more information about their financial situation, the "well-known fact" about the wealth of the Catholic church became a well-known myth.[14] A Catholic institution here and there, such as a university, may enjoy the cushion of a large endowment, but generally the various agencies of the Catholic church live on a tight budget. In fact, some organizations, such as the religious orders of women, are in terrible financial shape; the retired sisters, many of them in nursing homes, have to be supported by a relatively small "base" of working sisters.

And yet, the myth of the Catholic church's fabulous wealth remains as strong as ever. One reason for the persistence of the myth is art. People look at the marble, the gold leaf on the columns, the substantial buildings (on prime real estate); they conclude that all of this is "wealth." Only a religion run by millionaires could have produced such symbols of conspicuous spiritual consumption.

This "wealth," sad to say, does not produce cash. The gold candelabra, resting upon the marble altar with intricate carvings, will not pay the electric bill. Indeed, this "wealth" costs money to maintain; an average parish may spend a small fortune every year to keep the temperature and humidity of its church reasonable, just so the plaster will not crumble.

16. In some older Catholic churches the letters IHS are used as a decorative motif. High up on the ceiling or embroidered on the altar linens or carved on chairs, these letters seem to signify an important matter.

When I was young I remember being told that IHS stood for "I have suffered." The popular thinking was that God the Father, through His Son, had shared the suffering of the human race as a way of showing repentance for all the misery in the world — a misery for which God was somehow responsible. (The theology here was, it goes without saying, garbled.)

That was then. I do not know what the popular thinking is today, but probably just a small number of Roman Catholics realize that the letters IHS are from the Greek alphabet. IHS was an abbreviation for the name Jesus, a Greek version of a Hebrew name that is rendered as Joshua in English. Greek was the most widely spoken language in the ancient Mediterranean world. The writers of the Gospels may have recorded sayings and dialogues that were originally spoken in Aramaic, but they used the Greek language to make sure that their message would have a large audience. The letters IHS, therefore, represent Christianity's oldest written link to the name of Jesus.

I think of this "IHS misunderstanding" (the original meaning replaced by the popular reinterpretation) whenever I hear some professional liturgists describe what worship is and what it is supposed to do to the laity. Give these liturgists the right kind of art and music, give them a free hand to redecorate the building, give them the right texts, and they will transform the faithful. No longer will people be dazed by aesthetic nonsense, by pretty things; instead, they will at last *see* what everything means. For example, the faithful will realize that a procession is not a procession but (as it has sometimes been explained) really an epiphany of the presence of the Lord moving among the faithful. Put that Eucharistic table right into the midst of the congregation, and everyone will understand the meaning of a priesthood of all believers. Get all of those details absolutely right and the result will be full, conscious, and active participation.

So beautiful. So hopeless.

Centuries ago, the Catholic church realized that you can't win. The faithful see a beautiful procession or the position of the altar or the letters IHS and they make up their own explanations. They deal in emotional and aesthetic intuitions, not theologically correct formulas. God understands. Some of the liturgical theoreticians do not.

There is a tendency among many Catholics in positions of leadership to forget that true "catholic" worship will always be a very sloppy procedure; the congregation — men, women, and children, all at different levels of understanding and attention — is a crowd of diverse, imperfect people; nobody in the congregation, not even the most highly educated theologian, really *understands* the mysteries of faith. Long ago, the church recognized that it had the job of leading these imperfect people — the universal, "catholic" multitude — to higher things; it had to "shock" them with moral values that are above the norm. This "shocking" process also involved (at least occasionally) liturgical art and music that are above the "popular," above the comfortable lowness of kitsch. But that same church, with the wisdom that comes from centuries of experience, also realized that people cannot be "educated" so that all will reach the same state of theological "understanding." Any attempt to make the church building a place where identical clones all reach identical versions of full, conscious, and active participation is literally inhuman — or maybe it is some militaristic fantasy that a congregation can be turned into soldiers marching on parade.

Think of a place in our society where our participation can be vividly full, conscious, and active: a dentist's chair — with the drill going and no pain-killer. Think of a church building designed so that the worshiper will never be distracted by a moment of meditation, private thought, or the "aesthetic experience." Think of the postconciliar liturgy that uses a steady drilling of words spoken or sung into a microphone in order to silence any deep thought or emotion. This may be somebody's idea of correct, participatory "understanding," but it is also worship as dentist's chair.

17. A new building was going up along the side of a busy road. "Isn't that the new Catholic parish church?" I asked a friend.

My friend thought it was going to be a synagogue or church for a Pentecostal denomination.

The exterior walls were finished and the roof was put on; perhaps it was beginning to look like a store or a skating rink. It was hard to tell.

A sign appeared. The building would be the headquarters of a local company that distributes home heating oil.

In "contemporary culture" it is now hard to distinguish some houses of worship from — just about anything. I am not going to imply that all churches should have towers with crosses on top and stained-glass windows. I am only saying that many new churches, especially ones that go back to the 1950s and '60s, are undistinguished. They were built without care, without respect. Remove a few superfluous details from their exteriors and they would look like a small-town post office or the headquarters of a heating oil distributor — or like "nothing."

This is no cause for boasting about the freeing of religion from elitist art and its merging with the here-and-now, real life, today. The banal architecture is really an unhealthy sign, the result of a deliberate policy of putting up structures that have absolutely no character, no personality, because character and personality involve a little extra care about beauty, and that costs money. The undistinguished house of worship — the architectural equivalent of the cheap TV dinner zapped in the microwave — shows the world that this faith community has not wasted money on frills, on mere art. The ugliness is supposed to be a sign of true faith triumphing over false values.

With a lot of cleverness and a small budget, it is possible to build a church that is truly "distinguished" — set apart from the commonplace and yet pleasantly harmonized with the landscape. It has been done.[15] The "distinguished" new church and its art might be quite humble or a significant achievement in the history of architecture, but, whatever the case, the structure seems to say, "We are serious about our beliefs."

18. In 1991 the Environment and Art Study Group of the North American Academy of Liturgy issued a set of principles about space for liturgy.[16] These statements, unanimously approved by the group, contain some good, practical advice, but there are also a few strange moments. For example: "The assembly is primary symbol in liturgy. . . . Christian liturgical environment sponsors the mutual presence of the participants and therefore the real presence of Christ."

Statements like these are an example of words used as if they were perfume — sweet aromas that gently touch us and produce an agreeable feeling, yet never quite make it to the part of the brain that deals with coherent thought. But perhaps this is just as well. These perfume words, if someone thinks about them too long, could easily be misinterpreted to mean just about anything (such as, the only real presence of Christ, in liturgy, is the mutual presence of the participants, who receive primary importance).

Perfume is beautiful and somehow flattering to the person who exudes it. Unfortunately, much confusion could result if someone tries to transform these perfume words into the hard reality of architecture. Unless great care is taken, the result could be worship space that pushes neighborliness to an extreme — with each person in the congregation looking at the other persons to see what they are wearing, who they are with, how they look, and whether or not they "fit in."

The Art Study Group has an answer for this sort of objection: "People who are distracted by viewing faces of others in the assembly are not ready to pray/sing with their assembled fellow worshipers." It is true that you want to pray a little harder and longer when you see, in the assembly, a mother holding a sleeping baby or an old man who has come to church despite his infirmities or just a very nice family. Communal worship requires an awareness of the community. But, at the same time, one is entitled to a measure of anxiety concerning the idea that the worshiper's ability to pray while "viewing faces of others" means that he or she is mature enough to worship in an assembly (the "primary symbol").

Liturgical Renewal — including theories on what makes good ecclesiastical architecture — went through a "history phase," when the past was carefully studied by scholars for ideas and inspiration. Then it went through a "revolution stage," when many believed that one more set of changes, one more demolition job on something from the past would produce unbounded happiness. Now Liturgical Renewal is beginning its "poetry stage." What is supposed to be commentary on liturgy or an address at a Catholic convention sometimes comes across as a prose poem, with fervent yearning for a spiritual awakening. This could be a good, wholesome development. But trouble always begins if the poetry dissolves into verbal perfume (on, let us say, the subject of art and architecture for a postconciliar church). The function of the intoxicating perfume is to prevent you from noticing that the writer or speaker really wants to silence opposition and convey this message: "Forget history, tradition, experience, and even human nature. Forget all of that. Do it my way."

Chapter Four

DEPRESSING MUSIC
It Doesn't Belong

ON SEPTEMBER 8, 1990, Richard John Neuhaus, a Lutheran pastor and a highly respected author, became a Roman Catholic. The following September he was ordained a priest.

A few months after Neuhaus was received into the church, an interviewer for a Catholic newspaper asked him what he disliked and what he liked about Catholicism. "On the negative side," he responded, " . . . I find the liturgy and music of contemporary Catholicism depressing. But that is something I will have to bear with."[1]

I asked Father Neuhaus if his blunt statement needed amplification. In a letter he replied that he "did not become a Roman Catholic for the reasons cited by some — the attraction of liturgy, sense of the numinous, musical richness, etc. . . . No, the compelling reason I became a Catholic is that the Church of Christ most fully and rightly ordered through time 'subsists' in the Roman Catholic Church in a singular manner." Father Neuhaus praised the liturgy and music at a Catholic parish where he worshiped in Manhattan before his ordination; nevertheless, he readily admitted that the Liturgical Renewal "envisioned by Catholic leaders such as Msgr. Martin Hellriegel prior to Vatican II is better expressed today, generally speaking, in some Lutheran and Episcopalian parishes."[2]

The adjective "depressing," as used by Father Neuhaus, refers to the new, revised, updated, improved rituals introduced in the Catholic church after the Second Vatican Council. What could be called the "official line" is that these rituals have been successful beyond all expectations. But cradle Catholics I know tend to look at things another way. Ages ago they learned to bear with whatever form of worship the church offered them, successful or unsuccessful; they are resigned — which they interpret as being content. Maybe you have to be a newcomer, with unspoiled innocence, to see that something is not right. Maybe you have to be a pastor who has just converted from Lutheranism or a married Episcopalian priest who is now a married Roman Catholic priest to perceive, instantly, that it is not the revised rites but their *implementation* that is so often a mess; the liturgical life of the Catholic parish *too frequently*, but not always, can indeed be a depressing experience for anybody who has more than three grams of sensitivity in him or her and has seen better.

One does not have to be the conductor of a major symphony orchestra to detect the truth in the other observation made by Father Neuhaus: that the music of contemporary Catholicism (to a great extent but certainly not everywhere) is pretty depressing. Even those ever-enduring, never-complaining cradle Catholics will sometimes agree. In my book *Why Catholics Can't Sing* (1990) I described some of the reasons for this musical depression, which manifests itself in the tepid congregational singing — or at least I thought I did. Friends and correspondents, however, have politely informed me that I may have spotted a rotting tree here and there but I had completely missed the forest. I did not see the "big picture."

* * *

This "big picture," which helps to explain the depressing moments in the music of contemporary Catholicism, perhaps could be traced back to the late Middle Ages, when the worship life of the Roman Catholic church was — at least to those who were alert to what was going on — scandalous. The liturgical texts were thickly encrusted with all kinds of extra words called tropes, many of which were inappropriate. Various liturgical prayers mentioned the legendary (and unbelievable) exploits of saints. The handwritten missal in one parish did not agree with the handwritten missal in a neighboring parish. Many parish priests took a somewhat slovenly approach to the job of saying Mass. Their approach to their vow of chastity was also rather slovenly. No wonder the Protestant Reformers had very little trouble convincing many that the Church of Rome was hopelessly corrupt.

Pope Pius V (1504–72), one of the most austere of all the austere popes, devoted his pontificate (1566–72) to an offensive against Protestantism and against this corruption within the church. One crucial part of his militant battle was the publication, in 1570, of a new missal to be used in the Roman Rite throughout the world. Up until that time ritual books varied from place to place, but the printing press now made it possible for Rome to command the use of its own standard ritual book for every Latin Mass, with a few tolerated exceptions. The pope's insistence on liturgical uniformity was ignored in some places — the French, for example, did not abandon their Gallican rites until the nineteenth century — but the Missal of Pius V eventually became "the" Latin Mass.

The instructions at the beginning of this new missal prescribed in detail every gesture a priest had to make while saying Mass and they required him to read, without abbreviation or alteration, every single one of the required texts, including words that were really for the choir. The words "draconian" and "procrustean" describe, mildly, the thinking behind this new missal, but Pius V could claim, with some justification, that this was just the sort of thing the Council of Trent (1545–63) wanted when it initiated its own so-called Counter Reformation of the church.

If we look at this historical development from one angle, the structure of the Mass decreed by Pius V (which is now commonly called the Tridentine Mass) was a thorough modernization and exactly what was needed at the time. The clerics who put together this missal for the pope were bold modernizers; they threw out beloved liturgical songs (the sequences), the tropes, and ancient ceremonies, all in an effort to purge the liturgy of its medieval accretions and make it more modern. The new missal helped to restore the credibility of the church and it preserved the liturgy from further corruptions.

If we look at this matter from a slightly different angle, Pius V's missal was a disaster. It choked off a natural and normal evolution, it all but ignored the congregation's role, and (finally, I get to the point) it treated music as if it were something that did not belong to the *real* Mass. The instructions in the missal give the impression that the priest maintained the textual integrity of the Mass, while the choir only provided decorations, which were slightly more important than floral bouquets. In that big historical picture (beginning long before the sixteenth century), church music was supposed to float in its own parallel dimension *outside* the real business of the Mass ritual, which the priest administered. Music might belong *with* the church's rites but never quite *in* them.

A conspicuous example of this way of thinking can be seen not in a Mass but in a Vespers service. In 1610 the composer Claudio Monteverdi published a monumental setting of Vespers for feasts of the Virgin Mary. This lavish Baroque work for soloists, chorus, and instruments, according to the title page, was intended for liturgical use, not a concert, yet some of the words that Monteverdi set do not belong to any Vespers; other required words are missing. What Monteverdi composed makes no liturgical sense until we are let in on a little secret: The clerics in the sanctuary were expected to recite, quietly, every single word of the required texts; they would take care of the *real* Vespers prescribed in the liturgical books; the choir would sing a parallel approximation of the service with Monteverdi's music.[3]

Arcangelo Corelli (1653–1713) composed some luminously beautiful string compositions (*da chiesa*), which were played up in the choir loft by the local musicians, as a substitute for some of the words that the choir was supposed to sing. In effect, the string music was the community's form of participation — a kind of "dance" in church.[4] Wolfgang Amadeus Mozart (1756–91), following a custom at Salzburg Cathedral, wrote sprightly "Epistle Sonatas," instrumental compositions that replaced the choir's music between the Epistle and Gospel of the Mass. Maybe there were some who grumbled about this tradition of the priest doing "his own thing" while the musicians did "their own thing," but, according to the prevailing attitude, everything was in order as long as the priest read off all the words; the musicians, after all, only added occasional moments of artistic highlighting.

Because music did not "belong" in the real ritual (and was usually sung by people up in a gallery about a block away from the altar), a little mismatch between the music and the ceremony was tolerated. If a perfectly jolly Kyrie by Haydn did not seem to coordinate with the idea of "Lord, have mercy," which the priest was reciting privately, nobody worried. The music was not really *in* the actual ceremony.

Sometime near the beginning of the nineteenth century the little mismatch between the priest's "real" Mass and the music coming from the choir loft became more and more flagrant. For example, French organists delighted congregations with improvised "storm music" and Rossini's *William Tell* Overture (later known as the "Lone Ranger" theme song). The Sextet from Donizetti's *Lucia di Lammermoor,* fitted with the words of the Tantum Ergo, was a great favorite. In Ireland and parishes in the United States where Irish taste prevailed, the "choir" often consisted of a soprano soloist, probably with a fine operatic singing voice in the best *bel canto* tradition.[5] (My grandmother told me about the way that parishioners of one church used to brag to parishioners of another about their paid soprano soloist — a lady underneath a large hat — who could belt out a high C during Mass.) Even the pope's private chapel, the Sistine Chapel, was not immune to this musical mismatch. At the end of the nineteenth century, the repertory of this ancient organization was loaded with compositions by Giovanni Aldega, Luigi Pratesi, Paolo Tosi, Gaetano Capocci, and other contemporary hacks whose main source of inspiration was the Meditation or Prayer Scene that Giuseppe Verdi liked to put near the end of his operas.[6] Contemporary congregations, so the thinking went, needed contemporary music.

To be sure, there were complaints about the intrusions of contemporary theater music into divine services. The principal complainers, the followers of the Cecilian Movement, urged the church to return to its musical roots, to the distinctly anticontemporary music of Gregorian chant and Renaissance choral music (polyphony), but in some places the Cecilians were, so to speak, "outvoted" by the majority, which knew for certain that authentic Catholic church music meant something "contemporary" and "from our time."

Then, out of a clear blue sky, came a thunderbolt.

In 1903 the newly elected Pope Pius X issued a *Motu Proprio* (the name for a document that a pope writes to put forth his own ideas) on the subject of music for the church. The *Motu Proprio* contained a number of ideas that had been "in the air" for decades, but now they were presented as strict pronouncements: Gregorian chant and Renaissance polyphony were models of true church music, although some types of new compositions were permissible; the modern operatic style, however, was absolutely inappropriate for church; the sung texts were part of the rite and therefore they could not be abbreviated or replaced with something else; women were not permitted to sing in choirs; congregations "should take a more active part in the offices, as they did in former times," by singing chant.

Later, Pius X reinforced the *Motu Proprio* with a whole series of decrees. (He did virtually nothing, however, to encourage the congregation's "more active part" in liturgical singing.) The pope also made every effort to "rescue" Gregorian chant, which was almost in a state of ruin in 1903. (The musical editions were full of errors; the style of singing this music had become ponderous and dull.) He commissioned definitive editions of chant and eventually endorsed a chant "singing style" that had been developed at Solesmes Abbey in France after years of research.

The *Motu Proprio* produced results rather quickly. Soon after this document was issued, some Catholics were noticing drastic changes in church music and what sounded like a "new Mass" when the choir sang. Women were exiled from many choirs (until Pius XII invited them back); the number of boys' choirs multiplied. Monks, nuns, seminarians, brothers, and children in the parochial schools were singing Gregorian chant according to the "historically correct" Solesmes method. In some churches, especially on the European Continent, music of the late Renaissance masters (especially Palestrina) astounded worshipers with its rare beauty.

Now, we should keep in mind that all of this old music was so unknown and "different" that it was considered *très moderne* in the years before the *Motu Proprio*. (In 1892 the Impressionist composer Claude Debussy, who was never known for piety, took a great interest in the subtle sound of the "new" Renaissance music and "new" Solesmes chant, which he heard in one Parisian church; he was so intrigued, he invited friends to come with him and discover this unusual singing at Mass.[7]) In my younger days — let us say, the 1950s and early '60s — the men and boys choir with lots of chant and a couple of Renaissance Mass settings in its repertory was still considered to be way out there in front, on the cutting edge, especially if the children in the parochial school joined in the singing.

Alas, the unintended and unfortunate results of the *Motu Proprio* must also take up a big portion of the "big picture." Most chant melodies and Renaissance music, which the pope had so warmly recommended, proved to be unrealistic for many churches; in the United States, most parishes either gave up (and virtually abandoned choral music) or sang mediocre concoctions that were described as "liturgically correct" and "approved." The women soloists were replaced by poorly trained choirs of boys. The women had once reminded the congregation of great things as they soared to the top of their vocal range; the boys often reminded everyone of pernicious anemia in its final stages. Where the *Motu Proprio* was treated as a wonderful invitation to discover the joys of God's creation, the landscape blossomed with musical beauty; where it was treated as yet another papal attack on the evils of Modernism, the *Motu Proprio* left scorched earth.

Into this "big picture" fits the somewhat smaller picture of music in the Catholic Church, U.S.A.

THE CLOSETS

In the older Catholic parishes of the United States, the closets and cupboards near the organ would delight any archeologist. These holding places, where *passé* music is dumped and forgotten, contain layer upon layer of musical "civilizations" that came and went with amazing rapidity. Sifting through this rubble tells us a lot about the past, of course, but it also reveals patterns that indicate why music in most American Catholic churches may remain "depressing" far into the future.

At the bottom layer in the closet we find the broken fragments of a composition known as "Mozart's Twelfth Mass." From the 1830s until perhaps the 1930s, many Catholics in the United States regarded this as one of the most prestigious of all liturgical compositions — a "must" for important occasions.[8] Protestants liked it too.[9]

A largely immigrant church edifying its members with the angelic music of the angelic master — this sounds rather impressive, until we discover three awkward facts about the Twelfth Mass: (1) Mozart definitely did not write this music; the composer is unknown.[10] (2) The music has some flashy moments, but most of it sounds hollow and superficial compared to Mozart's authentic works for the church. (3) Most nineteenth-century choirs probably sang this repetitive, long-winded composition in a very abbreviated form. I own a copy that once belonged to a Catholic parish in Philadelphia; it contains numerous pencil marks that indicate cuts; in a few places, pages have been glued together (!) to get the singers past the more drastic cuts. In this process of shortening, whole sections of the text disappeared. Technically, the lost words were no problem because the priest recited everything and, besides, the music really floated outside of the "real" Mass.

Not everyone, of course, was pleased with the florid gaiety of the Twelfth Mass or its chopped-up words. This explains why we find in our archeological dig, just above the pseudo-Mozart layer, music that gets away from bombastic grandiosity and has somewhat smaller proportions. You might come across a copy of chant published by the firm of Pustet in Regensburg, Bavaria — "traditional" and much shorter than pseudo-Mozart but not that appealing. You are more likely to come across the works of Albert Henry Rosewig (or RoSewig), widely considered to be the heroic genius of American Catholic church music. Rosewig's music made a strong impression on James Frederic Wood, archbishop of Philadelphia, who took the extraordinary step of writing a warm letter of recommendation for the *Concentus Sacri* (1877), Rosewig's anthology of music by himself and other composers; the archbishop's letter was displayed right after the title page. In 1901, Rosewig received a doctorate, *honoris causa*, from a Jesuit college in recognition of his musical greatness, or at least for having written concise, brief, religious music in a pleasant "contemporary" style.[11] (All of his music sounds like something from *Pirates of Penzance*.)

But why did the compositions of Albert Henry Rosewig, honorary Doctor of Music, end up in the closet, the archeological trash heap? Two reasons: (1) He wrote lousy music; all the ecclesiastical endorsements in the world cannot extend the lifetime of lousy music. (2) His compositions horrified the leaders of the St. Gregory Society.

In 1914 the Society of St. Gregory of America was formed in order to promote the purest, the most Roman interpretation of Pius X's *Motu Proprio* on music. We have to remember that when this organization started out, it saw itself as a small group of courageous missionaries surrounded by musical savages. The Gregorians were determined to do something about this situation. They would bring the difficult message of repentance and reform (i.e., chant and Renaissance polyphony) to the ignorant savages. The savages, however, decided to remain ignorant (invincibly so) and stuck out their tongues at the dour Gregorians.

Then, in 1922, the St. Gregory Society, to use a current expression, decided to play hardball, and it issued *The Black List: Disapproved Music.*[12] That did it. That sounded serious. The American church paid attention to an Index of Prohibited Music.

In this directory of "disapproved music," the Society blacklisted the much-performed operatic Masses by Giorza, Farmer, Mercadante, and others as "clearly antagonistic to the principles enunciated" by Pius X. It singled out four beloved songs as especially "disapproved": "Good Night, Sweet Jesus," "Mother Dear, O Pray for Me," "Mother Dearest," and "Mother, at Your Feet Is Kneeling." Without explanation, the St. Gregory Society also banned the well-known Ave Marias by Gounod and Schubert, the wedding marches of Wagner and Mendelssohn, and (for good measure) all the Masses composed by Haydn, Mozart, Beethoven, and Schubert. There among the condemned composers is the name of Albert Henry Rosewig: all his religious works, without exception — *Anathema.*

The writers of *The Black List* really had no reason to panic about the authentic music of Viennese masters like Mozart, because only a rare American Catholic parish went near this repertory *circa* 1922. The real problem was most of the other items on the *Black List:* imitation opera, imitation operetta, imitation pop songs with religious words (music that sounds like *She's Only a Bird in a Gilded Cage*) — a huge pile of musical sludge. The Catholic church in the United States must have been astoundingly naive about liturgical music; it clearly needed some direction, but, unfortunately, the St. Gregory Society's direction was down a blind alley. The dead end was something called the *White List.*

Every now and then the society would issue a document entitled the *White List* of "approved" music. On the pages of this publication (endorsed by various bishops and updated regularly) was information about fine editions of chant and masterpieces by Renaissance masters. But the neighborhood choir directors, baffled by such exalted musical purity, tended to avoid the ancient repertory and concentrate their attention on the easier "approved" music by contemporary composers: Pietro Yon, Nicola A. Montani, Father Carlo Rossini, and many others. Most of this repertory was all very respectable, but a lot of it suggested a bowl of overcooked noodles, unflavored. The cold noodles on the *White List* only made people lose their appetite for any church music.

*   *   *

There are surprises in some of these old closets: traditional religious "folk" songs (especially in Polish and German) that congregations used to sing from memory during the Low Mass in the ethnic parishes; a setting of the Mass by the sixteenth-century composer Palestrina, probably in a Midwestern parish with a German heritage; instrumental parts from the days when a little orchestra accompanied some choirs; choral music, in an inoffensively modern style, written by Flor Peeters, Jean Langlais, and others in the 1950s. And then, after the earthquake of the Second Vatican Council, the surprises come rapidly; the layers of musical "civilizations," which used to be rather deep, are now rather thin. The *Black* and *White* lists were tossed into the closet soon after the council ended, along with chant books. Above them, in the next layer, is a homemade hymnal, filled from beginning to end with illegally duplicated material. (We smile today; such innocence.) "Michael, Row the Boat Ashore" and "Kumbaya," thank heaven, are now at rest in the closets, but so are the useful compositions of Father Clarence Rivers, in "Negro spiritual" style. Those psalms by Gelineau and Deiss, with a few exceptions, never really caught on; most of this music was entombed in the closets a few years ago. There might be some stray copies of songs by Ray Repp (in his early phase) and other folk composers, who were once considered to be just a little higher than the angels. There will also be a copy of an excellent hymnal/songbook, which is now out of print. Et cetera, et cetera — and the strata, like the trends they represent, keep getting thinner.

*   *   *

Stop. Ponder.

Think about the closets and their forgotten contents. They are a monument to fads that came and went, to reforms and good intentions that quickly evaporated; they represent the grand and

the profound, as well as the lowest and cheapest kind of sentimentality that the human race is capable of producing. What is
interesting about the American Catholic closets is the patterns
they reveal: (1) The sense of a "quality" musical tradition is very
weak. (2) The craving for Romantic sentimentality is persistent,
whether it is the older kind of sweet musical syrup, like "Mother,
at Your Feet Is Kneeling," or the newer syrup, like "Eagle's Wings."
(3) American Catholics frequently look for heroes, Great Men
of Music, who will bestow upon them the great liturgical music for which they have been yearning; in other words, there is
a tendency to "buy the name" (usually male) rather than "buy
quality."

Every now and then, the American church "cleans house" —
throws out the old musical fads and brings in new ones. The
American Catholic of, let us say, 1850 probably did not hear much
music that was around in 1800. Certainly, the Catholic of 1950,
thanks to the *Black* and *White* lists, heard very little music that
was the rage in parishes *circa* 1900. The Catholic of 1970 had
to forget most of the music that was described as "immortal" in
1950. The pattern of "create and destroy" continues.

To be sure, libraries contain shelf after shelf of first-rate religious music that had its day and then became obsolete. Most
religious music, even great music, only has a certain shelf-life. But
the odd thing about the American closets is the meager amount
of music that remains outside of them. To see what I mean, let us
visit the Protestant church across the street.

The closets of Protestant churches are just as full as the Catholic ones. Every few decades, the denominational headquarters
will assemble learned music editors who will revise the denominational hymnal; outdated hymns will be sent to the closets; new
hymns will be added. Things are in a constant state of change, and
yet there is a continuity — almost a capitalist sense of accumulat-
ing, investing in, and living off of a musical wealth (i.e., hymns
that become enduring classics). One generation passes on at least
a little musical capital to the next.

If the closets in American Catholic churches reveal anything it
is the constant flitting from one musical fad to another. Musical
wealth usually does not survive long enough to get passed down to
the next generation.[13] Even the revival of Gregorian chant, in the
Solesmes manner, alas, was treated as if it were just another fad.

The closets are a symbol of a spendthrift mentality at work. Spend, spend, go bankrupt, then start all over again.

*   *   *

I know a gentleman who had worked for several happy years as a music director for a Protestant church. His full-time job as a teacher kept him busy, but he still managed to develop remarkable things at the church where he worked part-time: a thriving adult choir, a children's choir, and a bell choir. On Sunday, the walls of the church vibrated from the sound of the joyous singing, congregational and choral.

Unfortunately, his teaching job was eliminated and he had to take other employment miles away; this meant that he also had to quit the church job. The members of the church gave him a large and tearful send-off party.

Once he and his family had settled down in their new home, he presented himself at a local Catholic parish, the Church of St. Gargantua the Less, Patron of Suburbanites. He asked if the parish could use his talents. The pastor, impressed by the man's broad experience, hired him on the spot, after first giving him a lecture on the goals and ideals of Vatican II. *Build*, the musician was told, *build big*, because thousands come to this prosperous suburban church every weekend.

The very first week of his employment, my acquaintance received a tense telephone call from the pastor. What was that thing the congregation sang last weekend? It sounded like Gregorian chant. Throw it out, the pastor demanded. Nothing that remotely resembles chant is allowed.

Soon thereafter the pastor decided that there would be no choir at St. Gargantua's. Choirs are forbidden, except maybe to help out a little during Holy Week, but definitely not for Easter Sunday. My startled acquaintance explained to the pastor that a choir is the musical cheering section that boosts the assembly's singing; at his old church (a plain, no-frills place), the choir supported the congregation with harmonized parts and an occasional descant. The pastor smiled contemptuously; such things, he said, are "a concert in church."

My very startled acquaintance next referred the pastor to documents of Vatican II and other church pronouncements that emphasized the value of a choir. The pastor brushed this aside. Liturgical music belongs to the assembly, he said, not to an elite group of musicians — as the liturgists have been telling us for years.

Other orders from the pastor followed: All the music for the weekend liturgies had to be identical from Mass to Mass. The music for 7:30 P.M. on Saturday, when nobody sang, had to be absolutely identical to that used on Sunday at 11:15 A.M., when there was a little more participation.

After a while, my acquaintance realized what was going on: The pastor wanted to run the liturgical equivalent of McDonalds. (The hamburger you get at noon in McDonalds will be exactly the same as the hamburger you get at midnight.) But at this ecclesiastical McDonalds, the identical music was somehow supposed to act as a stimulant that would force the congregation to be enthusiastic. Therefore, the music had to sound Protestant, of the tent-revival variety — except for times when the congregation would be treated to the more drowsy "hits" by the St. Louis Jesuits, Michael Joncas, and the other "contemporary" favorites.

Congregational singing barely exists at St. Gargantua's; even those yummy "contemporary hits," which everybody is supposed to love, get only a faint response. The music, in spite of my acquaintance's expertise, is farcical, almost hateful. What really demoralizes him is the knowledge that every neighboring Catholic parish has virtually the same policy — to keep the music as routine and depressing as possible.

The routine and depressing music in so many Catholic parishes can be traced back to the pastor and the policies that he carefully maintains. In a few rare cases the pastor might be a mental case (such as the one at St. Gargantua's), but most of the time you will find agreeable, conscientious men who, with great care, always make sure that their parishioners will be regularly and mercilessly punished by the most routine and depressing music in Christianity. Why do they do this?

A snobbish answer would be to say that the typical Catholic pastor is just a *parvenu, nouveau riche* in the matter of church music, a real hick. A more sinister answer might be envy. In his autobiography, *Confessions of a Parish Priest* (1986), Father Andrew Greeley, the sociologist and novelist, comments on what he calls the poisonous sense of envy that can corrupt the clergy.[14] (Actually, envy corrupts every profession, not to mention the whole human race.) Maybe Catholic pastors are so envious that they cannot stand competition — from the choir that sounds more impressive than they do, from the music director (and his or her loyal "constituency"), from the traditions that carry more weight than the pastor's opinions.

My own impression is that various shades of depressing music in Catholic churches are not always the fault of a pastor who is naive or envious but one who is just overwhelmed. At St. Gargantua's, like so many parishes, there are more souls than there are students at a nearby university, and every one of them wants salvation, renewal, and uplift, quickly and cheaply. All of the overwhelmed pastor's instincts tell him to standardize, routinize, and reduce to the lowest common denominator, the l.c.d. (or, to be more precise, *his* version of the l.c.d.). Moreover, he insists that, if you give one congregation fancy music at 11:15 A.M. on Sunday morning, pretty soon the people on Saturday night will complain about being shortchanged.

My acquaintance at St. Gargantua's reports that he too has come down with a bad case of the l.c.d. disease. Just to get through the overwhelming ordeal of providing music for so many Masses every weekend, he conserves his energies by keeping the music perfunctory and at a minimum. The result is very depressing. Even he admits it.

One way or another, the pastor at St. Gargantua's will eventually be replaced. A new overwhelmed pastor will take over and immediately toss his predecessor's idea of the musical l.c.d. into the closet. The new man, with the most noble intentions, will "begin all over again" and maybe hire a new music director. But, like his predecessor, he will base his musical policies on the sure knowledge that the large, overwhelming mob in the pews is not very bright and is best served by using not-very-bright music. The pastor will be new and the closet will have a few more items in it, but the musical result will be the same: rather depressing.

The different "layers" in the closets very often indicate a new dynasty: the precise time, in the fossil record, when a new pastor has arrived — or the old one has suddenly changed his mind.

*   *   *

A few years ago I received a nasty letter in which I was denounced for putting too much emphasis on "traditional Catholic hymns," like "Praise to the Lord" and "The Church's One Foundation." I fell off my chair. In my return letter I informed my youngish correspondent that these hymns are Protestant in origin. I can remember the time when such music (even some Christmas carols) was about as welcome in the American Catholic liturgy as a Ku Klux Klan rally.

I should send another letter, a postscript, and confess that I was partially wrong. These and many other Protestant songs have now indeed *become* "traditional Catholic hymns." The fads are flying past Catholic congregations, but the Protestant repertory (with some German and Austrian Catholic contributions) remains constant. "Praise to the Lord" and "The Church's One Foundation" now supply the musical continuity in most Catholic parishes. They are the only musical "traditions" that some parishes have.

The same could be said about the "Top Ten," the indestructible "contemporary hits": "Be Not Afraid," "One Bread, One Body," "Let There Be Peace on Earth," "Eagle's Wings," "Yahweh, I Know You Are Near," "Here I Am, Lord," and so forth. They too will be around for a long, long time, even though most of these melodies go through such difficult contortions that the majority in a typical congregation will not even attempt to sing them. But these technical problems are not taken into account because this music has become *obligatory,* rather than beloved. This is now *required* music. To affirm their hipness, their with-it acceptance of the postconciliar church, parishes feel that they must drag out something from this "Top Ten" repertory, on an unending and punishing cycle, every week, every occasion, again and again. Actually, the "Top Ten" died a few years ago — from sluggish tempos, overexposure, and the indifference of bored congregations; these tunes deserve a decent burial in the closets. But that is not to be; the mummified corpses will remain on display for years and years to come, because "Be Not Afraid" and the other "Top Ten" hits are among the few musical "traditions" that many parishes are permitted to keep.

* * *

If two or more trained, conscientious church musicians get together and they work for the Catholic church, they invariably play a game called "I've Got a Better One." The conversation goes like this:

"Did you hear about the parish where a man dressed up like Santa Claus leads the procession for Midnight Mass."

"I've got a better one: a parish where Santa Claus came down the main aisle on roller skates."

"Did you hear about the priest's funeral? 'Danny Boy' was sung as the casket was taken out of the church. His name was Dan." (Now, what's wrong with "Peg O' My Heart" for Margaret's funeral?)

"I've got a better one: funerals where somebody sang 'Mama' (a Connie Francis hit) or 'I Did It My Way' (a Frank Sinatra hit) or 'In Your Easter Bonnet' ('with all the frills upon it'), for a man!"

"Don't forget the weddings. There was the case of 'Goin' to the Chapel,' a hit by the Dixie Cups, being used as a wedding processional. Sometimes the music that couples pick for their wedding could be used later as grounds for an annulment."

"Well, I've got a better one: the Mass on a Marian feast day when the congregation sang 'The Battle Hymn of the Republic,' that old war whoop, but everybody was told to ignore the words 'Glory, glory, hallelujah!' and, instead, sing, 'Ave, Ave Ma-riii-a.' "

That's a good one. That wins.

Do not play "I've Got a Better One" in the presence of some liturgical specialists. They do not even crack a smile. Usually, they become very grim and announce that Liturgical Renewal must begin all over again, from the bottom to the top. Get it right this time. (Oi veh! Guys, not again, please!)

Sensitive Catholics are truly upset by "I've Got a Better One." They do not like to be reminded that silly antics and pop songs in church have a way of pushing Christ and his message right out the door.

The overwhelmed pastor and music director respond defensively: "What can you do? This is what people want. Besides, we are not going to start an argument with a couple about their wedding songs or with a grieving family about funeral music." (A somewhat reasonable point, in the case of weddings and funerals.)

Musicians — the ones who play "I've Got a Better One" with especial bitterness — have their own insights about the game. They know (from the archeological record of the closets) that they are working for a church that destroys its own musical identity, the good and the bad, every few decades. They are angry about working for an institution that, at the parish level, often has no standards about music and has given its people no sense of direction. The musicians have no reason to hope that all of their best efforts will ever lead to a new stage of development, to growth; sooner or later, everything (even people) gets thrown into the closets; the good work comes to nothing. The musicians weep.

Now, before someone splatters the pages of this book with tears, let me interrupt the weeping with my own interpretation of "I've Got a Better One." The game is harmless, merely an innocent way of relieving the tension produced when you have to deal with people who are independent-minded, beautifully naive, unintimidated by traditions, uninformed, and absolutely confident that they have reached the summit of perfection, that is, a substantial portion of the American Catholic population (but not the majority).

Years ago, the better church musicians realized what they were up against: the many American Catholics (clergy and laity) who had become convinced that real religious music was something that caused a sweet, glowing sensation in *their* breasts, music that touched them with poignant memories about *their* mothers and perhaps *their* personal relationship with God or the Virgin Mary. Yes, official, orthodox, traditional music for ritual existed, but the evidence in the closets suggests that it was often outnumbered, ten to one, by sweet, gooey "personal" music. We should never forget that the dear old song "Mother, at Your Feet Is Kneeling" personally spoke to people *here and now*, in their daily lives, *today*; its quivering sentimentality was *relevant*; its style was once *contemporary*. But, to cite one example, the Gregorian chant Sequence for the Easter Sunday Mass (between the Epistle and Gospel) spoke to people about other, "higher" things that had transformed their destiny. That kind of a message (Latin or the vernacular) was a rude, *irrelevant* interruption if, in your opinion, liturgical music is essentially a dialogue with yourself.

Not many Catholics have grasped the implications of the concept that the music in church is actually part of a serious act. Great numbers of Catholics in the United States, after all the pronouncements to the contrary, still think of liturgical music as a song that is really outside of the ceremony. Moreover, the external importance of this song is largely electrical; music in church is like jumper cables for a car — you clip them on to the congregation and, every now and then, turn on the juice. The songs jolt the throat muscles into an involuntary spasm that is called "participation." In my conversation with some Catholic laity I get the impression that church music is supposed to be a personal, "relevant" experience, and for them "relevant" means whatever makes them feel good at that moment in their lives. Put all of these attitudes together and you have an environment that will always provide abundant material for a long and bitter game of "I've Got a Better One."

*　*　*

The brash, bumptious television evangelist struts from one side of the stage to the other, microphone in one hand and Bible in the other. This man takes orders from nobody. He has all the answers — but he will fall on his knees in terror when confronted with a powerful totem: the denominational hymnal. He must submit to this symbol of tradition; he, meek pussycat, must accept the accumulated musical wisdom of the ages, "answers" devised by other people. (I exaggerate slightly.)

Modern American Catholics have no such totem. The musical fads from the past are all stacked up in dusty piles and decaying in the closets. Those old traditions, all failures, intimidate nobody. The Catholic priest, the pastoral musician, and the whole Catholic population struts.

There is something to be said for a benign anti-strutting factor called "intimidation" — the feeling that you are just part of a huge family, a continuum, and not the center of the universe. This used to be called humility.

"I've Got a Better One" would disappear, so would "depressing" music and a long list of liturgical stupidities, if more Catholics were to become aware of and humbled by something that is not in many closets: their musical heritage, their crown jewels.

THE CROWN JEWELS

Want to start a fistfight? Walk into any American Catholic seminary or conference of professional liturgists and drop this question: Should Mozart's *Coronation Mass,* with orchestra, be heard, on rare occasions, at liturgies in some Catholic churches and cathedrals? After all, the Second Vatican Council decreed, "The treasure of sacred music is to be preserved and fostered with very great care" (Constitution on the Sacred Liturgy, Article 114).

Brace yourself for a furious reaction: "Blockhead! Latin art-music handed over to elite musicians! Have you forgotten everything that Vatican II decreed? Have you no shame? Modern people won't buy that sort of escapism today. Besides, crown jewels — Gregorian chant, Mozart Masses, and all the rest — belong in museums, and Christ established a church, not a museum."

Pace, I respond. Relax. This is just a theoretical question for debate. We can learn a great deal by debating theoretical questions.

*   *   *

Nobody knows exactly when or where it began, but sometime in the Middle Ages, somebody who was in charge of choosing the chants for Mass must have decided that a particular Kyrie seemed to go with a particular Gloria. In time, the chants for the choral parts of the Ordinary of the Mass (texts that often stayed the same from one liturgy to another) were being grouped into sets: a Kyrie, a Gloria, a Sanctus, and an Agnus Dei, which all seemed to be related. In the fourteenth century, composers of polyphony (music that could be described as "singing in harmony") began to write music for these same sections of the Mass as a unified whole, with a Credo added. Thus began one of the towering art forms of Western civilization: the choral setting of the Mass, a musical suite with five related sections. Shelf after shelf in the library contains copies of these works. Some are modest, well-behaved enhancements of the Mass text, and yet brimming with ingenuity. A few are colossal summations of an era (e.g., the *B-Minor Mass* composed by the Lutheran J. S. Bach for his Catholic monarch); their elephantine size makes them impractical for liturgical use.

The history of the choral Mass as a unified suite — maybe a thousand years old, if you include chant — supposedly came to an end with the Second Vatican Council. The council itself said nothing specific about the matter in its documents, but subsequent commentaries by the Vatican itself and liturgical specialists imply that choirs may no longer "deprive" congregations of their right to participate by singing "concert" music like Mozart's *Coronation Mass*. The Catholic bishops of the United States seem to have settled this issue (nailed the coffin shut, as it were) in their authoritative statement on church music: *Liturgical Music Today* (1982), a pamphlet issued by their Committee on the Liturgy. The modern liturgical practice of the church, it says in this document, "no longer envisions the performance" of Mass-suites sung by a choir. Modern people do not need that sort of thing. That settles that.

Or does it? Think about the following:

• On June 29, 1985, the Feast of Saints Peter and Paul, Pope John Paul II celebrated a solemn pontifical Mass in St. Peter's Basilica, Rome. The principal music for this liturgy was Mozart's *Coronation Mass*. Herbert von Karajan conducted the Vienna Philharmonic and chorus. The congregation, which came from many nations and spoke many languages, resoundingly sang the responses, including the Our Father, in Latin.

• The Roman Catholic cathedral in a large American city is deservedly famous for its excellent liturgical music. About twice a year, the choir sings, at a liturgy, all or part of a brief choral Mass by a Renaissance composer or Haydn or Mozart. The cardinal-archbishop (who is often put in the "liberal/moderate camp") does not object; the laity who attend have no problem at all with this music, if we can judge from the smiles on their faces. Some liturgical specialists in this archdiocese, however, can barely conceal their outrage. They plot revenge.

• I was invited to hear the youth choir of a church sing portions of Mozart's so-called *Sparrow Mass*, accompanied by a chamber orchestra. The music blended in perfectly during the service in this small Presbyterian church.

• On June 4, 1991, during a communion service at the 203rd General Assembly of the Presbyterian Church (U.S.A.), held in the city of Baltimore, a choir, accompanied by orchestra, sang the Requiem Aeternam and Kyrie from Mozart's Requiem during the Offering; later, during the Distribution of the Elements, Mozart's Ave Verum and Laudate Dominum were sung. (The year 1991 was the two hundredth anniversary of Mozart's death.)

• On Christmas day, the choir at a church I know sang three sections of a Mass by Mozart. This was truly sung prayer, and it sounded just right for this small Episcopalian church, which is so militantly Low Church it is almost Baptist.

Do not tell the above anecdotes to the red-hot promoters of Catholic-congregational-participation-at-all-costs. They simply cannot process the information; nor can they comprehend the reality that congregational singing can be quite spectacular in places where the choir (one section of the assembly) is occasionally delegated to "take over" for a moment. The fact is, congregational music and choral music nourish one another. Mozart's *Coronation Mass* or any good choral setting of the Ordinary of the Mass makes perfectly good sense, but only under the following conditions:

• *The congregation consists of consenting adults (and children).* Everyone realizes that time will move a little more slowly; those who do not wish to come have been warned and can go to another Mass.

• *If various sung parts of the liturgy "rightfully belong to the congregation," that same congregation has the right to let one section of the assembly do some of the singing. After all, if you own a car, you have the right to let someone else drive it.* This has to be the understanding, the "social contract," behind the use of the choral Mass-suite.

• *The music helps to build community; it creates the impression of a great coming together.* The whole community senses that it is part of the project (the rehearsals, the planning, the fund drive to pay for the parish's music, the involvement of the children). When the church or cathedral is a place where many ethnic groups come together, this music has a great practical value.

• *The music helps to show the flag.* Sometimes the Catholic church needs to demonstrate to a hostile world that it is alive, well, and worthy of respect. The musical crown jewels command respect. For example, near Harvard and Stanford universities there is a Catholic church where the traditions of Catholic choral music flourish. The non-Catholic students and faculty at prestigious universities snicker at the parish folk musician crooning "Be Not Afraid" but they will become quite respectful (grudgingly) when confronted by a little chant or portions of a Renaissance Mass sung well at a liturgy.

• *The music fits the resources.* The talent, parish commitment, finances, acoustics, and innumerable other resources have to be in place — and that is unusual.[15] If this constellation of resources is not right, stay away — *far away* — from the ambitious choral repertory.

• *This "universal" music is a way of reaching out to people, especially those who do not belong to tightly knit communities.* "Well, I really had not gone to church in years, but I thought I would just come back to hear the choir sing, and then one thing led to another." The music welcomes the stranger.

• *The music must be reasonable for the liturgy.* This is the most important condition. The music has to fit. Blockbuster extravaganzas, like Vivaldi's popular *Gloria,* would throw everything off balance. Long settings of the Sanctus and Agnus Dei leave the priest stranded behind the altar and staring at the congregation (unless the priest is at a "sarcophagus/shelf" altar).

*   *   *

There are two churches in England where one can hear the great Roman Catholic Mass-suites and other masterpieces sung with special sensitivity: King's College Chapel in Cambridge and Christ Church Cathedral in Oxford, both Anglican establishments. I do not know what is done today, but in 1988 Christ Church provided worshipers with a booklet entitled *Guide to the Sung Eucharist,* which was based on a similar guide used at King's College Chapel. The "Introductory Note" in this booklet is worth quoting here:

> The settings for the *Kyrie, Gloria, Sanctus, Benedictus,* and *Agnus Dei* are longer and more complex than those composed for congregational use and are sung by the choir, not the congregation. This may well seem frustrating to those who are accustomed to taking a more vocal part in the service and its pace may seem to be slow. But this way of celebrating the Eucharist has its own advantages. Many of us do not have much opportunity to stop talking and being talked at, to silence the chattering of our own minds and be still. By our own quietness in this service we may be freed from the necessity to select words and shape phrases. We may then be free to hear the voice of our own deepest needs; free to remember those for whom we wish to pray.... Christians have been led through this service to a rich and diverse pattern of response. This, in view of the wide range of human personality, is both natural and right. The personal space offered by the choral settings of the prayers of the Eucharist makes room for everyone to turn towards God in his or her own way.

"Personal space"! Those words have probably caused some readers — liturgically correct and advanced Catholics — to shriek in horror. The very idea! But let us all remain calm and examine this proposition.

Before the 1960s, the Roman Catholic church was very reluctant to intrude into the "personal space," the individualism, of the worshiper. Each member of the congregation was like an independent farmer cultivating his or her own plot of land; at the sung Mass, the Mass-suite and other music helped to symbolize the communal participation of the independent farmers. This way of doing things was, without any doubt, taken to extremes, and in the 1960s it was corrected . . . by going to another extreme: the forced collectivization of the independent farmers and the abolition of personal space. The same kind of mind that thought up the idea of the collective farm also gave the world the intrusively communal (and "depressing") parish liturgy.

* * *

A few years ago, I attended a workshop given by the director of music at a Catholic cathedral. He described a handsome church surrounded mostly by empty lots and burned-out buildings. The cathedral parish was small and poor, yet the choir was in great shape. Loyal volunteers showed up every Sunday morning at 7:00 A.M. for rehearsal; later, they sang at Mass. What got the volunteers out of bed early on Sunday, the music director told us, was the *pleasure* of singing chant, Renaissance motets, lively arrangements of hymns, and other good music, including a couple of choral anthems in jazz style. The multiethnic congregation caught the spirit of this *pleasure* and sang very well. (Musical pleasure is infectious.)

At the conclusion of this talk there was a discussion period and members of the audience (mostly musicians) described how they too had enlarged the size of their choirs and increased the strength of congregational singing by using some "crown jewel" choral music, but in very small proportions.

All during this lecture and the friendly discussion afterward, two people sitting behind me — my instincts told me they were diocesan officials somewhere, but not priests — boiled with anger. "A concert in church!" they muttered. "This is a disgrace, a complete distortion of what Vatican II wanted!" (I thought that one of them was going to slap the speaker in half.) Whispering loudly, they ridiculed the speaker's tape recordings of music used in the cathedral; they ridiculed the comments from the audience. Finally, the more imposing of the two discontented ones behind me stood up and blasted away: "Don't you think that people like you, who provide music for the church, should really be motivated by a sense of *mission*, not by this artistic *pleasure.*" The speaker, stunned by the bitterness of the comment, was saved when somebody told him that time had run out and everyone had to go to the next workshop.

This little episode illustrates what is going on. The great majority of the Catholic laity feel honored and important when they are asked to sing the easier examples of chant, in the original or the vernacular. They know that participation means every fiber of your being, not just the motion of the vocal cords; they know that sometimes the "individualist" act of listening is a profound form of participation. But these tolerant people are bossed around by authoritarian dictators who, in so many words, fiercely assert: We can't hand over to choirs the music that *rightfully belongs to the assembly*; we can't lull the faithful into nice complacency with artistic beauty.

Very stern rhetoric, very dramatic — and you can't argue with it. You can, however, try to visualize the consequences of such thinking. To do that, just imagine a large pile of books that contain folk songs and children's songs: "Twinkle, Twinkle, Little Star," "On Top of Old Smokey," "Home on the Range," "She'll Be Coming 'round the Mountain," and so forth. Add "The Star-Spangled Banner" to the pile and some old pop songs, like "As Time Goes By" and "Stormy Weather." Now, with scissors, diligently cut up all of this music into little squares. Throw all the cut-up squares into a barrel and mix thoroughly. At a Catholic liturgy, place the barrel next to the organist, who reaches into it at various points of the ceremony, pulls out a square at random, plays the music on it, and then throws the piece of paper away.

This, alas, is what "rightfully belongs to the assembly" in countless Catholic parishes: disconnected scraps of music that seem to come out of nowhere and then disappear into that same nowhere. No wonder the result can be "depressing."

*   *   *

Musical "crown jewels" rightfully belong to any Catholic congregation, if they are used reasonably, judiciously, and with the greatest sensitivity to the liturgical action. They belong not because of their artistic merit or their historical importance but because they help to keep everything honest. When the choir, in the name of the community, has worked very hard to learn the Hallelujah Chorus or a Gregorian entrance song (an Introit), chances are that the priest will prepare his homily with great diligence and the congregation might pay a little more attention. Moreover, "crown jewel" music seems to pull together and ratify the goodness in any good congregational music (old or new) used in proximity to it.

"Crown jewel" music is like having the bishop at Mass. It puts everybody in the best-behavior mode.

*   *   *

"Should Mozart's *Coronation Mass*, with orchestra, be heard occasionally at liturgies in Catholic churches and cathedrals?" And what about all the other great choral music, in Latin? The most prudent answer would go something like this:

Slow down. Be realistic. Know your limits. The simpler "crown jewels" — yes, of course. The bigger projects — here and there, under *optimum* conditions. And make sure it looks like another aspect of the congregation's prayer. (The choir is part of the assembly, too.) If the Roman Catholic church can allow liturgical dancers in leotards to dash madly about the sanctuary and writhe all over the furnishings, while the congregation participates by watching, it can surely find a place for a little Gregorian chant and at least portions of a Mass-suite, like Mozart's *Coronation Mass*. But remember, a lot of more important things come first.

AGING HIPPIES

I met a musician who had been on the staff of the seminary of a huge archdiocese. While he was working there, this layman taught his students how to sing a few Gregorian chants, standard hymns, and a whole range of modern music for the church. He told me that some seminarians were intrigued by the chanted Mass, which they had never heard before, and wanted to know more about it, but then new bosses took over, *circa* 1990, and put a stop to that nonsense. The seminarians were to be taught "contemporary" songs almost exclusively; guitars and synthesizers were preferable to the organ, the music director was told. These seminarians had to be prepared for the future, not the past.

The music director soon quit and went off to a less restrictive job working for a Protestant church. He was not especially bitter about his bad experiences at the seminary — the open contempt for his "outdated" craft; the constant shifts in music fads and liturgical theories; the supervisors who had absolutely no idea of what they wanted. But the thing that really rankled him, he said, was having to deal with aging hippies on the seminary staff. I knew what he meant.

There are aging hippies all over the Catholic church — priests, nuns, musicians, lay people who were in their prime back in the days when the "folk Mass" was so deliciously naughty and they had trim waistlines; they never quite managed to mature, to grow up, to get hit with the realization that they are not the sun around which everything orbits. They seem to be forever stuck in adolescence, or maybe in the 1960s and '70s.

Some of the aging hippies love so-called "contemporary" music by the St. Louis Jesuits, Michael Joncas, and all the rest, because the words and the butterflies-in-the-breeze style have a way of giving the impression that the individual worshiper really is the center of all creation. Other aging hippies have gone beyond all this, they say, to newer and much more advanced forms of "contemporary" music (which sounds just like the old, original brand to me). Whatever the case, they agree on one thing: Chant (Latin or English), solid choral music, and "classic" music for congregation must go, because that stuff puts God front and center. They find this highly annoying.

But what motivates these aging-hippie Catholics? What makes them tick? I have heard several explanations: self-loathing, a kitsch mentality, resentment against anything that seems "above" them (anything that "outclasses" them), a violent reaction to their overly disciplined and overly scrupulous youth, the need to be the center of attention, and so forth. I do not know the answer, but this much I have seen again and again: They yearn for that perfect utopia, that Future Kingdom, just beyond the horizon — they can almost see it gleaming in the distance — and this land of perfection is the parish, the faith community, which is one big support group for the chosen few.

Love, reassurance, mutual encouragement, warmth, hospitality, self-discovery — all of this can happen in group therapy (Alcoholics Anonymous, a bereavement group, a feminist support group, a male support group); all of it can be healthy and strengthening. Architects, as we have seen, are trying to make Catholic chapels and churches intimate places where a super-sized support group can heal itself in its own warmth. The aging hippies campaign ceaselessly for the same thing, for the environment that suggests a special, intimate group at work or early Christians in the catacombs. The trouble is, "intimacy" (for the intimate ones) and "corporate worship" (for everybody) repel one another.

The aging hippies would not cause so much damage if they just went off by themselves and formed separate support groups, "intentional communities," that worshiped separately, in quasi-secret cells. This secession of the chosen few, who will worship only among their own kind, is really what some liturgists are working to achieve (although they are the last to realize this). But the flower children do not want to go off peacefully; their first obsessive goal is to get rid of any style of corporate worship that includes everyone who walks into the building. They are fanatically determined to transform every parish congregation into a small, touching, and feeling support group. The aging hippies will use the small, touching, and feeling sounds of "contemporary" music to accomplish this transformation.

*   *   *

The Master Guru arrives and takes over the job as director of liturgical music at a church for Catholic students near the campus of a big nonsectarian university. He (these types are usually men) announces immediately that the religious songs favored by his predecessor are nothing but romantic marshmallow candies. The predecessor was a nice guy, but he knew nothing about true liturgical music — the real stuff that grabs you by the shirt collar and shakes you into submission with its social message, with its honest language about today. There are going to be big changes now, the Master Guru declares to his docile and frightened disciples. None of this mumbo-jumbo elitist music for the Vatican curia and trained musicians. From now on, the music in this faith community will proclaim social relevance, not artistic values.

He hands out multiple copies of songs that he has composed. *This* will be the relevant music for the community from now on. He does allow some music by other composers, but week after week the community is never allowed to forget the deathless songs of the Master Guru. He regularly denounces the church music of the past (i.e., the Pre-Master-Guru era of error) and is not always charitable about his contemporaries. To put it another way, he takes every opportunity to slam the competition.

The Master Guru is masterfully ingenious. That must be said in his favor. Somehow he has managed to pass off his determination to eradicate all competition as the Gospel in action. Somehow he has cleverly combined the worst features of capitalist monopoly with the best of Christianity. (The federal government really should investigate to see if he is violating antitrust laws.)

I wish I could say that this story is a single aberration, but it is really a pattern that has occurred in a few places I have heard about. The frightening thing here is not so much the Master Guru, but his disciples, the Little Gurus who go out into the world and depress the Catholic faithful with their own version of musical monopoly. Their dictatorial tendencies, which are quite alarming, come out in the music — which usually features a soloist.

*   *   *

The setting: a poor parish in Massachusetts, but an impressive old church building with an impressive old pipe organ. A new pastor asks a new music director to do great things in the church and the parish school; at the same time, *he makes it clear that the parishioners have to raise the money to pay for the music.* Within a few months, the music program in the parochial school has all the children singing. The choir of men and boys is an overnight success; they sing lots of music with the congregation but also Gregorian chant and an occasional choral masterpiece at a genuine sung Mass nearly every week. Parishioners who used to be lethargic about the parish suddenly take an interest; they raise money to repair the organ and to pay the music director; they feel "empowered" — as if they are really a part of things. The school is thriving; it almost hums with music-making every day. The "bad kids" in the choir and school become reasonable. The slow learners begin to learn faster. The boys express an interest in entering the priesthood. In a town with so much despair and poverty, the parish becomes a beacon of hope.

The pastor is reassigned. A new one walks in. New policy: "Modern people today want modern music." The sung Mass is discontinued. The music director is told to stop using that old stuff and, instead, concentrate on music that people really want, like "Be Not Afraid." He quits. Parents pull their children out of the parochial school; enrollment plunges; within a few months the pastor announces that he has to close the school. The parishioners just give up. Hopelessness returns.

The aging hippies strike again.

*   *   *

"Mr. Day, you don't know me, but I would like to talk with you for a few minutes about a problem I have."

I might receive a telephone call that begins this way, or maybe at a conference a stranger will come up to me and begin with those same words. I listen.

"Mr. Day, you see I am a music director in a Catholic church. We were doing splendidly for a long time. The congregation sings energetically, the choir is thriving. We also have a children's choir and a bell choir. I attribute our success to the standard song book, which we use for the core of our parish repertory" (which means a publication like *Worship III, Hymns, Psalms, and Spiritual Canticles, The Collegeville Hymnal,* or *American Catholic Hymnbook).*

I interrupt: "And a new pastor has taken control or, even worse, a rabidly determined member of the parish council has asserted his/her authority; you are being pressured to shift the emphasis of the parish repertory to 'contemporary' slush. This is creating havoc because most of the 'hit' music is junk; the congregation really doesn't sing it at all well. In the past, you have always used some 'contemporary' music on a regular basis, but this is not enough for the aging hippies. They want total control. You know perfectly well that the flower-children will not rest until you quit and take your music with you."

"How did you know all that?"

How do I know? I have become a kind of national repository — an oral history memory bank — for stories like the above. Actually, the plural "stories" is not quite correct. What I have heard is really the same story, with variations, over and over again.

*   *   *

Mr. Timorous, a nervous twig of a man, happens to be a great human being and an excellent organist for a Catholic parish. Early on Sunday morning he plays for a Mass — and then, as fast as he can, he clears out to make room for the folk group, which performs at the next liturgy. If Mr. Timorous does not get out fast enough, he runs into the folk group's presiding guru, an aging hippie with laser eyes and a tense jaw. Encounters between the two men are not pleasant.

"Still playing these antiques?" asks the guru as he flips through the pages of the organist's music. He smiles; he shakes his head, as if to say, "When will you people ever learn."

Mr. Timorous almost fainted when the aging hippie said to him one morning (quoting Nikita S. Khrushchev's comment on the United States), "Someday, we will bury you."

STICKER SHOCK

It is time to buy a new car. The consumer, who has put off this purchase for as long as possible, visits a car dealer, takes a look at the price stickers on a few cars, and is stunned that the costs are not what they were just a few years ago. Sticker shock.

A form of musical sticker shock has hit the Catholic church. It is rather severe. Examples:

• In the 1970s I received a telephone call from a pastor. His parish needed a new organist, he said. Could I suggest some names?

Before I could say much, the pastor went into a long discourse on the importance of congregational music in the church after Vatican II. He was aiming high, he emphasized. He wanted strong, vibrant music in his parish.

I was impressed. This man had big plans. I knew that he did not need a cathedral-type conservatory-educated professional, and so I gave him the names of a few people in the area with the right qualifications. I also told him that he should contact the diocesan office for liturgy and even the American Guild of Organists. For a salary — and this was a fairly demanding job — I recommended something less than the cost of the smallest, cheapest subcompact car, used.

He started to laugh.

"Wait a minute," he interrupted, "You've got me all wrong. We just want some kid."

"Some kid" raked up the leaves around the church. "Some kid" answered the telephone in the rectory. "Some kid" would play the organ in the church — once on Saturday night and four times on

Sunday, plus Holy Days, plus this, plus that. "Some kid," cheap labor, would be worked like a mule.

• An "ethnic" parish — a booming place with eight (yes, 8) liturgies each weekend — was confronted by the problem of a decaying old church that needed serious repairs. With their usual cheerful generosity, the parishioners went to work and raised a fortune to fix up the beloved building and to give it a completely new "postconciliar look" inside. The pastor reminded everyone that music was also important in the parish — and so another fortune was raised from these middle-class parishioners to restore the building's majestic pipe organ.

Shortly before all the work on the church was completed, the parish's organist retired. Just as well, the pastor concluded, because he wanted some big changes. He put out a few feelers, made a few inquiries, and placed a couple of ads. Very quickly and very clearly the "music community" gave him a polite response, which could be summed up in two words: "Drop dead."

The trouble was, the pastor wanted somebody who would provide thrilling postconciliar music for his postconciliar church, seven (maybe eight) times on a weekend; he wanted music for Confirmations and Feast Days and Penance services; he wanted at least two choirs; he wanted the moon and the stars — and for all this, he was willing to pay what amounted to minimum wage. The organist, he explained, could make good money by playing for weddings and funerals, but this meant that the musician had to be available seven days a week and could not possibly hold down another job.

When somebody explained to the pastor that what he really had in mind was perhaps three music employees who were paid reasonably, he was appalled. This would mean that there would be more musicians than clergy on the parish staff and the budget for music would be larger than the salaries for the priests.

• A young woman, a very good organist, graduated from a music conservatory in New England and soon got a job playing organ and conducting a choir in an "Italian parish." Now, it is (or was) the custom for parishioners in such places to have memorial Masses, with music, for their departed relatives. At one point, this poor woman had to play for at least a dozen memorial Masses during weekdays, in addition to a half-dozen Masses on the weekends; choir rehearsals and planning sessions also took up hours

every week. She had no time to practice. She had no time even
to think. The constant playing, in addition to the back-and-forth
commuting between home and church, left her totally drained.
And for all this she was paid, per hour, less than what a "pump
technician" earns at a gas station. The church job, with everything figured in, amounted to exhausting full-time work, and she
could not even pay the rent.

When she explained the situation to the pastor, the man could
not follow her reasoning. She was, after all, just an hourly employee, a typist of music. (Put a piece of music in front of her, and
the fingers go.)

She quit.

*   *   *

Before the Second Vatican Council, the entire music budget
in many American Catholic parishes was probably much lower
than the budget for brass polish. One of the sisters in the convent
may have done an outstanding job directing the choir of children
from the school; maybe a kindly woman who had some spare time
donated her services as an organist for the occasional High Mass
and, as a form of payment, got the exclusive right to provide the
music for weddings and funerals.

After Vatican II came the shock that the "music thing" — no
longer an occasional nicety but now a regular feature of worship —
required the planning, expertise, commitment, and time of at
least one person, a music director who cared for the *ministry* of
music. This was not like volunteering to be an usher when you
felt like it; this was a real job. But wait! There was a hitch. The
Roman Catholic priest, according to diocesan regulations, might
receive a token stipend of a few dollars for saying a Mass. The
newfangled music director who played the organ for that same liturgy might, in contrast, be paid according to the pay-scale at the
nearby Protestant church and receive several times the priest's
token stipend. The arrival of this new and *expensive* "pastoral
musician" has caused uneasiness.

In January 1992, a diocesan newspaper printed a letter from
an uneasy Catholic pastor. His words:

> Far and away church musicians are the highest paid minis-
> ters in the church employ. Minute for minute and hour for
> hour, church musicians are receiving anywhere from a dollar

a minute to four dollars a minute depending on whether they are playing and singing at a wedding, funeral or weekend liturgy. No other employee at any level of Church administration even comes close to such an hourly rate.[16]

He maintains that he cannot, in justice, pay these outrageous wages to musicians when parochial teachers and even diocesan officials earn much less per hour.

The letter did not go unchallenged. Musicians, including the priest in charge of the diocesan liturgy committee, wrote to the newspaper and gave the other side of the story: (1) On average, the pay for musicians in Catholic parishes is significantly (maybe disgracefully) lower than the pay in Protestant churches and Jewish synagogues, and yet the amount of work required is usually much greater. (2) One hour of playing might involve several hours of preparation, planning, and practice. (3) Many parishes demand a back-breaking amount of work from their music director, and then pay for it in pennies; the musician is supposed to pick up the "real" money at weddings and funerals. In effect, the bride and the groom and the family of the deceased are paying a surcharge, which is the musician's salary. (4) No matter what a church musician earns, it is probably less than the cost of having a mechanic come over to the rectory and work on the broken dishwasher for a couple of hours.

Providing just one hour of music for a church is strenuous and sweaty work, a nerve-fraying public "test," which exposes every little mistake. Whether the parish music director is a brilliant organ virtuoso or someone who just has modest competence reading music, this is also "professional" work — a job that you bring home with you, work that does not end when the factory whistle blows.

*   *   *

The following paragraphs tell the story of two churches that I have known since pre–Vatican II days. Their socioeconomic profiles and sizes are almost identical; both have parochial schools. As I watched the liturgical music in them develop over the years, I realized that these two churches were like a controlled scientific experiment on what happens when parishes face up to or avoid the sticker shock of hiring someone to run the music ministry. These two churches also help to explain why music in one Catholic parish sounds so good, so hopeful, and why, in a comparable parish next door, it is so depressing.

The Church of St. Deiniol, a great suburban establishment with thousands of souls, had a long history of dreary church music. The reforms of Vatican II only brought out, in very vivid colors, a bad situation that had been allowed to deteriorate for years. Then, in the 1980s, the pastor decided that the time had come to put the music on track. He hired a man who is a very cooperative, competent musician, but not a virtuoso organist; he offered him a modest yet reasonable part-time salary for a reasonable amount of work.

Within a year, the music at St. Deiniol's was booming. The congregation sang. The choir became so big that it could not fit into the loft; a second choir needed to be formed. Behind the success was a pastor and, under him, a musician — who maintained musical quality and continuity. (A weekend Mass without any music also contributed to the general parish happiness.) There are no other big secrets here, except that the congregation's music mostly consists of plain, straightforward music from one of the best hymnals, in addition to a few "contemporary" songs. The choir does sing a challenging anthem on occasion, but the music director wisely decided that it would be unrealistic to struggle with the more elaborate "crown jewels" of music.

The music pulled the community together; it created a "positive atmosphere"; it gave prayer a depth that both surprised and pleased people of all ages. And this brings us to a phenomenon familiar to every Protestant minister but still unknown in most Catholic parishes: that is, when the music seems to respect people's intelligence, they give more to their church. Every nickel spent wisely on good church music brings back a dime in extra revenue.

A short drive from St. Deiniol's is the Church of St. Bertram, another great suburban establishment with thousands of souls. In the days before Vatican II and in the matter of liturgical music, St. Bertram's was, to use a popular expression, the pits. Oh, what an abomination and desolation! The mooing of cows had a more appealing sound, and faster speed, than the singing that emerged from that choir of six dedicated volunteers. (And they called it "traditional music"!)

The pastor was indifferent. Any music was great, in his opinion, as long as he did not have to pay for it. He got what he paid for: nothing.

Well, to be precise, he usually got about six volunteers in the choir — a magnet for frustrated crooners, vaudevillians, opera stars, screamers, musical psychopaths. It was indescribable. Now, good reader, these were not volunteers who get together and produce a "basic" sound that is functional, although not very polished. (That would have been perfectly acceptable.) No, this was a choir of *soloists*, each one showing off to the audience in the pews below.

St. Bertram's was fairly typical of the music that existed in many American Catholic parishes before Vatican II. The emphasis was on the solo voice, and, if there were six singers in the choir, they were all soloists vying for attention. There was no paid minister of music to keep them in line.

I have revisited the postconciliar St. Bertram's. Everything has changed but everything has remained the same. The soloists are still there, entrenched. At one Mass, a man with a trained voice sings; the microphone is practically against his molars. He is up front and it is his show; the congregation, his audience, watches in silence. At another Mass, the folk group sings, but this is really a solo performance by another man, with some light backup by the group; again, the congregation listens in silence. Behind the failure here — the soloists out of control, the congregation a captive audience — is sticker shock. The clergy in this parish simply could not face the prospect of paying a competent music minister, somebody who would direct and guide the musical energies that are there (and keep the soloists on a leash).

To justify this fear of having another type of professional on the premises, a new philosophy of church music has evolved and it goes something like this: The People of God are the church. Therefore (?), any volunteer who wants to take over the music at a particular Mass is the "grassroots," the authentic representative of the People of God. The church does not need trained musicians, these hirelings who want money. The church needs enthusiastic volunteers, who cost nothing.

The philosophy works. Sure enough, the volunteers do show up — from out of the woodwork, from underneath rocks. In most cases, they are vocal soloists who need an audience for their personal therapy. Sometimes a soloist will have an excellent,

well-trained voice, which is flaunted before the congregation for
something less than an hour. But most of the time, the soloists
are what could be called militant amateurs, a very dangerous
breed.

I am not referring to the gifted amateurs who, with a lot of dedication and effort, do a great job in organizing the music of a parish.
I mean the militant amateurs who take pride in being untouched
by knowledge. Somewhere (maybe in their college or university
folk group) these characters were indoctrinated by aging hippies
who told them, *ex cathedra*, that genuine religious music can
only come from the "grassroots," from the untutored and innocent children of nature, from amateurs who are musical illiterates.
From the way they talk, you would think that "skilled," "professional," and "educated" musicians are the servants of Beelzebub
himself.

*   *   *

Militant amateurs and most of the cantors in Catholic
churches have a lot in common with bodybuilders. Both the liturgical soloist and the bodybuilder get a thrill, a glow of reassurance,
when they pose in front of a crowd and show off the beauty they
have developed. Both use the approval of an audience as a form of
self-medication. The bodybuilder violently squeezes and strains
his/her shoulders, in order to bring out the intricate network of
veins and tissue in particularly well-developed deltoids; the audience roars with approval. The vocal soloist at the Catholic Mass
is supposed to be leading the congregation in a hymn but he/she
lingers for an extra moment (with shimmering vibrato) to show
off a well-formed note or slows up to bring out the sensitive interpretation of an important phrase; the audience, out of respect,
stops singing.

Those poor people at St. Bertram's parish. For decades now,
they have been forced to endure a musical bodybuilding contest
every week; they have been at the mercy of any volunteer soloist who poses in front of them. The "folk music" is a vehicle for
featured solo performers who constantly change the repertory, in
order to keep the congregation bewildered and silent; the "standard music" is a vehicle for failed opera stars and crooners. Choral
music is absolutely unknown in this parish, probably because that
type of singing, done correctly, does not glorify soloists.

*   *   *

I could not believe what I was hearing, but there it was, as congregational music: the famous "Lord's Prayer" by Albert Hay Malotte (the Our Father with that soaring climax at the words, "For Thine is the kingdom... ").[17] This more than anything else convinced me that the music in some Catholic parishes is not just depressing, it is depraved. The Malotte song is, of course, an inspirational solo aria, a slightly kitschy *morceau de concert* (and sometimes, if requested, it could be inserted before or after a liturgy), but asking a congregation to sing it is naive — and sick.

"Oh, but you would be surprised how people just *love* it. Why, some parishioners belt out that song with their whole heart and soul."

The pastor thinks it is just fine. He would not care if the congregation blew police whistles during the Presentation of the Gifts, as long as some people in the congregation were really excited by police whistles.

But that well-trained, expensive "minister of music" (or, if you wish, "pastoral musician") will become most wildly upset by the Malotte "Lord's Prayer," as congregational music, because this type of song is not for group singing. The vocal line is too operatic, too difficult; it convinces most people in the congregation that they should just be quiet and let the show-offs take over. In addition, the Our Father is not the moment in the liturgy for an atomic blast of musical power. And so, the minister of music protests — and is overruled, or fired, or never hired in the first place.

How appropriate it is that the Malotte "Lord's Prayer" will usually be framed, on either side, by "contemporary" songs like "Eagle's Wings" or "Yahweh, I Know You Are Near." Peas in a pod. Listen to those songs, to the way the singer hesitates dramatically at one point (as if lost in reverie) and then reaches for those sweet moments of high musical poignancy. Ah, such beauty! But tricks like that are for soloists, for singers showing off their voices.

It is true that some "contemporary" composers, in early editions of their music, may have specified that the more difficult parts of their songs (the verses) were for the featured soloist and the rest was for the congregation, but such distinctions are rarely made today. The congregation is expected to sing everything, because everybody is a soloist, everybody can sing the Malotte "Lord's Prayer."

In the last few decades, many (maybe most) American Catholics have been trained to believe that "congregational singing" really means the overpowering sound of a soloist (behind a microphone), accompanied by some light background music and a few soloists in the congregation. A competent, sensitive music director would immediately put a stop to this kind of musical bodybuilding contest and try to develop something that has a more communal sound — and for this reason he or she is deeply hated by some people.

*   *   *

Besides sticker shock there is also culture shock.

Back in the 1960s, some American Catholics went into severe culture shock when they attended an ecumenical service (that indescribably novel experience) in a Protestant church and heard such self-assured, commanding music, the likes of which they had never encountered in their own churches. A little embarrassed, they went back home, threw all of their musical traditions (good and bad) into a closet, and began the process of imitating that Protestant success with music. But there would be adjustments in this imitation, of course. Protestants use very good hymn books, support the singing with a strong pipe or electronic organ, confine the music to just one or two services on Sunday, establish a repertory and stick with it for years, use a choir to lead the congregational singing, and hire a respectably talented minister of music to organize everything. Catholics, however, would sing throwaway music in throwaway missalettes, use guitars (or synthesizers), water down the music so that it could cover four, five, six liturgies every weekend, flit from musical fad to fad, pretend that the soloist behind a microphone is really a choir, and perhaps put the congregation at the mercy of unpaid volunteers.

*   *   *

If somebody ever writes a definitive history of music in the Roman Catholic church after Vatican II, an appropriate title would be *Insane Ambitions* — or perhaps *Insane Expectations*. Just sit down with a parish organist and, with pencil and paper, figure out what the typical parish is trying to do. The colossal proportions of the undertaking will astound you. With a musical staff of one overworked, part-time person, the Catholic parish is trying to do what three or four Protestant churches would do with five or six employees. Resources have been stretched beyond the breaking point. In many cases, the music that comes across as "depressing" is really the result of exhaustion.

"But, sir, you must understand the economics here. Only a rare parish can afford the luxury of a minister of music, and we have to pay for parochial schools, for missions abroad and at home.... "

"A new age is dawning, an age where all of your old worn-out notions about the church and its music will be as obsolete as the horse and buggy. Get with it. We need musical artists who will make us aware of the imminent presence of Christ in our lives, now, today; we don't need paid musicians who are going to recreate the past.... "

"The poor come first, not a parish's cultivation of fine music.... "

And so forth.

The excuses, the rationalizing, and the hand-wringing are formed into eloquently sincere sentences. They are uttered with genuine emotion. But no matter how convincing the argument may sound, it could be demolished with just five words: *Put up or shut up.* If you want to have a parish school, you have to put up the money and hire somebody to run it. If you want to fulfill these colossal ambitions and imitate the glossy, triumphant musical sound of the televised Protestant service, then you have to pay for it; if you cannot, then accept music that is much simpler or become accustomed to the beauty of silence. Over the years, the cheap approximations of glossiness will only cause a credibility problem.

Poor parishes, churches in remote areas, and isolated chapels, it goes without saying, have to keep the music budget extremely low. They can, however, cultivate a very credible yet inexpensive form of music: a real sung Mass, with plain, unaccompanied singing, helped by volunteers who are kept away from microphones. The rest of the churches, the great majority, can surely afford the sticker price of a "minister of music" — at least the basic model, which comes with the following features: (1) A competent, spiritually motivated musician who is (2) paid the local "interdenominational rate" for (3) supervising the church's entire music ministry, (4) providing music at only two, possibly three, weekend liturgies, plus other occasions, and (5) rehearsing a choir. A most important feature is that (6) the musician must keep the congregation's music close to the repertory in one of the best

Catholic hymnals. (This will insure continuity.) The music minister's income does not depend on weddings and funerals; they are a separate issue.

Now *that* would be a "revolution in church music" for many American Catholic parishes, and it would produce good, practical results. There is, to be sure, a severe shortage of organists and even trained musicians who have the skills to serve the church's needs; many parishes are lucky if they can find someone who can pull together a choir and manage a few things on a keyboard. But Catholic parishes will be able to cope with shortages and budget problems if they lower their ambitions and if they take that revolutionary step of employing a "minister of music" who is paid the going rate for the exhausting job of supervising the music at a small number of liturgies on weekends and holy days. This might mean totally abandoning all music at certain Masses.

* * *

I happened to say, in passing, that Catholic parishes are spreading their music pretty thin. They would be much better off if they just left singing out of some liturgies — and millions of Catholics would be grateful for the absence of music.

A priest who was there became indignant. "If you think I am going to go in front of all those people without some music to back me up, you've got another thing coming."

I sympathized with him. In the revised rites, with the altar turned around, the priest is alone and awkwardly conspicuous up there; so much is expected of him. He needs music to "back him up," to acknowledge the force and effectiveness of his presence.

But, at the same time, I did not sympathize. Music as just a backup sound for the priest — to get him into the sanctuary, to occupy the congregation while he does something else, to hold people in the pews so that he can exit with some dignity — that used to be called "travel music" in vaudeville. In church, "travel music" only trivializes the congregation's role.

* * *

Let me sum up briefly:

The Catholic laity tend to think that liturgical music is like free tap water — something that is always there and it does not cost a cent. The laity need to be introduced to the idea of paying for what they want. There is no free lunch. If they insist on having all the music that is available at the 11:00 A.M. service at the nearby Protestant church, but (for their convenience) six times on a weekend, then they have to put up the cash for a music budget that is six times the music budget of the nearby Protestant church, or else they have to live with something much simpler.

Many members of the Catholic clergy are downright uncomfortable about working with another professional, a "minister of music" who, in a real sense, educates the community and takes care of the "ministry of music." They would rather put up with the soloists, night club performers, and militant amateurs (who are all out of control in some places) than deal with a "minister" who is going to establish long-term plans. The soloists and hacks can always be treated as if they were external entities "out there" and not part of the "real Mass." The "minister of music," however, has to be a close partner. Too close.

Yes, absolutely — a musician, no matter how qualified or pious, must be moderated. The pastor must make sure that the musician's creativity is both encouraged and yet harnessed. There are two very effective ways to do this: (1) regular staff meetings and (2) staying close to the repertory in the best hymnals for the congregation's music. But such things — working hard to use creative energies productively and surrendering to the "authority" of a good book of song — always involve a combination of humility and mutual respect. That is a high price which some musicians and clergy refuse to pay.

INCULTURATION INFATUATION

The liturgy and music in a particular parish are well below the level of vile. You describe the situation to the more doctrinaire liturgists (aging hippies, usually), and you notice that they are not even listening. When you finish, they respond with a prepared speech that usually sounds like this: *Blame everything on the Roman Rite,* that imperialist tool for enforcing a universal uniformity; all problems will just go away if the Roman Rite is virtually abandoned and replaced with rites that are carefully inculturated to fit the local cultural values. In the United States this means that you must use only music that comes from the culture of the citizens in the pews, and that cultural ancestry might be Korean, Vietnamese, Hawaiian, Aleut, Panamanian, Northern Californian, Southern Californian...

The chic word here is "inculturation," the adaptation of ritual to the cultural values of different peoples of the world — something that Vatican II specifically recommended, without really going into detail. This is where the aging hippies have stepped in; they think they know all the details. They swoon rhapsodically as they describe their vision of the truly inculturated worship of the future. In Africa, inculturation means drums and tribal dancing; in Asia, gongs; and in Western countries...

Watch what happens when the aging hippies turn to the civilization of Western Europe and its extension in other continents. Their blood freezes. As far as they are concerned, the West represents corruption, imperialism, colonialism, arrogant missionaries trying to foist the Roman Rite on innocent converts, and, worst of all, Western music. The ruinous influence of Western culture and European standards of taste must be stopped.

It is hard to follow the reasoning here. Inculturated worship — which is a very fine idea — must be brought to Africa and Asia, to certain ethnic groups in the United States, to women, to children, but apparently not to any part of the world shaped by European civilization. Elementary logic would require that once you accept the idea of inculturation (and the good in all the cultures of the world), you must also accept the reality that the Catholic faithful in the West might pay closer attention if they sometimes encounter the sung Roman Rite, Gregorian chant, classic hymns, excellent organ music, and other respected traditions from *their* received culture. When a choir sings, let us say, a Mozart Mass, with orchestra, in the churches of Austria, Bavaria, and a few other places, it is an example of the purist form of inculturation and perfectly valid — as valid as drums and dancing in an African Mass. Both the Mozart choral music and the African dancing are revered tribal customs (which cannot always be transplanted to other cultures).

This kind of reasoning makes the aging hippies irritable, but there is one fact that pushes them into a state of fury: Western Europe (like India, Japan, Iran, Java, and so forth) developed a "high art" music, which is sophisticated, carefully studied, and capable of a wide variety of expression. Oddly enough, this "high art" music of Western civilization, far from sounding unapproachable and remote, can often be "fun." The rich and poor, educated and uneducated, from Lithuania to Alaska, have found meaning in this music; it has gone all over the globe and (for better or worse) mixed in with different kinds of musics. Some "high art" music of the West is probably "understood" by more peoples of the world than any other music. A Catholic from a remote corner of Asia or Africa can probably walk into the solemn liturgy at Notre Dame Cathedral in Paris or St. Peter's Basilica in Rome and find moments when the music in this European pan-tribal ceremony sounds "familiar." No other kind of religious music on the planet can claim such a broad "recognition."

Catholicism's more radical inculturators — who are indistinguishable from the more extreme multiculturalists in the field of education — have a standard put-down for any favorable comment about Catholicism's rich tradition of music in the West: There is no such thing as a "high art" music, they insist, and all the musics of the world are equal. (Watch the magician's tricks with language here.) The Peking opera is just as good as a Native American war dance which is just as good as a rock song or a Gregorian chant. All the cultures of the world, in the opinion of inculturating multiculturalists, are separate from one another and each one is isolated in a hermetically sealed compartment; since they are all equal, they all demand a liturgical equality. It is supposedly undemocratic, insulting, and evil to contaminate the purity of one culture with something from the culture of another, especially with irrelevant "high art" music from European Catholicism's past.

The musical cultures of the world are indeed equal, in the sense that each one must be judged on its own terms; each type of music must be given the courtesy of "equity"; apples and oranges should be recognized for what they are and not be subject to snobbish comparisons. But as the music critic Edward Rothstein astutely pointed out, many multiculturalists are so abysmally naive about the cultures they wish to protect from contamination that they completely pervert this idea of equal treatment.

Multiculturalism condescends to the very cultures for which it demands "equity," because it refuses even their own distinctions. Precisely which music a group plays, and the aesthetic or social meaning of that music, are largely matters of indifference to the multiculturalists, who are fixated single-mindedly on the music's provenance. In most other cultures, multiculturalist notions would be dismissed as an expression of patronizing ignorance. The puzzle is why they should be taken so seriously in the West.[18]

... or in the Catholic church. So many of the church's avid promoters of inculturation and multiculturalism are really tourists who want "other" Catholics to remain picturesque and contented peasants. When they get their hands on an "inculturated liturgy," the result is sometimes a tourist's or Hollywood producer's idea of "local color," but far removed from the type of music that the local population actually respects. Catholicism's inculturating multiculturalists come across as such lofty-minded heroes of equality, such democratic chums, but look closely at what they are saying. Behind the facade, you will find the worst form of aristocratic condescension — that patronizing attitude which sees the "others," as limited little children who shall content themselves with the weaving of baskets, the wearing of gaudy costumes on feast days, and the singing of their own inculturated music in church, because the poor dear things are capable of so little. Multicultural inculturation is frequently a form of racism, with a smile.

History would have been so different... if St. Patrick had decided that the Irish, backward tribesman, should not have their culture spoiled by Latin liturgies and other imports from the Continent... if St. Boniface had decided that the newly converted barbaric Germanic tribes, in the interest of multiculturalism, should keep their own primitive form of worship and not be introduced to foreign ways... if Rome had realized that the multicultural approach of the Jesuit missionaries in China was right and the "high art" of Chinese culture was indeed a better basis for a local rite than something European.

The history of music would have been so different, so dull, without some cross-pollination from one culture to another. A few examples: That family of Latin chants called "Gregorian" owes a good part of its greatness not to a cultural purity but to a mixing of traditions. In chant there are elements and influences that come from Jewish, Byzantine, Italian, French, German, and other sources. African-American music uses instruments, scales, and harmonies that were familiar to Bach and Beethoven. In some of the best popular music of our time, white, black, Caribbean, and Latin American influences are piled one on top of another.

*   *   *

Centuries ago, Roman Catholicism faced the problem of running a multicultural church. The difficulty was this: how do you reassure an "ethnic group" that God hears its prayers and blesses the best in its culture — without encouraging the worst kind of ethnic chauvinism, without setting up a system of sub-denominations that become antagonistic to one another? This is a long story and its plot begins to thicken in the sixteenth century.

During the Reformation, the singing of vernacular chorales and psalms became a symbol of a victorious Protestantism, and very popular. The Catholic church (notably the Jesuits) responded to this challenge by encouraging congregations in Central and Eastern Europe to sing a kind of "folk Mass." The priest quietly went about the business of reciting the Low Mass in Latin, while the congregation sang memorized songs, which might have had texts that paraphrased the words of the Mass. This "folk" music in German, Polish, Czech, Slovak, and so forth was not always pretty and sometimes the words were inappropriate, but it sympathetically vibrated with the cultural soul of a people. And then, as a balance to the ethnic "folk Mass," there was also the Latin High Mass; its music reminded these same people that they belonged to a universal church that worshiped the God of the whole human race. In the United States (and years ago), some ethnic parishes continued this dual, "bilingual" tradition of a "folk" Mass, with religious songs from the Old Country, and a Solemn High Mass, with "high art" music in Latin. The Mass with songs in the vernacular was an example of inculturation. The sung Latin Mass, if done properly, was an example of the church showing that it was not patronizing, not condescending. This ceremony had a way of saying to the faithful, "You are capable of great things. In God's eyes, you are on a par with aristocrats in a court chapel or a bishop in a cathedral. This music belongs to you too."

English-speaking Catholics, unfortunately, never developed a tradition of a "folk" song for church. They really do not know what you are talking about when you mention a tradition of simple, sturdy congregational music, often sung unaccompanied. Today, Catholics in the United States (and certainly elsewhere) need to build this same kind of "primitive" tradition; they need an abundance of plain, *low-tech* music but, instead, they keep on producing commercial products called "contemporary" songs, which try so hard to sound like a cross between the 1960s folk ballad and the theme song from *Gone with the Wind.* That kind of folk-Romantic hybrid (e.g., "We Will Rise Again" by David Haas and anything by Sebastian Temple) must be propped up with high-tech support from synthesizers, guitars, pianos, and, most of all, amplified soloists; the music is not easy for a congregation to sing.

American Catholic parishes would reap enormous musical benefits if they pushed the "contemporary" song to the side and, at least occasionally, imitated the traditions of low-tech music that developed in Eastern and Central Europe. These parishes would also benefit by using the kind of low-tech congregational singing found in the Orthodox churches and Eastern rites. What does all of this mean in practical terms? Use one or two first-class hymnals for the repertory; make sure that the congregation learns simple, "primitive" chants, hymns, and other music that can stand on its own without accompaniment; on a regular basis, sing at least some music without instrumental support; unplug the microphone for the song leader or choir; keep the repertory stable and "repetitive." (Caution: Something like the chant version of the Our Father, unaccompanied, can be repeated every week and still remain fresh. "Lift High the Cross" and music of similar exalted grandeur, repeated every week, would lead to a rebellion in the pews.)

This unpretentious, low-tech music would certainly sound honest and "authentic"; it would come across as "inculturated," something from the very soul of the people; it would also have the advantage of being low-budget. (Save the "high-budget" music for one or two weekend Masses.) Unfortunately, the lack of gadgets, gimmicks, and loud volume in low-tech music might strike some as terribly Third World, and inappropriate for technologically advanced people who drive to church in their own cars. That primitive sound of low-tech music also makes enemies among the fanatical multiculturalists, because this type of singing could (oh paradox!) be confused with the imperialist "high art" of Gregorian chant.[19]

* * *

It is sad to see what is happening today. In some places, the "high art" music of Roman Catholicism is starting to be segregated as something exclusively for "Anglos."

I remember the parishes where the "Anglos" (maybe predominantly Irish) and the "others" (maybe Italian, Latino, or African-American) did not always get along, but they could come together for the High Mass. The acolytes and the children in the choir were a "rainbow coalition" of ethnic groups. The ceremony symbolized a unity, of sorts. Now I am told about parishes where the "high art" musical traditions are becoming the property of the "Anglos." (That heavy emphasis on English hymns, which must be read from a book, does not help matters.) The inculturators and multiculturalists have convinced the "others" that they really should not be seen in the same church at the same time with the "Anglo" cultural oppressors; they should worship by themselves — and if that is not possible, then each parish liturgy must incorporate a whole menu of assorted music and words to accommodate every single ethnic group in the assembly.

* * *

On Saturday, September 26, 1992, in the city of San Francisco, California, eighty people attended a workshop devoted to the subject of Latin Gregorian chant. It was a bit of a surprise when a crowd of about fifteen hundred showed up at the end of the conference for Mass in St. Mary's Cathedral. The congregation and choir sang the *Missa de Angelis* — chant melodies that, until the 1960s, were familiar to many Catholics. The choir alone chanted the other, more difficult parts of the Mass.

A correspondent who was at this liturgy told me that the choir sang all these beautifully austere chant melodies in Latin — these supreme examples of "high art" music — and there in the pews you had an incredible mix of humanity: the "Anglos," from all kinds of backgrounds, and also people of other ancestries, including Mexican, Filipino, and African. The multicultural congregation was obviously responding to something multicultural in the music.

An interesting story, but it should not be told to the dogmatic inculturators. It would shatter their illusions.

* * *

When the Spanish and Portuguese colonized the New World, they brought their traditions of European art and music with them. From California to the bottom of South America, the colonizers built missions and cathedrals; they installed pipe organs in them; they were printing music in the New World and singing choral music in their churches before the Puritans settled in New England.

So much of that cultural transplanting has disappeared. Thanks to the climate and the termites, the pipe organs that the colonial powers had installed eventually became rotting ruins. The heritage of European "high art" music for church never developed strong and lasting roots in Latin America. What will replace it is anyone's guess.

But maybe the real issue here is not a disappearing musical heritage but a disappearing church. What is going to replace Catholicism itself in that part of the world?

All the statistics show that Latin America is rapidly becoming Protestant — mostly the Pentecostal, Evangelical, Fundamentalist varieties of Protestantism. In fact, Catholics in Latin America are converting to Protestantism at a faster rate and in greater numbers than Catholics in Europe during the sixteenth-century Reformation.[20]

These Protestants offer the advantages of fellowship, a network of like-minded believers, and a virtuous lifestyle; their religious services provide abundant opportunities for emotional release and for the assurance of strong, even authoritarian preaching. The music for these services is simple, energetic, and accompanied mostly by guitar.

Roman Catholicism can barely compete with the new Protestant denominations. People in Latin America still associate the church with the worst features of Spanish and Portuguese colonial rule. There are not enough priests, and many of the ones who are working in the parishes are foreign missionaries, outsiders who speak the local language imperfectly. (Brazil, the largest "Catholic country" in the world, has more full-time Protestant ministers than Catholic priests.)

The Catholic church does respond to the challenge. It sends in Pope John Paul II for yet another visit — and the crowds are not always as large as expected. It sends spies to Protestant services, in order to bring back songs that Catholic congregations might like.

Will musical inculturation help to rescue Roman Catholicism in Latin America? Should the church use more guitars? Songs from the Protestant sects? Castanets? Probably the best answer is not yes or no but another question: "Is anybody really being serious about inculturation?" Inculturation is not an attractive decal that is pasted onto a surface of a structure; it goes much deeper than that. If Roman Catholicism were truly serious about inculturation in Latin America, it would begin not with songs and guitars but with the issue of a married clergy. In the cultural values of Latin America, celibacy is given a very low ranking.

*　*　*

Someone told me about the time she and her husband went to Mass at the Shrine of Our Lady of Guadalupe in Mexico City (a church visited by millions of pilgrims every year). She was very disappointed by the "unconvincing" music — especially when a visiting band in the congregation, apparently without authorization, played "Anchors Away." I, too, remember seeing a similar occurrence during a televised Mass from the same church. This time, a visiting mariachi band in the congregation filled in a blank spot with a colorful fountain of sound. The dance music they performed seemed to fit in perfectly, and it relaxed the tension caused by the overcrowding in the church, but you have to ask: Has inculturation come to this? Is that all there is?

Maybe Latin America does not need another visit from the pope. Maybe it needs musical missionaries who will reintroduce people to some of the enduring traditions of European music for congregation and, at the same time, greatly expand a tradition of liturgical song that is simple, very impressive, and mostly sung from memory. These missionaries would achieve remarkable success and confound the inculturating liturgical specialists by promoting low-tech music that can stand on its own without accompaniment (if necessary) and — imagine this! — does not try to affect a phony, inculturated "Spanish sound." Some congregational singing with a "catholic" (non-Latino) "sound" would help to convince people in Latin America that the Catholic church is a strong, confident institution with its own impressive history behind it.

If, however, the church in Latin America would rather give the impression that it is weak and pathetically unsure of itself, then it should discard all that is useful in the European Catholic tradition of music and substitute peppy songs borrowed from Pentecostal Christianity.

*　*　*

Now and then I will come across a television broadcast of some "Hispanic Mass" in the United States. The guitarists are strumming vigorously; there are recognizable Spanish-sounding clichés in the music. Yes, this looks like certified inculturation . . . and you want to reach for the antacid tablet. It is a farce.

Maybe the problem is that somebody at the diocesan office of Latino matters thinks that people whose ancestry is Mexican, Cuban, Puerto Rican, and all the rest can be edified by a kind of generic-brand "Latino music." Maybe the inculturating bureaucrat responsible for the "Hispanic/Latino Mass" subconsciously believes that these good, decent people are really brainless.

The more the Catholic church pushes musical inculturation as a form of cultural *segregation* for Latinos, or any other group, the more it increases distrust and alienation. At a certain point, inculturation begins to look like second-best for the second-rate. But a practical blending of useful "folk" traditions with some "high art" music (and that could be a simple little chant) is a way of reminding people that they are equal and highly *respected* members of a large and happy family. If the Catholic church wants to use music as part of its evangelization program among Latinos, it should play its ace: some good, red-hot, "high art" music — maybe something as plain as a Gregorian litany, sung in the vernacular, or as exalted as a choral work from the sixteenth century (with the local children in the choir).

⋆　⋆　⋆

Marie Antoinette, Queen of France, was bored by the frosty formality of the court at Versailles. To get away from it all, she and a few of her ladies-in-waiting would retreat to a *faux* farmer's cottage on the palace grounds (the hamlet, built just for the queen) and pretend that they were but simple shepherdesses and country girls. There, away from the pressures and responsibilities of the royal court, they would milk cows. (One imagines Bo-Peep costumes, much lace and crinoline, Limoges porcelain bowls for the milk.) Today we would call this slumming.

The Catholic church now has more than its share of Marie Antoinettes (male and female) — usually white people who are trying to get over their repressed younger days. They are bored; they want to unbutton their collars, to visit the Arcadian landscapes, where life is simpler, more relaxed, so free of responsibilities. If they cannot have a picturesque hamlet, at least they can escape to the sylvan glades of love and sinlessness, as found in the "contemporary" songs of the missalettes. In this musical land of sacred casualness, they can pretend that they are simple folk, with their simple synthesizers and simple "latest hit" commercial songs. There is such sweetness in pretending — especially among certain theologians and liturgists who, bored with the formality of Western liturgical traditions, long for that unbuttoned music of the Future Kingdom church. They tell us that the only real, positive contribution to liturgical music after Vatican II has come from a handful of "folk/contemporary" composers. They hint that the African-American parishes are closest to the type of church that Christ wanted.

My cousin and his wife, who are both white, get in their car on Sunday morning and drive a long distance to take part in the liturgical life of a predominantly black parish. They love the spirituals and the total physical involvement in the singing, but they also love the parish's commitment to the poor in the neighborhood. They cannot stand what passes for music and "relevance" in the white suburban parishes near their home. I understand their reasoning.

In the African-American parishes, the music, the real thing (roots, tradition), is not pretending. In some white parishes, the music is not the real thing, because the Marie Antoinettes have taken over; these white Catholics want music that will help them to pretend that they are lounging in a warm, carefree landscape, where everyone has escaped from the bother of history and culture, where everyone can forget inherited traditions and live in a perpetual celebration of "now" — their time, their moment in the sunshine, their "contemporary hits." The Marie Antoinettes know very well that "crown jewel" music for church ruins the whole pretty illusion; just twenty seconds of that music (maybe a majestic classic hymn or a congregation chanting responses at Mass) will expose the whole idyllic pretending for the fraud that it is. That music of the "high art" Western tradition can come across as brutally honest — the real thing — and just as honest as African-American music. "Crown jewel" music, even at its simplest, is not the easy way out; every note of it demands a sense of responsibility, commitment, and indebtedness to those generations that kept the faith through the centuries.

Maybe someday, the whole thing, the whole pretending fraud, will end in revolution and the guillotine.

*   *   *

One of the better Catholic hymnals published in the United States after Vatican II is in Polish: *Śpiewnik Stulecia: Orchard Lake* (1990).[21] This book, whose title means "Century Hymnal" in English, contains old Polish "folk" songs for church, a good selection of service music for the revised liturgy, a few Latin chants, and a few inescapable examples of "contemporary hits" (such as "Be Not Afraid" in Polish). A large amount of the music in this book is low-tech.

I thought about *Śpiewnik Stulecia* and its old, solid traditions of inculturated congregational singing when somebody sent me an Order of Service for a "Polka Mass" (dated November 9, 1991) in a Polish-American parish.[22] The music for this Mass (accompanied by a polka band) begins with "Chapel in the Valley," drifts into the kind of "contemporary" slop that embarrasses even the more respected "contemporary" composers (e.g., "Let There Be Peace On Earth"), and finally ends with "You Are My Sunshine."

The Polka Mass: Warsaw, Poland, meets the Grand Old Opry, Nashville, Tennessee — and this, too, is an example of inculturation.

I sometimes think that when an immigrant enters the United States (and this includes some of my Irish and Italian ancestors), an agent from the Customs Service whacks him or her on the head with a hammer. At that moment, all the best traditions of the Old Country are forgotten; the descendants of the immigrant then begin to replace the lost heritage with a sentimental, Americanized fabrication, an invented memory, all in shades of pastel. The forgotten traditions were not charming keepsakes; they were an ethnic record of struggle, sorrow, and an enduring faith. The kitsch American substitutes — "memory" sprinkled with powdered sugar — are symbols of comfort, superficiality, and suburban niceness.

Good-bye to the charming old Polish "folk" songs for the Mass. Good-bye to the Latin repertory, which is also a part of Polish cultural history. Hello to the Polka Mass, a Polish joke.

*   *   *

Sometimes inculturation produces freakish results when it is based on decadence, self-centered ethnic pride, and the innocent contentedness that comes with ignorance. Sometimes inculturation backfires.

THE BISHOPS SQUEAK

It has been said (or whispered) that the more the Catholic bishops of the United States are ignored by their flock on matters of faith and morals, the more they poke their noses into matters that are beyond their "jurisdiction." According to this theory, the bishops are spending too much of their time in Washington, in the committees of the United States Catholic Conference (USCC) and the National Conference of Catholic Bishops (NCCB); they issue pronouncements on the Palestinian problem and nuclear weapons, but they should be at home, minding the store.

A better evaluation of the situation is that the Catholic bishops, as a group, certainly do have a right to "exercise their pastoral mission of sanctification, teaching, and leadership."[23] Their "jurisdiction" is broad. They have an obligation to speak out, bravely, on vital issues of our time, as a group and not just as individuals.

The one area where they have done relatively little speaking out — in fact, where they have displayed a bit of cowardice — is church music. They really ducked this one.

"But when you think about social justice, poverty, nuclear war, and all the social ills of our time, is the small matter of liturgical music really worth the attention of these busy men?"

You bet it is. The typical Catholic spends more time singing (or supposedly singing) in church than listening to sermons. A lot of teaching and sanctification of the faithful is done through musical notes, yet the leadership of the bishops in this area is ... (what is the right word?) ... fuzzy. Extremely fuzzy.

The reasons for this fuzziness go back to the late 1960s, the years after Vatican II finished its business. In those days, there was serious talk about a National Catholic Hymnal — a book, published by the bishops, with a basic collection of congregational music for Catholic parishes. ("Hymnal" is, of course, shorthand for "a book of service music and songs for congregation.") The book would set standards; it would establish a common, familiar repertory; it might provide an income that could go to the church's pastoral needs. After all, bishops in some other countries were

planning to issue their own national song books. Why not the
United States?

The talk did not get very far because there were valid objections: "We need more time...we are too diverse...an official
song book would stifle creativity...there is no consensus out
there," and so forth. Another complication was that all kinds
of priests, nuns, diocesan officials, and laypeople were running
around and denouncing "standard" religious music of the past as
an abomination. The future, said the Catholic futurists, belonged
to "Kumbaya" and other "folk" music. They sounded very angry,
these futurists. Would they revolt — set up their own secession-
ist parishes — if the church ever tried to establish a "standard"
repertory in an "official" book?

The bishops must have sensed that anybody who poked his
nose into this matter ("good" and "official" church music) would
get a bloody nose.

It must be said, however, that the bishops have shown leadership; they have said something. In 1972, through their Committee on Liturgy, they issued a pamphlet called *Music in Catholic
Worship*. Another pamphlet on the same subject, *Liturgical Music Today*, followed in 1982. There are inspiring moments in both
pamphlets — exhortations and ideals, insights into everything
from recorded music in church to compensation for the music director; but the tone of the prose is so weak, so cautious. After you
finish reading both pamphlets — once — you expect the pages to
crumble into dust, right in your hands.

The bishops were probably afraid that clear, decisive language
on the matter of musical taste might anger somebody. (The clergy
can safely denounce whole categories of wickedness, and the
faithful take it with pious docility — but make one unflattering
remark about musical taste, and be prepared for war!) Certainly
the bishops gain nothing if they antagonize one of the many
factions out there in the pews just waiting to be antagonized:
the musical traditionalists, conservatives, conservationists, futurists, radicals, reactionaries, sentimentalists, and all the rest.
Also, the bishops must realize that no matter what they say, the
local pastor will do exactly as he pleases. In effect, the fuzzy, cautious, and inoffensive leadership of the bishops on the matter of
church music is their way of admitting that nobody is paying
attention to them; and so they have stepped aside and let the

private sector take all the flack, all the risks — as well as all the profits.

What is called "the pastoral music scene" in the Catholic church of the United States is something that is pushed and pulled in different directions by businesses that exist to make profits. What is called "folk/contemporary religious music" and the "grassroots revolution in church music" is a commercial undertaking for profit. Yes, there are good intentions and religious motives, but the music still has to come to the parishes through the private sector, which needs a profit to survive — and economic survival means the following realities: (1) A company only makes a quick, one-time profit by selling a song book that will just stay there in the pews for thirty years. (2) There is little money to be made by selling music that is old and has no copyright protection, no matter how good it is. (3) The only way to survive (i.e., to keep the cash flowing in) is by constantly selling music that is garbage. Musical garbage, from an economic point of view, is the best music, because it becomes obsolete very fast.

* * *

In the downtown area of a large city in New England there is a Catholic church that prides itself on its mod and ceaselessly experimental liturgies. Somewhere near the altar there should be a banner that proclaims this church's motto: "What will we think of next!"

There are no hymnals or missalettes in the pews of this church. When the time comes for the congregation to sing a song, a beam of light from a slide projector cuts through the air and the congregation finds the words of the song flashed onto a surface behind the altar.

The video song book! Is this the greatest invention since popcorn at the movies? Is this a dopey stunt? Let us put such questions to the side for the moment and, instead, concentrate on one disconcerting aspect of the giant video image behind the altar: the top billing, what you see above all the words to be sung — *the big name.* There, above the priest's head, above the text of the song and in a space that suggests exalted importance, you see the words (let us say) "MARTY HAUGEN," a "hit" composer of our time. Later on, the words to a familiar old hymn might be projected onto the mystical space above the altar but, in cases like this, no composer's or author's name is indicated.

Now, immediately, I must rush in with a clarification and say that Marty Haugen should certainly receive recognition for his liturgical music; some of it is very pleasant. (One unpleasant example would be "Gather Us In," which, because of its chatter-box, yackety-yack repetitiveness, can cause migraines.) My only point is that this mod church bases its whole musical life on the assumption that postconciliar Catholics shiver with excitement when they sing "hit" songs by the "hit" composers of today.

Who needs a National Catholic Hymnal? Who needs a book with a lot of music written by people who are not "hit" composers? Today's celebrity composer, of course, will soon become yesterday's has-been — so, why put music by the soon-to-be has-beens into a durable book? Instead, project the music, or at least the words, onto a screen. Everything disappears when you want it to disappear. In the Future Kingdom parish, this may be the only way to deal with the built-in obsolescence, that is, the problem of getting rid of rotting garbage, fast.

* * *

The bishops have virtually "deregulated" liturgical music, something intimately associated with everything they are trying to teach; they have allowed it to be controlled almost totally by commercial interests. Parishes and chapels are trying to express their prayer and their religious convictions in musical sounds; they seek guidance — and who provides most of it? The publishers, who are in a feeding frenzy for customers. The bishops, powerless, watch from the sidelines. Maybe this has frequently been the case throughout history.

It would be so useful if one brave bishop could say out loud, "Let the buyer beware." Beware of the publishers who issue planning guides and reviews that are really promotional advertising for their products. Beware of the Master Gurus and other composer hucksters who cry, "Lord! Lord!" in public but are really trying to get another message across: "Ignore the competition; buy my music." Beware of anyone who thinks that the Catholic faithful would be so much happier if they totally surrendered themselves to the *today* music of Bob or Dan or John or ... "Well, they're old-hat now, but there's this *brand-new* group called something-or-other ministries and I think they have finally hit upon the *real* liturgical music of our time." Beware of this commercial enterprise, this liturgical music industry. Its motives are not always pure.

Pure or not, private enterprise, it must be said, does work sometimes. A few excellent, first-rate Roman Catholic song books have been published in the United States since the Second Vatican Council. Some are no longer available but, among the survivors, the best would include the following, in alphabetical order: *American Catholic Hymnbook* (American Catholic Press), *The Collegeville Hymnal* (Liturgical Press), *Hymns, Psalms, and Spiritual Canticles* (BACS), and the third edition of *Worship* (G.I.A.); in addition, there are a few good selections in *Gather* (G.I.A.). I have heard speculation that all of these books are doomed; they will soon be out of print. This would be a very sad loss.

I have also heard speculation that, when the dust settles, the *de facto* "National Catholic Hymnal" in the United States will probably be *Today's Missal*, a missalette published by Oregon Catholic Press. I wish it the best of luck.

To understand the secret of this missalette's success, you must imagine a roulette table (an odious comparison, I admit). The management of *Today's Missal* is like a gambler who distributes chips all over the table, in the hope that at least a few numbers will be winners. In the pages of this missalette you will find weepy old Victorian hymns like "Mother Dearest," a few Gregorian chants, a good selection of hymns, and — this is where the money is — great, huge mounds of "contemporary" songs, most of which are instantly forgettable. You hit the jackpot when one of these mod songs becomes a "hit." Suddenly, everybody must have it.

The editorial committee of, let us say, a hymnal for Presbyterians or Lutherans has the task of discovering what music is securely popular within the denomination and what would be beneficial for the faithful; by using standards of religious values, taste, singability, and quality to determine what gets into the book and what does not, the committee provides leadership. (For diplomatic reasons, a few weak specimens of music are allowed into the hymnal.) In contrast, the management of *Today's Missal* and other Catholic publishers moisten one finger, as it were, and check to see which way the wind is blowing. They follow; they do not lead. *Today's Missal* regularly surveys its customers to find out what's hot, what's not. One of its letters to parish music directors sums up the philosophy: "We're following your lead."[24]

They certainly are not following the lead of the bishops, who are not even in the picture. When it comes to music, the lambs lead the shepherds.

*   *   *

Where does all the money go? All of those missalettes and song books for sale — we are talking about hundreds of millions of pages, millions of dollars. Some publishers, it is true, lost their corporate shirts when they decided to promote their own tasteful song collection, but other publishers, as well as composers, are hauling in money by the truckload.

Where does all the money go? "To charity," I am told, to monks in Vermont, Jesuits in St. Louis, the poor, and a diocese in Oregon.

Today's Missal is published by the Oregon Catholic Press, which is listed in the *Official Catholic Directory* as an agency of the diocese of Portland in Oregon. As such, it is tax-exempt and nonprofit. The tax-exempt status must be infuriating to the commercial publishers, who have to pay taxes. The nonprofit status is rather hard to believe for a company that markets its products so aggressively.

Where does all the money go? They asked that question earlier in the twentieth century, when the monks of Solesmes Abbey in France were responsible for editing chant books that were used all over the world. The *Liber Usualis* and other chant publications were all skillfully (even brilliantly) prepared at Solesmes, on the basis of immense scholarly knowledge, and the general presumption was that the abbey must have collected a part of the profits on these publications. This financial arrangement was all perfectly proper, but, unfortunately, it would eventually create an undercurrent of bad feelings.

That was the past. Where does all the money go now? To commercial interests. To businesses, to publishing companies that follow a marketing strategy attributed to H. L. Mencken: "Nobody ever went broke underestimating the taste of the American public."

(*N.B.* I, the author of this book, receive royalties on the same. They are strictly of minor-league proportions.)

*   *   *

The Lutheran pastor buys a hymnal. He knows that the book contains "Silent Night." He also knows that this beloved old

Christmas carol will be available in the pews for the life of the hymnal, maybe twenty or even forty years.

The Catholic pastor makes out a check for a missalette — every year. He knows that, every year, he gets another copy of "Silent Night." (The previous year's copy is thrown out.) For the foreseeable future he has to buy a new copy of "Silent Night" every single year. This is a very good deal for the publishers, when you think about it.

*   *   *

Here is an idea that sometimes comes up in discussion:

The Catholic bishops, or perhaps a prestigious nonprofit foundation, should publish a National Catholic Hymnal — a basic collection with "Silent Night" and other standard works in English and Latin; there would be a parallel volume in Spanish; both would contain some excellent service music and some very "primitive" chanting, for churches with limited musical resources. These "official" books of song for a parish would give some sense of confidence and continuity to congregational singing. Any profits from the sale of these publications would support a retirement fund for clergy and religious orders or other laudable projects. But the "official" books would be only half a hymnal. Parishes and chapels would put into the pews a companion volume, something like a missalette, which might have the latest "hit" songs or specialized music for a particular community; the contents of this booklet would change from time to time and be left to the ingenuity of private enterprise. (Hymnal publishers would be allowed to incorporate the "official" repertory into future editions of their own song books.)

It sounds like a good idea — the obvious next step — until you realize that there is no acknowledged Catholic leadership in this area. (Remember that educated musicians are frequently excoriated for being irrelevant elitists.) If the Catholic bishops were in charge of such a publication, there is the danger that they would put everything into the hands of eager underlings, aging hippies who would proceed with the following policy: (1) For tradition, allow some rousing old Protestant revival hymns. (2) For the good of the faithful, destroy anything that even suggests a connection with Gregorian chant. (3) Make "Be Not Afraid" the model of what all liturgical music is supposed to sound like, from now until the end of time.

*   *   *

A large parish sits in the middle of a residential area of a large city. Over the years, the parish's music director, a talented organist, has trained the congregation to sing a fairly standard repertory from a standard hymnal. The congregation, securely familiar with the music, sings well.

The music director quits, in order to take a less hectic job elsewhere. He is replaced by a husband-and-wife team; neither can read a note of music; neither can play the organ. The team, overnight, wipes out almost all of the music that the congregation has learned. They replace most of it with songs they have composed. The bewildered congregation barely makes a sound. The team and their associates, thrilled with the relevance of their postconciliar accomplishments, sing on and on from their position around a piano in the sanctuary.

True stories like this make you realize that a National Catholic Hymnal (or even an official National Catholic Repertory) is desperately needed: to provide at least a little continuity in the parishes and to swat those annoying pests, the militant amateurs.

*　*　*

In all fairness, I have to add that many of the bishops in the United States have made sure that the music in their cathedrals is exemplary — but in the parish right next to the cathedral, pastor and people ignore the good example and do exactly as they please. The bishops have set up all manner of commissions, workshops, and offices that issue very useful guidelines, directories, and sample contracts for musicians — but it is the rare pastor who can just find the time to read all this paperwork. Maybe the bishops have not spoken out much on the subject of music because nobody is listening.

One bishop has spoken. Archbishop Rembert Weakland of Milwaukee — a graduate of the Juilliard Conservatory of Music and a respected scholar — gave a speech in 1991 and declared, "Today there is no Catholic poetry, no outstanding Catholic church music."[25]

FOR FURTHER MEDITATION AND GROUP DISCUSSION

1. In the comedy film *Sister Act* (1992), Whoopi Goldberg, who is black, plays the role of a singer who entertains the patrons of a gambling casino. One night she happens to walk into a room during a mob killing. The police, who need to protect her as a witness in this murder case, hide her in a convent where she dresses like a nun. Instead of blending in quietly with the other sisters, she becomes the conductor of the choir of nuns and turns that hopeless bunch into a swinging, hand-clapping, dancing soul-music group; the new black-influenced music she has taught the choir brings in hundreds of new parishioners; then she persuades these cloistered nuns to go out into the city, where they improve the lives of the poor, children, and society's rejects.

Sister Act is an enjoyable comedy. It has to be seen as a piece of fictional entertainment . . . and yet, the parts of the film that deal with music deserve further analysis as fact.

The main bad guy in *Sister Act* is Whoopi Goldberg's mobster boyfriend, but the second villain is what the mother superior in this film calls the "time-honored sacred music" of the Catholic church. When we first hear the choir of nuns in this film, they sing music that is supposed to be "time-honored" and very Catholic: a horribly deformed, dissonant rendition of "Hail, Holy Queen Enthroned Above." Later, they think about rehearsing "Crown Him with Many Crowns" (a mighty, stick-out-your-chest Protestant hymn that was unknown to most Catholics until the 1970s). Conservative, cloistered nuns such as these would have maintained a tradition of Gregorian chant, sung exquisitely, or else they would be developing a form of chant in English, but this convent knows only songs in a missalette.

Sister Act, a mixture of comedy and fantasy, is based on a sad premise: American Catholics are poor cultural orphans who have no real musical traditions or roots of their own; they must be rescued — by using exuberant music from black culture, by abandoning their hopelessly irrelevant traditional music, if such a thing even exists. Many American Catholics have no difficulty accepting this musical premise behind *Sister Act*, because, in their experience, "traditional" music for the Catholic church now means the following: two perfunctory stanzas of a Protestant

hymn, meandering "contemporary" songs, and that awful missalette music that makes you think you are eating styrofoam when
you sing it.

What would have happened if Whoopi Goldberg's character
had been hidden in one of those rare convents where the nuns
chant the Divine Office and Mass in Latin every day, or in a parish
where the best traditions of "European" music for the Catholic
church flourish in all their resounding, affirming glory? I would
like to think that her soul music and the "European" tradition
would have happily coexisted side-by-side — two very different
and very strong ways of doing the same thing. One "way" would
learn deep respect for the other "way."

2. A friend of mine toured Europe recently and went out of
his way to hear the best church music. In a great cathedral he
heard choral singing of indescribable beauty. In an even greater
basilica the organist's playing left him speechless. Oddly enough,
one place that also impressed him, he told me, was a poor Catholic
parish in the north of England.

My friend happened to be at Mass on a weekday morning.
The singing was led by a man in the pews (someone delegated
by the pastor and the organist). Without a microphone, he just
said, "Let's sing number so-and-so in the book." He then started
off the singing and most of the congregation joined him, without
any accompaniment. The singing was not ready for Carnegie Hall,
but my friend reports that it was one of the most inspirational
examples of liturgical music he had ever encountered.

The weekday Mass in this church should be videotaped and
shown to Catholic parishes throughout the world. This is what
the foundation of liturgical music should look like — and on
a foundation like that you can build a skyscraper. Nobody is
saying that churches should copy exactly the musical routine
in this parish; rather, it is the general *principles* here that are
worth imitating: simplicity, living within your means, reasonable expectations, low-tech music, and even the value of musical
sophistication.

Yes, sophistication. Behind the simplicity in the music for
that weekday Mass there was a good hymnal, a pastor and organist who had set up a program to be followed, and a volunteer
song leader who knew what he was doing. (The "live" acoustics

also helped.) Music like this, which sounds so "natural" and "organic," does not happen by accident. It is always guided by very knowledgeable people.

How refreshing it would be to walk into a Catholic parish on a quiet Saturday evening or early on Sunday morning and sense the honesty of lowered expectations, an unwritten social contract that sounds like this: "Look, if you want choirs and an organist and all that, come back at another time. We cannot afford an around-the-clock music program. We cannot drive our music director until he/she drops from exhaustion. We're doing the best we can with what we have." If there is singing, it is low-tech and unaccompanied: a couple of hymns, a few chanted items (like Lord, Have Mercy and the Our Father), and an exceedingly plain psalm or two; the emphasis is on memorized music which does not have to be read from a book; the leader of song (assisted by a few volunteers) perhaps stays in the pews and goes near a microphone only for announcements.

But I am dreaming. Postconciliar Catholics are supposed to get the music of a cathedral ceremony when they go to Sunday Mass, except that all of it is miniaturized for purposes of speed. Or else they are supposed to be romantically embraced by "contemporary" songs — which need the expensive backing of soloists and instruments to make musical sense. (Try to have a group sing "Be with Me, Lord" or "Eagle's Wings" in a low-tech fashion, without accompaniment, and you will not be able to keep a straight face.)

3. "At our Catholic college in the Midwest, we plan our liturgies — oh my, do we plan! — for weeks ahead, and it pays off. Let me tell you, when people leave those liturgies, they are exhausted, I mean totally drained from the experience, from the constant participation in song!"

Admirable, I replied. In measured amounts, exhilarating high-tech congregational singing is great, but if used too much, this type of music (even good music) wears out faster than a pair of cheap sneakers.

The clever old Catholic church of the past had appropriate music for great feasts and for times when the mood of "quiet routine" prevails. The unwise Catholic parish of today tries to turn every weekend liturgy into a New Year's Eve party. Just as the athlete should beware of overtraining, the parish and chapel must beware of musical overkill, burnout.

A friend of mine, a nun who is a church musician, puts it this way: "You can't stage the Second Coming every weekend."

4. Church A and church B; any denomination. The music in both is "traditional" and outstanding. Why, then, do I feel comfortable in A, while the music in B makes me want to scramble over the pews and run for the exits?

The answer has to do with . . . wrinkled skin . . . patina . . . hair in the armpits . . . sweat . . . grit.

In church A you sense that the music is expressing the profound and deep prayer of real human beings who are conscious (however dimly) of their religion's place in destiny; in church B they are trying to be historically and artistically correct.

5. Singing in a church with thick carpeting all over the floor is like singing with a pillow against your mouth. Part of the "joy" of music — e.g., singing in the shower — comes from our own physical vibrating with the resonance of the sounds we create. (Does this remind us of our fetal development in the womb?) Take away the reverberations, and the music can lose its physical "joy."

6. Not long after Vatican II ended, a new abbot was elected at an abbey in France. Convinced that the place needed to be brought up-to-date, he persuaded the monks to end the time-consuming practice of chanting the Mass and Divine Office for hours each day.

Within a short time, a strange malaise began to afflict this monastic community. The monks were always exhausted. One medical specialist after another was brought in to examine them but nobody could determine the cause of the constant fatigue. Finally, in 1967 the monks asked Dr. Alfred Tomatis to examine them.[26] This specialist, who treated the throat problems of professional singers, found seventy of the ninety monks "slumping in their cells like wet dishrags," but they were not suffering from a disease known to modern medicine.

Dr. Tomatis decided on a radical procedure. He told the monks to return to their original schedule of chanting (which went on for hours every day). They did, and within a few months nearly all the monks were feeling fine again, thanks to the chant.

Dr. Tomatis believes that certain types of music (e.g., Gregorian chant, Tibetan chant, Mantra yoga, and the music of Mozart) charge the body with energy ("energy food"); some other types of music discharge energy and can leave us exhausted. The whole body takes in musical stimuli, while the inner ear transforms the musical sounds into electrical messages sent to the brain. "We are creatures of sound," he says. "We live in it, and it lives in us." Our bodies become part of the music, even if we are not performing it. "The music rubs against you, it manipulates you, and therefore it's important that it be of good quality."

A crackpot theory? Who knows. The doctor mixes scientific fact with insights and a mysticism that cannot be proved. Perhaps the theories will receive greater attention if they help to explain, *partially*, why so many religious communities and seminaries pushed the self-destruct button soon after they stopped singing chant of any description.

7. In the seventeenth and eighteenth centuries, German Lutheranism split into two factions: the "orthodox" and the Pietists.

The "orthodox" Lutherans believed in worshiping with thoroughness. At a Sunday service, the minister, with learned reasoning, expounded on the readings of the day; a cantata and chorales further probed the implications of the readings; communion took more time and called for the singing of more musical items. This kind of patiently thorough and traditional service went on for hours.

The Pietists denounced such goings-on in church. They wanted religion of the heart, not the brains; they wanted services with emotional appeal, not intellectual thoroughness. The only music appropriate for worship, they insisted, was the plain, sentimental song (the more sentimental the better). "Elaborate" church music of any sort had no real place in their services. Pietists at the Lutheran church in Mühlhausen made life very difficult for their organist, Johann Sebastian Bach; sensing that his talents were absolutely unwelcome, Bach quit as soon as he could.

Pietism, in one form or another, has been flourishing in Roman Catholicism for centuries, but, until recently, the church had always managed to keep it under control with a conservative, "orthodox" liturgy. Now, with nothing to restrain them, the Catholic

Pietists have taken over in some places; they have driven many fine, dedicated musicians right off the property.

8. It is interesting to chat with people who graduated from Catholic high schools that, starting in the late 1960s, began to use recordings of rock songs for liturgies, especially the graduation Mass. (The rock group Chicago was a favorite.) The school administrators ran out of breath congratulating themselves on their cleverness. Yes sir, they had found the way to make religion meaningful and relevant for these kids.

History has played a joke on these clever ones. The alumni who had experienced these meaningful and relevant ceremonies with the rock songs (supplemented by the "contemporary" religious songs) look back and laugh. The phrase that the alumni often use to describe their memory of these exercises in trendiness is "so stupid."

By the way, never patronize "kids." They like music that respects their intelligence. A special Kiddie Mass, at which the children sing cutie-pie songs, might look so terribly darling to the parents, but twenty years later (when the children, grown up, recall the event) the cuteness begins to look "so stupid."

9. In 1903, Pius X — saint and patron of church music — issued his *Motu Proprio* on music, a document that set off an avalanche of words. For the next fifty-five years, the popes issued all manner of exhortations, allocutions, and decrees, in order to strengthen the ideals of the *Motu Proprio*.

When consulting the authoritative prose of these papal documents, never forget one fact: During the reign of Pius X and up until recent times, the Vatican's choirs produced vocal tones that stank. It was not just a case of honest singing from a poorly trained choir (a sound that can be quite agreeable). No, these were deliberately and aggressively repulsive noises.

Father William J. Finn (1881–1964), a Paulist priest and director of the Paulist Choristers in New York, visited Rome in 1912, during the reign of Pius X. In his autobiography, Father Finn described the music he heard in the Vatican, and it is interesting to observe how he tried (in print) to keep himself from blowing his top.[27] One gathers from reading his memoirs that this highly respected priest, appalled by the execrable racket that came from the papal choirs, shook with rage as he listened to the vocal desecration of one "liturgically correct" composition after another.

The papal choirs continued to stink for decades after Father Finn heard them in 1912. (Recordings attest this.) There was improvement, however, beginning in the 1980s.

As you listen to an old recording of the Sistine Chapel Choir, remember that the squawking boy sopranos and the basses sliding lazily from note to note are singing some of the most magnificent choral music ever written. Stunning, beautiful music — and the singers are brutally forcing it through a musical meat grinder.

We have to wonder: Has the Vatican sometimes interpreted the New Testament, the "Greatest Story Ever Told," the way it has interpreted some of the greatest music ever written?

All of those solemn papal pronouncements on music would have been so unnecessary if, let us say, the Sistine Chapel Choir had been able to produce the agreeable tones of a second-rate provincial choir in France or England. One good example hits with an impact that is stronger than ten encyclicals. This is called practicing what you preach.

10. Two Jesuit stories. The first, from 1986, concerns a Jesuit seminarian who was living is a "house of studies" run by that order. One day, he happened to come across a recording of chant in the house, and he decided to play it. (He knew almost nothing about chant.) The sound of the music drifted through the halls of the building and came to the attention of the rector, who immediately stopped what he was doing and tracked down the source of the music. When he found the seminarian listening to chant, he gave the young man a dirty look and left.

From that day on, the ex-seminarian told me, he felt he was under special surveillance. He was taken aside and it was made clear to him that the church had entered a new era. Anyone who showed curiosity about the music of the old (and discredited) era was not quite trustworthy. Worship reached perfection in the liturgies celebrated in the common room of this house, with the rector in the center and everyone around him. The repertory of songs composed by the group known as the St. Louis Jesuits would supply most of the liturgical music he would ever want to know.

The second story is about a man who sang in the large folk

group of a church connected with a Jesuit university in the Midwest. Sunday after Sunday, for every possible occasion in the church, the folk group sang from the musical canon of the St. Louis Jesuits and a few other "contemporary" composers. Rarely was anything else permitted. Indeed, members of the group were taught to ridicule music outside the canon. After he graduated, this man saw what was going on in the rest of the world and realized that he had been subjected to four years of promotional advertising.

These stories are *typical* — in the sense that you can find similar instances in all kinds of Catholic seminaries, convents, and institutions of learning. The common theme running through stories like this is determination: Certain Catholic individuals (in positions of power) are determined to prove that they have arrived at the moment of true spiritual perfection; they have nothing to learn from the past, from a church that had worshiped in a way that was wrong, from top to bottom.

Sometimes you can see this determination in the printed Order of Service for a priest's first Mass or for a liturgy at which a nun takes her final vows. There is not one speck of music written before the 1960s. The choice of "contemporary" music to the exclusion of everything else is a symbol of open contempt for something that is bigger, older, and much more impressive than the determined ones.

But there are signs that maybe the tide is turning. For example, some music that predates the St. Louis Jesuits is now used at the church next to the Jesuit university mentioned above. They have let in the competition. If any organization can lead the Catholic church out of that determined, narrow-minded intolerance called "contemporary" music for liturgy, it is the Jesuits.

11. To learn how to play a Bach fugue on the organ or how to conduct a great choral work, one must spend long, lonely hours practicing. This requires dogged determination and/or an obsessive-compulsive personality.

After years of this relentless struggle toward the perfection of one's craft, there is sometimes the risk that one will display alarming antisocial tendencies when dealing with congregations and clergy (e.g., making an assembly sing until everybody is hoarse or insisting on the most unyielding interpretation of liturgical custom or acting out a Mad Scene if the sixteenth-notes are not sung precisely). Advise these perfectionists to cool it or get lost.

12. A current conspiracy theory sounds like this: "Back in the 1980s, Pope John Paul II began to appoint these reactionaries as bishops. That was the beginning of the conservative backlash. You can see it in some of the newer priests coming out of the seminaries. They are more conservative than the old conservatives of yesteryear. You can see it in the attempts to silence liberal theologians. You can see it in the return to old church music — you know, back to chant and all that."

Baloney. If a congregation shows an interest in singing a chant melody, if some old choral music is heard in the local cathedral, the reason is not always a severe conservatism trying to reassert its authority. Sometimes, the old tunes just happen to be more endearing and enduring than the latest fad songs.

Besides, "conservative Catholicism," in the United States and elsewhere, usually does not express its conservatism by promoting a "conservative musical tradition" (which now means the church's heritage of music). There are notable exceptions, to be sure, but "conservative Catholicism" has a long history of talking about the church's musical traditions with pious reverence and then treating them as if they were hated in-laws.

13. Not long ago a Catholic parish in California "went hillbilly." Every Sunday at the 10:00 A.M. folk Mass, they sang one old Protestant Gospel hymn after another: "Rock of Ages," "What a Friend I Have in Jesus," "In a Garden," "The Old Rugged Cross," and all the other favorites of this type. For a "Catholic balance," the congregation also sang "contemporary" songs from *Glory and Praise.* (It is very revealing that the music of the St. Louis Jesuits and other "contemporary" composers would be considered the perfect complement to the Gospel-song favorites.) This Catholic parish was always packed for its Old-Time-Religion Mass. People were standing in the aisles. The place rocked with the powerful singing.

A discreet letter from the chancery office arrived; it requested that the Country & Western Mass be stopped. Use only music from *Glory and Praise,* the parish was advised. The pastor complied. People were heartbroken. Attendance at Mass dropped.

I love those old Bible songs and I never pass up an opportunity to sing them, but I also know that they can create confusion at a Catholic Mass. Their topic is "me" and what God does for "me." ("I" or "me" occurs in almost every line of "In a Garden.") At a Catholic liturgy, "we" come together to be part of a tremendous event; the music is part of our job.

14. In 1991 a Catholic bishop wrote an article about his experience as a choirboy in a parish near Chicago.[28] His choir director was Dr. Otto Singenberger, a distinguished church musician and son of John Singenberger, another prominent church musician. Under Otto Singenberger's direction the choir sang chant, Bach, Mozart, Bruckner, and other "greats." All of this music impressed the boy who would become bishop, but what impressed him even more was the sight of Singenberger — old, frail, and in terrible pain from rheumatism — getting down on his knees after the Consecration.

The bishop says that Singenberger is in heaven now and kneeling in adoration but no longer bothered by the rheumatism. "He moves his right hand briskly as though he were directing the Elgar and the Mozart, and he carefully follows the unfamiliar cadences and rhythms of the 'folk' Mass. He prays that church musicians understand that their music is to be inspiring, of course, but that they in their lives are to be inspiring as well. Sacred music is not just to be sung or played, he wants to cry down from heaven. It is to be prayed, and, even more, lived."

Chapter Five

WHAT DOES IT ALL MEAN?

OCCASIONALLY I RECEIVE a long-distance telephone call from a stranger who has read something I have written. The stranger begins with an introduction, proceeds to the topic of what is happening in the Catholic church today, and then gets to a matter that is bothering him or her. What do I think about it? What does it all mean?

One call, which I received not long ago, was from a particularly puzzled gentleman who told me about Mass in his parish church. When a certain priest presides, he said, the liturgical dialogue always goes like this:

Priest: May the Lord be with you.

Congregation: And also with you.

Priest: Thank you.

The man who telephoned me said that he could not explain to himself why he was so irritated by this addition of two little words ("Thank you"), but he was learning to endure it as a unique eccentricity; then, one Sunday, he happened to go to another parish in another diocese and there it was again — the thank-you non sequitur. The caller demanded to know: Is this becoming a trend? What does it all mean?

I responded by saying that I did not have the slightest idea, but maybe the next time he was hit by this doubtful improvement upon ancient tradition, he should shout, in a loud voice, "You're welcome."

A short time after that telephone call I happened to attend Mass in a wealthy suburban Catholic parish outside Philadelphia and, instead of praying, I kept thinking: What are they trying to prove? What does it all mean?

For at least one quarter of this liturgy the congregation sang, with support from a choir of about twenty-five and a fine pipe organ. But during every single moment of singing, what you really heard was the voice of a soprano soloist (behind a microphone) floating on top of everything. The congregation, choir, and organ were her accompaniment.

For perhaps another five percent of the liturgy we heard the voices of readers (also behind a microphone). For the rest of the Mass (maybe as much as forty minutes) what we heard, heavily amplified, was the booming voice of the priest: during his prayers and the homily, of course, but also during assembly prayers, such as the Creed and Our Father. I should add that his homily was excellent and he seemed like a perfectly fine fellow, but the cumulative effect of hearing one amplified voice after another — his, the lead singer's, the reader's — was deadening.

And then everything made sense. I saw what it all meant: the thank-you peculiarity, the constant emphasis on one amplified voice at a time. Everything made sense.

The reader is annoyed, justifiably. It does not make sense. To explain what it all means, I must first enter into a long digression.

*   *   *

For many centuries, the Roman Catholic church was a sprawling, ramshackle institution that appeared to be a collection of independent monarchies. It must have looked as if each bishop reigned supreme in his diocese. But in reality there were many checks on his authority. For instance, he had to work with something that resembled a board of trustees: a group of priests called the cathedral chapter. The priests on this board — they were called canons — received an independent source of income that was beyond the bishop's control. Sometimes the bishop could not make certain financial decisions without the approval of the chapter. At various times in history, bishops also had to contend with other factors that complicated their authority, such as ecclesiastical courts, meddlesome governments, noblemen who had the right to nominate pastors for certain churches, and some pastors who could not be easily removed from office.

In his cathedral, the bishop sat on an ornate throne that symbolized his authority in the diocese, but here again there were checks and balances. That episcopal chair (*cathedra* in Greek) was on the side, not at the center; the position on the side suggested deference and lesser importance. From the moment that bishop entered his cathedral for a Latin liturgy until the end, the rubrics denied him all authority; he was as checked and restricted as any parish priest.

When the different Catholic dioceses were established in the United States, starting at the end of the eighteenth century, the bishops consistently evaded their responsibility to set up a government structure of the sort described in Canon Law. They would not submit to local checks and balances on their authority. The American diocese would not have an independent cathedral chapter; instead, there would be a timid board of consultors, which consisted of clergy who were dependent on the bishop for their careers. For as long as they could, the American bishops resisted even the establishment of real parishes, as described in Canon Law — with rights and job protections for certain pastors; instead, they routinely designated their parishes as missionary outposts where the personnel could be easily switched around.

The story of how Roman Catholicism in the United States grew as an institution is a complicated one, but a large part of it can be simplified in one phrase: the concentration of ecclesiastical power in the hands of bishops. As early as the middle of the nineteenth century, an American bishop enjoyed more unrestricted power than the pope. Furthermore, in the American diocese the bishop is the sole owner of the entire diocesan operation: the cathedral, seminary, diocesan newspaper, some hospitals, parishes, cemeteries, every piece of property, every stick of furniture. In a few cases, such as the archdioceses of Baltimore, Boston, New Orleans, and Los Angeles, the Catholic bishop has the legal right to act as a "corporation sole"; this means that the diocese has all the legal privileges of a corporation, but the entire corporation is just one man, the bishop. In other cases, diocesan operations are owned by an interlocking system of boards of trustees, and the bishop controls all of the boards. For very practical economic reasons, he may even require individual parishes to keep all of their income — except for petty cash — in a central bank account, which is in his name. (The religious orders, colleges, and universities operate their own corporate institutions, but the local bishop has rights, in most cases, to intrude into their affairs.) What could be called the American System of ecclesiastical management looks so centralized that it is almost monarchical.

In the new Code of Canon Law promulgated in 1983, cathedral chapters lose virtually all of their power. There are provisions for committees, consultors, and even a senate of priests in each diocese, but their role is strictly advisory; moreover, these advisors will be men who are dependent on the bishop for their next assignment and perhaps their next meal. To put it simply, the Canon Law of 1983 makes the American System the model for the entire church.

This long historical development in Catholicism — the gradual concentration of power in the bishop — is, ironically, a result of a modernizing process, a streamlining of an institution hampered by too many medieval complications. Bishops can rightly claim that most of their power is not as absolute as it appears; today they have to make decisions with the consent and cooperation of those who work for them. If a bishop dares to act too monarchically, he knows that every loyal pastor and every loyal nun is skilled in the tactics of evasion and outright obstruction. The American System is monarchical only superficially.

Nevertheless...

Although the American System of governing the Catholic church may be a model of corporate efficiency, it is a catastrophe as a role model. With the bishop setting the example, each Catholic priest and each member of the laity now acts like a corporation of one, a religious enterprise owned by one person, who is a genius. The pastor, parish musician, liturgist, parishioner — they are all CEOs, independent bosses, freed at last from outmoded medieval traditions that restrict one's direct authority. Indeed, the influence of the American System is so pervasive in the Catholic church today that it could be called the new "Catholic style," which replaces the militant, defensive "style" of the recent past.

The beauty of the American System as a paradigm is its adaptability. The bedrock conservative and the liberal who has really drifted off into pantheism are both flattered by the idea that whatever stands in the way of his or her direct exercise of Christianity (as they see it) can be brushed aside as a useless me-

dieval remnant. This is not a simple case of "disobedience" —
independent-minded liberals once again refusing to follow the
church's explicit teachings, as interpreted in Rome. (When, in
history, have Catholics, in great numbers, not disobeyed Rome?)
Rather, the American System, as a bad role model, is all about
obedience: the belief that each individual has direct knowledge of
God's will, has absolutely nothing to learn from the past or other
individuals, and must be obeyed.

*   *   *

When we pick up the newspaper and come across yet another
report on the latest Catholic sex scandal (pedophile priests, bishops having affairs), we are actually reading about the American
System badly out of control. Again and again, in every one of
these sordid stories, we find the same pattern: A culprit, who
(1) never had to worry about anybody evaluating his ministry,
(2) was allowed to work with absolutely no effective supervision.
In the years before Vatican II, sexual transgressions among the
clergy were restrained by institutional despotism, augmented by
a strict routine of formal prayer and by an extravagantly developed Catholic sense of guilt. The postconciliar church, however,
has too often tried to find its "style" — maybe its identity — in
the very process of abandoning one restraint (i.e., tradition) after another. If the conscience of a transgressing priest is troubled
by guilt, he can rationalize the situation by saying that the modern Catholic is someone who yearns to get rid of useless medieval
restraints, such as archaic traditions and a few of the Ten Commandments. If thoughts of sinfulness enter his mind, they will
evaporate instantly whenever he throws himself into the role of
liturgical presider as centralized quasi-divinity — with all of those
people in the pews who must have come to reassure him, to ratify
his liberation from the silly old liturgical restraints of the past.

"See our new postconciliar church/chapel! See the clear glass
windows that open up liturgy to the world, to the universe! See the
new baptismal bath for total immersion! See the burlap banners,
the guitars, pianos, and synthesizers! See how we are seated so
that we see one another! See that there are no kneelers! See how
we are all offering the Mass together, since we stand during the
Mass, just like the priest. Hear the music, which is untouched by
traditions, by the discredited church of the past."

There are certainly things to see and hear, and many of them fall into the category of art. Individually, they are somewhat neutral, but collectively and "in action" they all seem to enforce the American System. Everything is structured so that the "spiritual experience" has to come from one person at the top: the priest. What the worshipers will "see," normally, is not the banners or the simplified postconciliar architecture or their important role, but one man talking at them for the better part of an hour. In many cases he is not "part of the scenery" — just one more "item" (albeit the most important one) in a complicated collection of human symbols called worship. He is not even a sign of Christ's presence. No, the priest, as a corporation of one and as an individual person, becomes the principal "item" to which all of the arts point — the human figure in the center of an elaborate cameo setting... unless, of course, there are some postconciliar musicians nearby. See how they use every trick in the book to push their way into the cameo. See how they sometimes force the congregation to pay attention to them. In the old days, a group of musicians could be straining their vocal cords to sing a Mass by Bruckner or maybe they were concentrating on the flowing line of a Gregorian chant, but they were hard to "see," because they were lost in all the ritualized chaos.

Sincere, dedicated liturgists and theologians write the learned articles and give eloquent speeches. See, they tell us, how postconciliar Catholicism leads the faithful to a new era, in which the people, during worship, become intensely aware that they are the church, they are one with Christ. Well, this may be the theology, but its practical application frequently suggests something entirely different — an "experience" in which everything is centralized in a priest or musician (or even a lay person substituting for a priest in a rural church). One centralized individual at a time "spoonfeeds" each prayer or song or even thought to the worshiper.

It would be misleading to think that this is a simple case of the bad guys doing bad things. Rather, the real evil here is good individuals being led into temptation by electronic technology. Modern people have been trained to spend hours looking at faces (important celebrities) on an electronic tube called television; this act of watching, unlike listening or reading a book, requires no imagination, no fantasy, no filling in the missing messages to the brain — in other words, no involvement. The celebrities on the tube supply everything. These same modern people have also been trained, this time by the entertainment industry and politics, to associate the privilege of controlling a microphone with power and authority. For all of these reasons, Catholics too often assume that worship is essentially an act of watching individuals who talk or sing to everyone and assert their power, with amplification, with microphones. What many Catholics experience as "liturgical participation" is really the worshiper meekly attempting to recite or sing something "underneath" someone else's amplified and authoritative voice.

The Catholic church, hundreds of years ago and long before amplification, was well aware that the priest, musicians, and congregation needed checks and balances to remind them that worship was not a solo performance. This is why the church invented the cleverly ambiguous dialogue, "May the Lord be with you / And also with you." Observe that the words "I" and "we" are not there. Singing that dialogue — in Latin or the vernacular — is an act of decentralization. When these words are repeated here and there in a liturgy, they do something that can best be described in metaphors: they refocus the lens, recalculate the equation, put the furniture back in place. At the beginning of a liturgy, this traditional dialogue very clearly removes any misunderstanding that the ceremony might be a case of "I" the priest, on one team, pitted against "us" the congregation, on the other; it establishes a mutual "together" right away. If a priest decides to dispense with this medieval tradition and, instead, substitute something else (such as "Good morning" or "Good evening" or "Hello folks" or even warm, welcoming remarks), he might really be trying to say, "*Ta-dah!* Here I am, the corporation of one." If he decides to top the congregation's line (if I may use an expression from the theater) with a sincere "Thank you," he is committing sabotage; he is trying to take over the sole control of the corporation.

One act of sabotage deserves another. Whenever a priest or bishop looks or sounds too much like a liturgical corporation of one (with customers in the pews), you might find that the cantor is graciously allowed a few minutes in the spotlight to sing something like "O, Holy Night," or maybe the choir sings a brilliant anthem — *and the congregation applauds afterward.* If anyone requires proof that the American System has helped to transform liturgy into a series of centralized solo appearances, it is the new practice of applauding great musical performances (classical or "folk").

*   *   *

Read through the papal encyclicals of the nineteenth and twentieth centuries. On one page you will find the noblest expression of Christianity and human thought. A page later you will come across cantankerous nonsense. For example, Leo XIII on the subject of workers and their rights is a heroic champion, a prophet, a saint. On the subject of governments and how the state should be organized, he displays an unseemly preoccupation with the church's worldly power; he remains indifferent to the presence of despots and dungeons, as long as a government makes Catholicism the state religion.

The devout Catholic who wishes to follow papal teaching does not have to worry about disagreeable moments in some encyclicals, because these letters were not proclaimed as infallible teachings, but a dilemma still remains: What sentence in the encyclical is eternal truth, or at least the most honest wisdom of Christianity, and what is just a medieval accretion, an outdated perception from a bygone era? When is the pope the pope and when is he just an opinionated Italian or Polish bachelor?

This dilemma, in a broad sense, has been the defining characteristic of Catholicism since Vatican II. How is a Catholic supposed to figure out what is right (or full of great practical value) and what is a useless holdover from the Middle Ages? The standard answer is that a Catholic is supposed to follow the authentic and unchangeable teachings of the church, but that is not really the way human beings operate. What we sinful, frail creatures really accept or follow is not teaching but intuition — a whole complex of hunches and emotional instincts. The theologian would say that this is really about God's gift, divine grace, at work; others might say that this is about a human need for a *style*, which is really an interlocking system of beliefs and customs (including the arts) that make sense out of the madness called existence. Whatever the case, faith without an expression in a style is God reduced to a fill-in-the-blanks test on dogma. Style without faith is recreation.

*   *   *

In perhaps the majority of Protestant churches, the style of the preaching is rather seductive; a minister, chosen by the community, lures the flock into a new life in Christ. What he or she says is as important as the enticing, attractive way it is presented. The artwork, however, tends to be matter-of-fact in most Protestant churches; the hymns might be uplifting and beautiful but their style is direct and devoid of seductive ambiguity. In Roman Catholicism, years ago, the liturgical ceremonies and arts were seductive — or at least supposed to be. With occasional exceptions, the preaching was relentlessly matter-of-fact, with emphasis on the word "is." ("This is this, that is that" may have been expressed coldly or intensely or even angrily, but not seductively.)

In Catholicism's new, postconciliar style, the tendency is to take the seductiveness out of both the preaching and the liturgical arts. The worshiper must function in the middle of a direct, utterly functional "is-ness." A message may be repeated in prayers and songs (amplified so that you will not miss the point), yet it is considered embarrassingly old fashioned to use anything, any style, that conveys this message to the nonverbal intuitions; as a result, the worshiper is informed, but not seduced.

Some liturgists rejoice in this. When older Catholics ask them, "Where did all the seductive beauty go? What happened to the beautiful Solemn High Mass and the Forty Hours devotion?" these liturgists reply that such questions miss the point. A lot of medieval baggage had to be removed so that the worshiper could understand the church and the Eucharist as they should be understood. We must not judge whether a liturgy is "good" or "bad" according to aesthetics (candles, vestments, singing, and so forth). Rather, a "good" liturgy "is one which transforms me and my fellow parishioners in such a way that men and women of today's society will see the full implication of the Sacrament of the Eucharist. And they will say of us as they said of the first Christians, 'See how they love one another! There is no poor among them.' "[1]

Liturgy as the gathering of beautiful, transformed Christians who love the poor, rather than liturgy as beautiful things: that is indeed the ideal; it was not unknown in the days of the Solemn High Mass in Latin, but, back then, at least everyone realized that the ideal could never be totally achieved. The problem today is that many of Catholicism's intellectual leaders want this same ideal — here and now, on earth, in this life — but they think that centralization (i.e., the American System) can achieve it. The result, too frequently, is worship in which one centralized individual, behind a microphone, hands out prayer; another individual hands out song. Sometimes the stylistic expression of this centralization comes in large, vulgar proportions. (For example, there are a few "modernized" cathedrals that have the episcopal chair dead-center, from which place the bishop presides; he seems to eclipse the altar in importance.) Sometimes centralization takes a milder form. (For example, the postconciliar funeral Mass — with the white vestments, cheery tone, and singing of "The Battle Hymn of the Republic" and "For All the Saints" — is supposed to celebrate a life that is changed, not taken away; but, let us be honest, it really looks like a triumphal celebration of the departed one's canonization, achieved single-handedly.)

The naughty word in Catholicism today is "individualism" — supposedly a new thing that is now ruining liturgy. But this does not tell the whole story. Catholic worship, pre–Vatican II, was truly individualistic and almost anarchic in the way each believer, all alone, was supposed to approach God. It would be more accurate to say that Catholic liturgy, post–Vatican II, has sometimes tended to become more centralized than individualistic. When modern postconciliar Catholics worship, they are frequently expected to surrender themselves not to a new life in Christ but really to a priest or musician or special group or guru. The only individualists are the ones who occupy the center and thrive on the idea of other people surrendering to them.

If some medieval liturgical obstruction — Latin, art, music — has been removed from liturgy, the reason given is that the old thing no longer makes sense in the modern world; but, in some cases, the old thing is really destroyed because its *beauty* competes with the centralized individualist's importance among others (who also begin to think of themselves as somehow centralized). All the talk about transformed Christians loving one another and about the poor can be a diversionary tactic: to discourage people from asking why beauty is out and the centralization of personalities is in. All the talk about the new style for a renewed, loving church usually comes from the same people who have set up worship so that nothing gets in the way of their centralized, individualist performance.

*   *   *

The late Mark Searle, a distinguished liturgist who taught at the University of Notre Dame, was an example of the modern Catholic struggling to find the new and elusive style that would symbolize a postconciliar vision of the church. His writings show that he was a man of extensive knowledge. His thoughts were the result of profound understanding of theology and orthodoxy. He respected viable liturgical traditions. He could comment eloquently on liturgical planning, community, goals, social justice, and theology. But in his writings, he perhaps displayed a small amount of uncomfortableness concerning the "form" that all of that liturgical commentary and theory would take. The problem is this: A community will want a liturgical "form" that is acceptable, right, and fitting; this leads directly into the idea of the beautiful (which varies from culture to culture). Beauty in worship — seductive, long associated with preconciliar Catholicism, irrational, intuitive, almost "feminine" — is a messy, uncomfortable proposition because it cannot be neatly fitted to any liturgical theology or theory.

In 1985, Searle spoke at a conference on liturgical music.[2] In his remarks, he stressed that liturgy was public worship, which is offered to God the Father by the whole body of Christ, head and members. This requires a full, conscious, and active surrender of oneself to Christ in the assembly, "that Christ may be present, may speak and may act in and through us." Searle observed that the repetition of fixed and familiar canonical texts helped a community to affirm its faith in Christ. He suggested that the proliferation of all kinds of liturgical music to accommodate many different musical tastes might only serve to divide the church.

All of these points — about matters theological and logistical — were "easy" for Searle to make. The real difficulty came when he had to confront the problem of the beautiful. Searle revealed little patience for what he called "religious folk music," as well as the "elitist pleasures" of Gregorian chant and Palestrina (a Renaissance composer but used here as a generic term for Latin choral music at its most ethereal). He maintained that this kind of artistic beauty comes close to "sentimentalism and entertainment which trivialize the liturgy of the Church by dissociating the joy of singing from the cost of discipleship." The "immediate gang-appeal" of the sing-along and the "aesthetic peak-experience of the concert hall" are the kinds of beauty that, in liturgy, allow people to "fake it," to enjoy the experience of feeling religious without actually being religious.

This is the stern reasoning of the prophet, and it sounds logical, but actually doing something about the problem of liturgical beauty — stopping the "sentimentalism and entertainment" — would require worrisome measures: such as placing, in every church and chapel, an armed guard who patrols up and down the aisles and shoots any parishioner who tries to "fake it" or enjoy the musical beauty without suffering the pain of discipleship.

Searle eventually found what he thought was the perfect style for a revitalized Catholicism. He and his family occasionally attended the liturgy in a small Melkite rite Roman Catholic parish. He was happy in this place. The ritual was sung from beginning to end, except for the sermon. There was no organ, cantor, choir, or guitar group. (It could also be said that there was certainly no effort to follow the advice of some modern liturgical theoreticians.)

For Searle, whose ancestry was British, the foreign unfamiliarity of the liturgical style in this parish may have released him from using the human emotions that have to deal with the familiar (and the inculturated). In other words, he did not have to respond to familiar ceremonies or art or Gregorian chant or hymns or "folk" music, which were all part of his cultural experience and wired to specific emotional reactions in his psyche. The "strangeness" of the Melkite rite allowed him to escape from the emotions of an overly familiar "Western" style of worship. (The familiar can appear to be incorrect or even immoral to someone who is satiated with it.)

Searle could also rejoice in the small size of the congregation in that Melkite parish — rarely more than twenty-five people. Quite a few modern Catholics, like Searle, are filled with nostalgia for that perfect Christian "style" of the early centuries: the chosen few (certainly no more than twenty-five) sharing their radiated warmth in the upper room or catacombs, the elect worshiping with rites that contradicted the pagan values of the multitude. These same modern Catholics become exasperated when they see today's big congregations, with the "cultural Catholics" and beauty-seekers, all of them trying to "fake it," to get a cheap mystical thrill, without going through the pain of true discipleship.

Someone should remind these nostalgic Catholics that the image of the early Christian communities as perfection itself is an illusion. Even in apostolic times — and this is clear from passages in the Pauline Epistles of the New Testament — those small Christian congregations were not getting it right, not always living up to the ideal of a Mystical Body of Christ visibly expressed in worship.

Perhaps the key concept here — which Searle missed — is sloppiness. A "catholic" church is, by definition, a sloppy church; its doors are open to everybody. In the past, Roman Catholicism very cleverly used structured, disciplined forms of beauty to keep the sloppiness under control and perhaps transform it. (If some undeserving people were using the beauty to "fake it" and feel religious, that was a matter for God to sort out.) Also, the beauty in worship was supposed to touch something deeply embedded in human nature — and this brings us to another one of those essential digressions:

* * *

Tens of thousands of years ago, two-legged creatures that looked like apes roamed the earth. Then something happened. These beings discovered fire and tools, but they also indulged in activities that had nothing to do with an animal's instinct for survival: they painted caves; they created music and dance. This artistic activity, which separated them from other animals, was not necessarily a sign of intelligence (which even dolphins have) but of a soul, a divine spark. The evolutionary development of *homo sapiens* is, in part, the story of two-legged mammals desperately trying — with poetry, metaphor, art, music, dance, ceremonies, and restless hearts — to define that mystical source of their creativity, their souls. God does not need all the forms of "art" but human beings do: to express praise, thanksgiving, and total bafflement about what it all means.

The advanced postconciliar Catholic has progressed beyond all that, beyond the uncertainty of mysticism and beauty. He or she has Jesus all neatly figured out; everything has been solved. It is all about community, people looking at people, hospitality, participation (full, active, and conscious), the poor, revised texts, and, above all, one individual rising to a place of central importance among other individuals. Religious art and music of the past must be abandoned, because they symbolize a communal acknowledgement of a sloppy human nature — sinful, imperfect, and forever struggling to express the meaning of this God who must have some connection with the good and the beautiful.

*   *   *

What does it all mean? One telephone call I received was from a man who was both upset and amused. It seems that he happened to attend Sunday services in a Lutheran church and saw something that almost totally monopolized his attention. The minister, choir members, and a big group of young children, all in the front of the church, had strings around their necks and hanging from each piece of string was a plastic fork. Prayers were prayed, hymns were sung, and plastic forks dangled. The congregation was without a clue.

Finally, the minister talked to the children and explained the symbolism of the forks.

"Remember those times when you were eating dinner and your mother told you to save your forks?"

Continued cluelessness from the congregation.

The minister, sensing that further clarification was needed, continued: "You know, save your forks for dessert . . . for heaven."

What does it all mean? First of all it means that Roman Catholics are not the only ones capable of liturgical nuttiness. Secondly, it means prepare for the worst. We must surely be living in a dangerous era when any religion begins to treat human beings as if they were little kitsch toys — without yearnings, without imperfections, without imagination, without the gift of a soul, without art. We would expect dictators, radical political theorists, and others who have a low opinion of people to indulge in amusing games with symbols, as a sign of their contempt for the idiots called human beings, but in religion this sort of thing is bad news. It means the end of that idea of a special, creating human "soul," and the beginning of an age when people in churches will be manipulated as if they were stupid machines — easily turned on or off (with a gimmick) by smart machines. It means head for the hills.

NOTES

Chapter 1:
AN INTRODUCTION TO A STYLE: Never Say Never

1. Quoted in James Hennesey, *American Catholics: A History of the Roman Catholic Community in the United States* (New York, 1981), 222.

2. Even though the council passed this decree by a vote of 2308 to 70, a very small number of Roman Catholics (and all the schismatic followers of Archbishop Marcel Lefebvre) still believe that the Declaration on Religious Freedom is an appalling mistake and really has no doctrinal value, because it breaks with the consistent teaching of the church. In his book *The Second Vatican Council and Religious Liberty* (Long Prairie, Minn., 1992), Michael Davies argues that the church must return to the ideal of the "Catholic state" proclaimed by all the popes before Vatican II (the sort of government that, if possible, keeps non-Catholic religions hidden from public view and restricted). Davies and others like him need to be reminded of reality: (1) About-faces on papal policy are nothing new; e.g., modern popes, in contrast to their medieval predecessors, do not condemn the practice of taking interest on loans. (2) The Natural Law of history is that monopolies — even religious ones — do not work properly; they inevitably become lazy, arrogant, and corrupt. (3) "The Reign of Christ the King" is a utopian ideal, but in modern times it has usually meant hypocritical right-wing dictatorships supported by a clergy that is more interested in its privileges than its people.

3. Helen Hooven Santmyer, *Ohio Town* (New York, 1962; reprinted 1984), 94.

4. Ibid., 130.

5. Decree 197. See Glen Gabert, *In Hoc Signo? A Brief History of Catholic Parochial Education in America* (Port Washington, N.Y., and London, 1973), 54. These decrees were issued in Latin, without an English translation.

6. Just one small example of Walsh's incompetence as an objective historian is found in the Appendix of this book (482), where he describes the eighteenth as the "lowest of centuries." He was so obsessive about discrediting the age that had produced the mocking anticlericalism of Voltaire and the anti-Catholicism of the French Revolution that he could not simultaneously entertain the idea that the eighteenth century might possibly have produced something good, such as the Declaration of Independence and the Constitution of the United States.

7. "Have We Any Scholars?" *America* 34 (August 15, 1925): 418–19.

8. Reprinted in 1978. Quotations are from 116, 117, 118, 172, 178.

9. This book was published by Our Sunday Visitor.

10. *Catholics and Scholarship*, editor's Foreword. Pages not numbered.

11. Ibid., 23. From 1885 to the 1960s, *A Catechism of Christian Doctrine*, commonly known as "The Baltimore Catechism," was the series of standard textbooks for teaching religion to Catholic youngsters in the United States. Question 514 of Book No. 3 in this series asks: "What excuses do some people give for not becoming members of the true church?" The second excuse is: "There are too many poor and ignorant people in the Catholic Church."

12. *Catholics and Scholarship*, 23.

13. Information on how O'Brien started this Catholic Foundation (later called the Newman Foundation) at the University of Illinois can be found in Winton U. Solberg, "The Catholic Presence at the University of Illinois," *Catholic Historical Review* 76, no. 4 (October 1990): 765–812, and Hennesey, *American Catholics*, 249–50.

14. "The Development of Catholic Writers," in *Catholics and Scholarship*, 220. Monsignor Smith, Ph.D., LL.D., Jour.D., was editor-in-chief of the Register System of Newspapers. In this same article he tells about a Catholic man who refused to allow his daughters to attend high school, because the only one in the area was public. (The theory was that the daughters would surely lose their souls in the public school, but they would be safer in the workplace, which was somehow free of temptations.) This man had one son and the boy was determined to go to high school. The boy, helped by his sisters, had to plead with the father for permission to attend this non-Catholic institution. Finally, the father relented; the boy was the only member of the family to go to high school — and he later became a priest. Without the high school education he could not have entered the seminary.

15. John Tracy Ellis, "American Catholics and the Intellectual Life," an address to the Catholic Commission on Intellectual and Cultural Affairs (formed in 1946), published in *Thought* 30, no. 118 (Autumn 1955): 351–88; published also in book format (Chicago, 1956).

16. Thomas F. O'Dea, *American Catholic Dilemma: An Inquiry into the Intellectual Life* (New York, 1958).

17. According to the research of Seymour P. Lachman and Barry A. Kosmin (both of the City University of New York) black Catholics, especially those who attend Catholic schools, are more likely than all Americans to complete high school and college. Black Catholics are 40 percent more likely to graduate from college than other black Americans; their income is likely to be higher as well. They conclude: "One reason why Catholic schools often enable their students to overcome class and racial handicaps is that they expect and reward academic diligence and personal development." These schools also "teach the rich, middle class and poor the same curriculum." Surprisingly, about 70 percent of the students enrolled in Harlem's parochial schools are Protestant ("Black Catholics Get Ahead," *New York Times*, September 14, 1991, 19).

18. Paul Scalia, "How Catholic Are America's Catholic Colleges?" *Campus* 3, no. 2 (Winter 1992): 9, 17.

19. In his book *Playing the Private College Admissions Game* (New York,

1979, 1986), Richard Moll included Holy Cross among the top selective colleges and universities in the United States (83).

20. *New York Times*, September 16, 1986, B2.

21. *New York Times*, February 23, 1992, 16.

22. Dennis Castillo, "The Origin of the Priest Shortage 1942–1962," *America* 167, no. 12 (October 24, 1992): 302–4.

23. Gabert, *In Hoc Signo?*, 88.

Chapter 2:
THE LATE LATIN MASS: Abolished Forever

1. Anecdotes mentioned in this chapter are reported in various issues of the *Newsletter*. The editor of this publication (Professor Anthony LoBello) and his associates may strive to keep it politically neutral, but they take every opportunity to indicate that the Latin Liturgy Association does not support the bigotry or the seething reactionary theories of people who use the Tridentine Mass as a symbol of angry defiance.

2. Xavier Rynne (Francis X. Murphy), *Vatican Council II* (New York, 1968), 65. Father Murphy's reporting on the council originally appeared in *The New Yorker*.

3. "Investigatio de usu linguae latinae in liturgia romana et de missa quae 'Tridentina' appellari solet," *Notitiae* 17 (1981): 589–611. This report, published in Latin and Italian, concluded that worship in Latin was neither frequent nor widespread. It also indicates that 108 of the 153 American bishops who reported to the survey said that they had received no requests for Masses in Latin. But what was not reported was the number of bishops who had let it be known that they would treat any request for any Latin Mass as an act of disloyalty.

4. "Worship in Latin Found to Decline," *New York Times*, December 31, 1981, B7.

5. *New York Times*, January 6, 1985, 18.

6. Reported in the *Newsletter* of the Latin Liturgy Association, no. 40 (March 1991): 15.

7. This unpublished study by Dean R. Hoge, Joseph Shields, and Mary Jeanne Verdieck is Report No. 3 in a series entitled *A Study of Future Church Leadership*. I obtained a copy by writing to the Department of Sociology, Catholic University, Washington, D.C.

8. See, for example, Edward T. Hall, *The Hidden Dimension* (New York, 1966).

9. These reactions are mentioned in Anne Roche Muggeridge, *The Desolate City: Revolution in the Catholic Church* (San Francisco, 1990), 155. It should be noted that in 1971 the Catholic bishops of England and Wales obtained Vatican-approved authority to retain the "old" Mass for certain groups. This concession spared Britain some of the turmoil that would hit Catholicism on the continent.

10. "Chronicle," *Worship* 60, no. 2 (March 1986): 168–71.

11. For a clear-headed appraisal of the Tridentine Mass in the United States

today, see Charlotte Low, "That Good Old Tridentine Mass," *Crisis* 5, no. 8 (September 1987): 13–18.

12. "The Latin Language and Gregorian Chant in the American Seminaries: Result of a 1985 Survey of the Latin Liturgy Association," reported in the *Newsletter* of the Latin Liturgy Association, no. 39 (December 1990): 13–17. According to a survey of seminary teachers, very few seminarians today have any interest in learning Latin, Hebrew, or Greek (the language of the New Testament). But this is only part of a "weak academic background" and general "lack of intellectual enthusiasm" among these seminarians. See Eugene Hemrick and Robert Wister, *Readiness for Theological Studies: A Study of Faculty Perceptions on the Readiness of Seminarians* (Washington, D.C.: Seminary Department of the National Catholic Educational Association, 1993), 29–30.

13. Quoted in Alec Lewis, ed., *The Quotable Quotation Book* (New York, 1980), 176. One early morning in 1978, Jimmy Breslin, another New York reporter, attended Mass in Notre Dame Cathedral in Paris. "The Mass was in French, which was wrong," Breslin wrote, "for the cathedral demanded a particular richness of language, a unifying connection with the past, in order to remind the one kneeling of his insignificance" (*The World According to Breslin* [New York, 1984], 29).

14. Interview with Father Godfrey Diekmann, O.S.B., "Vatican II: There's Been Nothing Like It in 1000 Years," *U.S. Catholic* 56, no. 11 (November 1991): 20.

15. It is interesting to note that Dorothy Day (no relative of this author) devoted most of her adult life to the poor and she lived among them, yet when it came to liturgy this Catholic socialist called herself a "traditionalist" and a "romantic." She wholeheartedly supported the change to the vernacular but she had no sympathy for experimental or nontraditional forms of liturgy. See William D. Miller, *Dorothy Day: A Biography* (San Francisco, 1982), 506.

16. Published in *Origins* (CNS Documentary Service) 21, no. 14 (September 12, 1991): 225–29.

17. At a conference for a small religious order of women (and I do not know which one), an afternoon prayer session was really a game of catch with a ball of yarn. The sisters were supposed to grab the ball and, while holding on to a piece of yarn, toss the rest of the ball to someone else. The resulting tangle of wool symbolized collective unity and prayer. At another prayer session, the participants were asked to get down on the floor, roll all over it, and moan. The woman who told me these stories was a member of this religious order at the time, but its domination by a few radicals convinced her to go back to the secular world.

The source of the difficulty is this: A small number of Catholic women in and out of religious orders honestly believe that liturgies and liturgical music that might in any way deserve the label "traditional" must be designed to keep them subservient to men in authority; the only way for these women to declare their emancipation from the male-dominated church is to find ways of worship whose suitability is measured only against two criteria: no men and no connection with the pre–Vatican II church.

Chapter 3:
PRIDE, COVETOUSNESS, LUST … AND MUSEUMS:
Edifice Wrecked

1. For an interesting commentary on Roman Catholicism's long association with kitsch statuary, see John Lyon, "Of Plaster Statues & Romantic Heresy," *Commonweal* 110, no. 6 (March 25, 1983): 170–75.

2. In videocassettes and printed material Father Baranowski discusses how to restructure a parish into small, basic Christian communities. This material is distributed by St. Anthony Messenger Press.

3. "Small Faith Groups Help the Good News Hit Home," an interview with Father Arthur Baranowski, *U.S. Catholic* 57, no. 1 (January 1992): 6–13.

4. Maginnis was born in Ireland and settled in the United States in 1885. He and the architectural firm he headed received numerous prizes and awards for their ecclesiastical and educational buildings. In 1948 the American Institute of Architects awarded Maginnis a Gold Medal for the outstanding achievements of his career. For more information on his work, see *Charles Donagh Maginnis FAIA 1867–1955: A Selection of His Essays and Addresses Selected and Edited by Robert P. Walsh A.I.A. and Andrew W. Roberts* (New Haven, 1956), privately printed; and *Liturgical Arts* 23, no. 4 (August 1955).

5. Letter from Elizabeth Maginnis, September 9, 1992.

6. See Morris Lapidus, *An Architecture of Joy* (Miami, 1979).

7. E. J. Applewhite, *Washington Itself* (New York, 1981), 308.

8. When the Shrine was being planned, the general rule was "one Mass, one priest." Everyone assumed that the building would have to have dozens of altars, one for each priest, and there would be a large number of them (visitors or priests associated with Catholic University). Concelebration was a rare exception in the Roman Rite.

9. Constitution on the Sacred Liturgy (Article 122).

10. *Musicae Sacrae Disciplina,* reprinted in Robert F. Hayburn, *Papal Legislation on Sacred Music: 95 A.D. to 1977 A.D.* (Collegeville, Minn., 1979), 348–49.

11. William S. Rubin, *Modern Sacred Art and the Church of Assy* (New York, 1961), 39.

12. As of this writing, the interior of the main church is no longer open to the public. Nevertheless, the Noack Organ Company has been hired to clean and restore the historic organ.

13. Søren Kierkegaard, *Kierkegaard's Attack upon Christendom 1854–1855,* trans. Walter Lowrie (Princeton, 1944), 175.

14. For a realistic appraisal of the Catholic church's wealth, see James Gollin, *Worldly Goods* (New York, 1971); Scott R. Safranski, *Managing God's Organization: the Catholic Church in Society* (Ann Arbor, Mich., 1985); Shawn Tully, "The Vatican's Finances," *Fortune* 116, no. 14 (December 21, 1987): 28–40.

15. See, for example, "First Church" (an article on the church of St. Therese, a Catholic parish in Winston, North Carolina), *Architectural Record* 180, no. 5 (May 1992): 112–17. Allen, Harbison and Associates was the firm that de-

signed this low-budget church, which blends graciously into the neighborhood landscape.

16. Reprinted in *Modern Liturgy* (November 1991) and *Pastoral Music Notebook* (January 1993).

Chapter 4:
DEPRESSING MUSIC: It Doesn't Belong

1. "Catholic of the Year," an interview with John Neuhaus by Mary Arnold, *Catholic Twin Circle* (February 24, 1991): 5.

2. Letter to the author, May 6, 1991.

3. See Stephen Bonta, "Liturgical Problems in Monteverdi's Marian Vespers," *Journal of the American Musicological Society* 20, no. 1 (Spring 1967): 86–106.

4. See Stephen Bonta, "The Uses of the *Sonata da Chiesa,*" *Journal of the American Musicological Society* 22, no. 1 (Spring 1969): 54–84.

5. In James Joyce's short story *The Dead* (from *Dubliners*, 1914), the elderly Julia sings a beautiful song for the guests at a party. We gather from comments made by her sister, Aunt Kate, that women "slaved ... all their lives" in the choir lofts of the churches to provide music for the liturgy in Ireland. But Pius X came along and in his *Motu Proprio* of 1903 declared that women could not sing in choirs. Aunt Kate says that "it's not just ... not right" that these hard-working women soloists should be banished and replaced by boy sopranos, "little whipper-snappers."

6. Listen to the dreadful musical nonsense on the recording *Alessandro Moreschi the Last Castrato: Complete Vatican Recordings* (Opal Records, produced by Pearl/Pavilion Records, England). By way of explanation: Alessandro Moreschi (1858–1922) was, because of some accident or disease, deprived of full male development and retained his boyish soprano voice all his life. He studied music, became a respected teacher of voice, and in 1883 was admitted as a member of the pope's choir, the Cappella Sistina. In 1902 and 1904 Moreschi, assisted by other singers, recorded some music that was performed in the Sistine Chapel, before the reforms of Pius X. Most of this music (religious arias in a pseudo-operatic style) is so atrocious it cries to heaven for vengeance. Even the better music is performed atrociously.

Castrati, men who had been castrated as boys in order to retain their soprano voices, were the rage in Italian opera from the middle of the seventeenth century to the middle of the eighteenth. This barbaric operation on children was against church law and civil law, but some impoverished parents subjected a son to castration in the hope that the boy would become a rich and famous castrato singer on the operatic stage. Castrati who were unsuccessful or whose voices had deteriorated got jobs singing in churches.

7. Claude Debussy, *Prelude to The Afternoon of a Faun*, ed. William W. Austin, a Norton Critical Score (New York, 1970); introductory essay, 11. The church that Debussy visited was St. Gervais, and the music director there was Charles Bordes. The music in most Parisian churches was bombastic and in-

fluenced by opera. At St. Gervais, however, the choir sang Renaissance music and the "new" kind of chant developed at Solesmes.

8. In my research I have come across references to the Twelfth Mass being used for the dedication of St. Peter's Church (1838) in Manhattan, St. Paul's Cathedral (1855) in Pittsburgh, and the Jesuits' Gesu Church (1888) in Philadelphia. The Twelfth Mass was sung, with orchestra, at the final liturgy of the Second Plenary Council of Baltimore (1866). When St. Paul's Church (Cambridge, Massachusetts) was first opened on Easter Sunday, 1923, the music for the first High Mass was the Twelfth Mass.

9. George Templeton Strong (1820–75) was a prominent member of New York society. In his massive diary he mentioned, more than once, his fondness for the Twelfth Mass. He even persuaded his parish, Trinity Episcopal Church (which faces Wall Street), to tilt a little toward Romanism and use the Gloria of this composition for a Christmas service. See Vera Brodsky Lawrence, *Strong on Music*, I, *Resonances 1836–1850* (New York, 1988).

10. In 1821 the German publishing firm of Simrock issued this composition in a series of Masses by Haydn and Mozart. Vincent Novello published the Mass in England as number twelve in a series, and in that edition it came to the United States. The Gloria is still performed; I heard it in an arrangement for women's voices at a public high school concert in 1991.

11. St. Joseph's College (now University) in Philadelphia. A commemorative booklet for this commencement (which celebrated the institution's fiftieth anniversary) was published afterward. It indicates that a visiting Cardinal Martinelli presided. As he presented Rosewig with a parchment copy of his honorary degree, the cardinal, speaking in a low voice, congratulated the composer on "his well deserved honor because of his achievements in the field of music."

12. Reprinted in Nicolas Slonimsky, *Music Since 1900* (New York, 1938), 530–33.

13. See Charles Hughes, Albert Christ-Janer, and Carlton Sprague-Smith, *American Hymns Old and New* (New York, 1980). As this study shows, American Catholicism between 1800 and, let us say, 1930 produced a large number of hymns for congregation, but only a tiny fraction of this repertory became a "heritage" that was passed down from generation to generation.

14. Andrew Greeley, *Confessions of a Parish Priest: An Autobiography* (New York, 1986), 133–36.

15. Most of the music in the Masses of Haydn, Mozart, Beethoven, Schubert, and Bruckner should not be used for a liturgy unless there is an orchestra of some sort to accompany it. The music will usually sound "wrong" or "weak" if an organ replaces the orchestral support that the composer originally had in mind. A parish that cannot get an orchestra together should not go near this type of music.

16. *Providence Visitor* (Providence, R.I.), January 23, 1992: 19.

17. Albert Hay Malotte (1895–1964) worked for the Walt Disney Studios. He composed music for Disney's *Silly Symphonies* and *Ferdinand the Bull*.

18. Edward Rothstein, "Roll Over Beethoven," *New Republic* 204, no. 5 (February 4, 1991): 32.

19. For a wider discussion of the need for simple, "primitive" liturgi-

cal music, especially in rural churches, see *Pastoral Music*, April–May and August–September, 1993.

20. For more information, see David Martin, *Tongues of Fire: The Explosion of Protestantism in Latin America* (Oxford, U.K., and Cambridge, Mass., 1990); David Stoll, *Is Latin America Turning Protestant? The Politics of Evangelical Growth* (Berkeley, 1992); Andrés Tapia, "Why Is Latin America Turning Protestant?" *Christianity Today* 36, no. 4 (April 6, 1992): 28–29.

21. Published by the Orchard Lake Schools, Orchard Lake, MI 48033.

22. For a sympathetic study of the Polka Mass phenomenon, see Robert Walser, "The Polka Mass: Music of Postmodern Ethnicity," *American Music* 10, no. 2 (Summer 1992): 183–202.

23. This phrase appears in the 1991–92 *Publications Directory*, documents issued by the bishops and other items that are sold by the United States Catholic Conference Publishing Services.

24. Letter to customers, July 3, 1991.

25. "The Church's Crisis of Culture," reprinted in *Origins* (CNS Documentary Service) 21, no. 4 (June 6, 1991): 68.

26. This story was recounted by Tomatis in an interview for the Canadian Broadcasting Company and was included in a special program on chant (May 1978). The program was also broadcast in the United States by National Public Radio and is available from PBS on a tape cassette (entitled *Chant*). A printed text of the interview was published in *Musicworks 35* (Toronto, 1986) and in a booklet issued by the Dom Mocquereau Foundation. See also Alfred Tomatis, "The Importance of the Ear," *Pastoral Music* 16, no. 5 (June–July 1992): 59–60.

27. William J. Finn, *Sharps and Flats in Five Decades* (New York, 1947), 115.

28. Most Reverend Edward M. Egan, Bishop of Bridgeport, "Music Lesson," *Fairfield County Catholic* (September 1991).

Chapter 5:
WHAT DOES IT ALL MEAN?

1. Thomas Richstatter, "The Sacrament of the Eucharist: What Happened to My Devotion?" *Catholic Update* (September 1992): 4.

2. Mark Searle, "Ritual Constraints on Liturgical Music," a speech given at the Milwaukee Symposium for Church Composers, 1985. Searle circulated copies of this speech. In a revised form it was published under the title "Ritual and Music" in *Assembly* 12, no. 3 (February 1986), and *Pastoral Music* 11, no. 3 (February–March 1987).

INDEX